C

Acknowledgments

While it is a standard convention to assert that a book would not have been possible without the help of many others, this is perhaps more literally true in my case than in most. In the years before voice-recognition technology was widely available, I was heavily dependent on the generosity of others to be my "hands." And so these people by right deserve my first thanks. While I cannot list and do not even know all the people who have typed for me over the past twelve years, I would particularly like to thank Ruth Roland, Alan Terlep, and my brothers William, Lawrence, and Robert Su. If to type for me means to love me, then they have loved me greatly. I would also like to recognize Jim Knox of the Adaptive Technology Site at the University of Michigan for introducing me to voice-recognition technology.

I have a great many intellectual debts to acknowledge as well. First and foremost, I would like to thank my dissertation committee at the University of Michigan for their tireless support, generosity, and assistance. Tobin Siebers, Simon Gikandi, Betty Louise Bell, and Margaret Somers have been and continue to be inspirations for me as a teacher and writer, and I hope some day to justify the countless hours they have invested in my education. Toby, above all, deserves my thanks. Any success I have had as a scholar can be attributed to his mentorship; any failures I have had I can only claim as my own. I would also like to express my gratitude to my colleagues at Marquette University, who have helped me to make Milwaukee a happy home these past four years. In particular, I would like to thank Tim Machan and Michael Gillespie for their support and friendship. A Summer Faculty Fellowship granted by Marquette was also helpful in providing time for me to write. Among the many others who have read and commented on parts of this manuscript, I would like especially to thank Andrew Sofer, Michael Lackey, Apollo Amoko, and Cynthia Petrites.

ETHICS AND NOSTALGIA IN THE CONTEMPORARY NOVEL

Images of loss and yearning played a crucial role in literary texts written in the later part of the twentieth century. Despite deep cultural differences, novelists from Africa, the Caribbean, Great Britain, and the United States have shared a sense that the economic, social, and political forces associated with late modernity have evoked widespread nostalgia within the communities in which they write. In this original and wide-ranging study, John J. Su explores the relationship between nostalgia and ethics in novels across the English-speaking world. He challenges the tendency in literary studies to portray nostalgia as necessarily negative. Instead, this book argues that nostalgic fantasies are crucial to the ethical visions presented by contemporary novels. From Jean Rhys to Wole Soyinka and from V. S. Naipaul to Toni Morrison, Su identifies nostalgia as a central concern in the twentieth-century novel.

JOHN J. SU is Assistant Professor of English at Marquette University. He has previously published in such journals as *Modern Fiction Studies*, *Contemporary Literature*, and *Modern Drama*.

ETHICS AND NOSTALGIA IN THE CONTEMPORARY NOVEL

JOHN J. SU

 CAMBRIDGE
UNIVERSITY PRESS

CAMBRIDGE UNIVERSITY PRESS
Cambridge, New York, Melbourne, Madrid, Cape Town, Singapore,
São Paulo, Delhi, Dubai, Tokyo

Cambridge University Press
The Edinburgh Building, Cambridge CB2 8RU, UK

Published in the United States of America by Cambridge University Press, New York

www.cambridge.org
Information on this title: www.cambridge.org/9780521123808

© John J. Su 2005

This publication is in copyright. Subject to statutory exception
and to the provisions of relevant collective licensing agreements,
no reproduction of any part may take place without the written
permission of Cambridge University Press.

First published 2005
This digitally printed version 2009

A catalogue record for this publication is available from the British Library

ISBN 978-0-521-85440-5 Hardback
ISBN 978-0-521-12380-8 Paperback

Cambridge University Press has no responsibility for the persistence or
accuracy of URLs for external or third-party internet websites referred to in
this publication, and does not guarantee that any content on such websites is,
or will remain, accurate or appropriate.

Finally, I would like to thank all my friends and family for their generous tolerance and unquestioning support of a project that has been my personal obsession over the past few years. Above all, I owe everything to Cindy, who has patiently read multiple drafts of chapters and offered me friendship and love. I hope to be able to return in some measure the gifts I have received from her.

Parts of this manuscript have appeared elsewhere in printed form. An earlier version of my discussion of Ian McEwan and three other paragraphs from Chapter One appeared as "Haunted by Place: Moral Obligation and the Postmodern Novel," in *Centennial Review* 42.3 (1998), 589–616. A previous version of the sections devoted to Jean Rhys and a few other paragraphs in Chapter 2 appeared as "'Once I Would Have Gone Back . . . But Not Any Longer': Nostalgia and Narrative Ethics in *Wide Sargasso Sea*," in *Critique* 44.2 (2003), 157–74. An earlier version of Chapter 4 was previously published as "Refiguring National Character: The Remains of the British Estate Novel," in *Modern Fiction Studies* 48.3 (2002), 552–80.

Introduction: nostalgia, ethics, and contemporary Anglophone literature

The longing to return to a lost homeland becomes a central feature of the Western literary tradition long before the term "nostalgia" was coined to describe it.[1] Homer's first image of Odysseus is of him sitting alone on the island of Ogygia, weeping, pining for his beloved Ithaca. Despite offers by the goddess Calypso to take him as a spouse and grant him immortality, Odysseus desires nothing more than to return to the place of his birth – even after Calypso foretells of the hardships he must bear before reaching his home. This first "narrative of return" establishes a pattern that continues to compel writers even now in the twenty-first century. In the past century, some of the most distinguished Anglophone writers from across the globe have rewritten the Homeric tale, including the expatriate Irishman James Joyce, the St. Lucian Derek Walcott, and the American Charles Frazier. Long after it has become cliché to say that "you can't go home again" – long after it has become widely recognized that nostalgic homelands frequently exist only in the imagination – literary texts continue to depict characters defined by their longing to return.

Although twentieth-century literary texts share the Homeric preoccupation with lost homelands, they are produced in environments in which nostalgia is subject to stark criticism. Perhaps the most widely cited academic study of nostalgia, Susan Stewart's *On Longing: Narratives of the Miniature, the Gigantic, the Souvenir, the Collection*, characterizes it as a "social disease."[2] What began in the seventeenth century as a physiological disease had become in the twentieth century a social ailment that leads to an obsession with kitsch and heritage in its most benign forms and fascism in its most extreme versions. Nothing in *The Odyssey* suggests that Odysseus should be faulted for his longing to return to his homeland; to the contrary, his crew criticize the inadequacy of his longing as he tarries on the island of Circe. But in the contemporary Western world, a diagnosis of nostalgia typically earns a writer or scholar condemnation; to be nostalgic is to be "out of touch," reactionary, even xenophobic. As Jackson Lears notes, nostalgia continues to be "the *bête noire* of every forward-looking intellectual, right, left, or center."[3] Unlike nostalgia in the Homeric world, which drives Odysseus to remember his past despite the lures of Calypso, nostalgia in the twentieth century is characterized as a form of amnesia. Thus, despite the surging interest in topics relating to memory within the humanities over the past two decades, the analysis of nostalgia has largely been neglected. To the extent that it enters such discussions, it typically functions as a foil. "Memory" signifies intimate personal experience, which often counters institutional histories; "nostalgia" signifies inauthentic or commodified experiences inculcated by capitalist or nationalist interests. Indeed, cultural critics like bell hooks have insisted that the study of memory demands a rigorous rejection of nostalgia, calling for a "politicization of memory that distinguishes nostalgia, that longing for something to be as it once was, a kind of useless act, from that remembering that serves to illuminate and transform the present."[4]

Such dismissals of nostalgia, however, risk occluding crucial aspects of contemporary Anglophone literature. Memory and nostalgia are intertwined, for example, in one of the most widely studied works written in recent decades, Toni Morrison's *Beloved* (1987). Early in the novel, the protagonist Sethe discovers that even the plantation on which she was a slave evokes a certain nostalgia: "and suddenly there was Sweet Home rolling, rolling, rolling out before her eyes, and although there was not a leaf on that farm that did not make her want to scream, it rolled itself out before her in shameless beauty. It never looked as terrible as it was and it made her wonder if hell was a pretty place too."[5] Sethe's reflections demonstrate the sentimentality and selectivity characteristic of nostalgia; later in the same passage, she notes that she can remember the sycamore trees around the plantation, not the lynched children hanging from them. As will become apparent in Chapter 1 of this study, Sethe experiences nostalgia throughout the novel, particularly for the gatherings of African Americans that occurred at the Clearing. Yet, there is no indication in the novel that Sethe should be condemned for these longings or that they are even avoidable. They constitute significant parts of her memory and experience. Who she is, how she acts, and the claims she makes upon readers cannot be understood without reference to her nostalgia.

This insight leads me to challenge the predominant characterization of nostalgia and the ways in which this characterization has influenced the study of contemporary Anglophone literature. Drawing upon a diverse array of authors including Chinua Achebe, Kazuo Ishiguro, Paule Marshall, Ian McEwan, N. Scott Momaday, Toni Morrison, V. S. Naipaul, Jean Rhys, Joan Riley, Leslie Marmon Silko, Wole Soyinka, and Evelyn Waugh, *Ethics and Nostalgia in the Contemporary Novel* examines how loss and yearning have shaped the ethical visions of literary texts in recent decades. Despite deep cultural differences, the novelists in this study share a sense that the economic, social, and political forces associated with late modernity have evoked widespread nostalgia within the communities in which they write. Whether these authors embrace or reject the nostalgia surrounding them, they all consciously exploit nostalgia's tendency to interweave imagination, longing, and memory in their efforts to envision resolutions to the social dilemmas of fragmentation and displacement described in their novels. My study thus questions the tendency by many scholars to downplay or repudiate the presence of nostalgia in contemporary Anglophone literature. In these novels, fantasies of lost or imagined homelands do not serve to lament or restore through language a purported premodern purity; rather, they provide a means of establishing ethical ideals that can be shared by diverse groups who have in common only a longing for a past that never was.

From the outset, it should be clear that this study makes no claims to analyze all forms of nostalgia, nor will it claim that nostalgia is necessarily ethical. Such a claim, of course, would be foolish. The longing to return to a lost place frequently conceals feelings of fear and anxiety, and nostalgia has been repeatedly exploited for commercial and nationalistic purposes. But the prevalence of nostalgia in contemporary societies across the globe demands greater attention. Indeed, a growing number of cultural critics argue that nostalgia is one of the defining features of the postwar era. Stuart Hall, for example, asks, "Who has not known, at this moment, the surge of an overwhelming nostalgia for lost origins, for 'times past'?"[6] The success of political movements in utilizing nostalgic constructions, from ultranationalism in Eastern Europe to the neoconservative "return to family values" in the United States, suggests that they are meeting some kind of need, albeit in an exploitative fashion. My own sense is that even the most ideologically compromised forms of longing express in attenuated fashion a genuine human need, and so I would like to ask the somewhat perverse question: can nostalgia ever assist ethics?

The analysis proposed here will require rethinking common biases against nostalgia in order to see its full range of complexity. Ever since the term entered the Western lexicon in 1688, nostalgia has provided a means of expressing resistance for individuals who otherwise lacked the power to change their circumstances more directly. The first nostalgics were the ill-trained and poorly fed military conscripts of seventeenth-century Europe, taken far from their homes and forced to fight battles in which they had little or no personal stake. Nostalgia provided not only a means of expressing resentment; more importantly, as an illness, nostalgia provided in some cases the only legal way for a soldier to be granted leave from military service. According to Marcel Rinehard, even after the French Minister of War ordered the suppression of leaves for convalescence in 1793, nostalgia was still exempted.[7] This example points to the fact that nostalgia is an historical phenomenon that arises in response to a set of specific cultural, political, and economic forces. In particular, nostalgia responds to the new ideas of time and space introduced by modernity; according to Svetlana Boym, "nostalgia is rebellion against the modern idea of time, the time of history and progress. The nostalgic desires [. . .] to revisit time like space, refusing to surrender to the irreversibility of time that plagues the human condition."[8] Boym's characterization encourages a fundamental reassessment of nostalgia as a mode of interpreting experience rather than a pathology. To view one's surroundings nostalgically means to interpret the present in relation to an inaccessible or lost past. Thus, to "indulge" in nostalgia need not imply an effort to escape present circumstances or to deceive oneself about the past; rather, it can represent the conscious decision to reject the logic of modernity and what Boym refers to as the "tunnel vision" of so-called progressive ideologies. It is here that nostalgia assumes an ethical dimension for Boym and Lears: no longer a disease, nostalgia represents in the late twentieth century an existential life choice for individuals who admire ideals associated with premodern societies.

This study will ultimately suggest a somewhat different role for nostalgia in contemporary literature, arguing that it facilitates an exploration of ethical ideals in the face of disappointing circumstances. But even at this point, it should be clear why I depart from Stewart's *On Longing*. My study aspires to provide both a theoretical investigation into the uses of nostalgia and a contribution to literary history that identifies crucial features of the various threads that constitute contemporary Anglophone literature. Stewart's psychoanalytic focus leads to a dehistoricized characterization of nostalgia as "sadness without an object [. . .] the desire for desire."[9] This focus certainly illuminates the function of nostalgia in literature and culture at certain moments in time, particularly the late nineteenth century; however, her transhistorical claims overlook how the forms nostalgia takes shift in response to changing historical factors. Nostalgics pine for very specific and concrete objects throughout the seventeenth and eighteenth centuries: the homelands from which they were separated. Likewise, expressions of nostalgia in post-World War II novels are consistently portrayed as motivated by a longing for very definite objects, even if nostalgic characters and their authors do not always articulate their images of longed-for homelands in precise or consistent terms. Narrative provides the space to work out and revise these images as characters become more able to recognize their disappointments and frustrations with their present lives. Nostalgia, in other words, encourages an imaginative exploration of how present systems of social relations fail to address human needs, and the specific objects of nostalgia – lost or imagined homelands – represent efforts to articulate alternatives.

Although *Ethics and Nostalgia in the Contemporary Novel* calls for a significant rethinking of scholarly attitudes toward nostalgia, this study recognizes that the conventional opposition between memory and nostalgia has played a central role in establishing the legitimacy of contemporary Anglophone literature generally, and ethnic/minority literatures more specifically. Since the early 1980s, a number of excellent articles and books have asserted the importance of studying these literatures in large part by claiming that they make available particular kinds of experience that readers would otherwise be unable to access. Satya Mohanty offers one of the most eloquent formulations of this argument. Drawing on the tradition of philosophical realism, he argues that a genuinely multicultural curriculum is essential to gaining greater knowledge of others and ourselves. "Since our deeper ethical and aesthetic concepts are necessarily theory-laden, ideological, and culturally inflected," Mohanty writes, "the realist can argue that the best form of inquiry into the nature of value, aesthetic or ethical, will need to be comparative and cross-cultural."[10] The scholarly focus on acts of memory or recollection within literary texts has been important in this regard, and fine work has been done exploring how novels such as *Beloved* reclaim and represent experiences that have been actively or passively forgotten. If "memory" becomes the term to describe these unrecognized experiences or perceptions of the world, then "nostalgia" signifies false appropriations of these experiences or efforts to recast such experiences within Anglo-American or European cultural narratives. As Renato Rosaldo notes, Western nations have historically concealed their oppression of other populations by appropriating their experiences and representing them in sentimentalized terms. The transformation of former Southern plantations into tourist attractions and the creation of popular fables of the noble but vanishing Native American represent but two examples in the United States of what Rosaldo terms "imperialist nostalgia." Such representations of the past do not question mainstream versions of history – as acts of memory can – but legitimize them by "conceal[ing] complicity with often brutal domination."[11]

The desire by many scholars of literary and cultural studies to distinguish rigidly between "genuine" and "inauthentic" representations of experience, however, is complicated by the fact that so many contemporary novels characterize representations of the past as inevitably partial, incomplete, and often actively revisionary. In the case of *Beloved*, for example, Morrison claims that the Middle Passage represents a defining experience for African-American communities generations after the slave trade and slavery itself were outlawed. The only character to have any personal memories of the transatlantic journey, however, is Beloved, who functions simultaneously as the ghost of Sethe's murdered daughter and as an embodiment of the former slave community's collective trauma. The challenge facing Morrison's fictional community, then, is the same that she herself faces as a writer at the end of the twentieth century: to establish a sense of coherence out of a set of unfathomable experiences without recourse to personal witnesses.[12] And to the extent that narrative reconstructions are motivated by the desire, in Kathleen Brogan's words, "to re-create ethnic identity through an imaginative recuperation of the past and to press this new version of the past into the service of the present," the notion of authentic experience becomes difficult to maintain.[13] Sethe's recollections of Sweet Home, cited earlier, hardly seem "authentic" even to her; yet, the ethnic identities envisioned by the novel are shaped by these and other similar images of the past – images that are sentimental, selective, and not entirely accurate.

While neither Brogan's distinction between Morrison's "recuperative desire" and "nostalgia" nor other similar attempts to distinguish rigidly between authentic and inauthentic memories may be sustainable,[14] her impressive book, *Cultural Haunting: Ghosts and Ethnicity in Recent American Literature*, identifies two theoretical problems that will face this study. First, if *Ethics and Nostalgia in the Contemporary Novel* is to build on the work of Brogan, Mohanty, and others, then it will need to make a case for how "inauthentic" experiences of the past associated with nostalgia contribute useful knowledge that can be employed by both characters and readers to redefine present identities and values. Second, it will need to show how the authors in this study use nostalgia in their literary texts without endorsing essentialism. As Brogan suggests, reconstructions of the past can efface historical knowledge not only when they are used to conceal the experiences of particular populations but also when they oversimplify or essentialize the material they depict. Drawing on the work of Michael Fischer, Werner Sollors, and other theorists of ethnicity, Brogan argues that the development of greater historical consciousness is crucial to the formation of healthy ethnic identities. Essentialistic portrayals of identity – which she links to nostalgia – inhibit such consciousness, promoting static and homogeneous identities that never existed historically. Such reconstructions are detrimental to ethnic communities because the assertion of a timeless and unchanging essence dramatically limits the ability of individual members or groups to feel comfortable redefining ethnic identities in the face of changing social circumstances.

Roberta Rubenstein's notion that literary narratives use nostalgia to "fix" the past provides at least a partial answer to the second theoretical problem. Focusing on contemporary American women writers, Rubenstein argues that nostalgia does not necessarily lead to regressive attitudes but can in certain instances enable characters and readers alike to revise their perceptions of the past in two complementary senses. "To 'fix' something is to *secure* it more firmly in the imagination and also to *correct* – as in *revise* or *repair* – it," Rubenstein argues.[15] To take her own analysis of Morrison's fiction as an example, Rubenstein argues that novels such as *Jazz* imaginatively reconstruct and thereby "secure" collective histories that have been lost to contemporary African Americans; at the same time, Morrison's narratives open up new interpretations of these histories and thereby enable characters and readers to "revise" their own longings in ways that enable more healthy relationships. The apparently stable or fixed pasts produced by the characters' nostalgic longings are thus not in fact essentialistic because the narratives in which they appear demonstrate a self-conscious awareness that the past is continually revised in the very process of telling. Hence, Morrison and her contemporaries create narratives that endorse a kind of constructivism that sees the past as produced and reproduced through subsequent retellings.

The notion of "fixing" the past does not directly address the first theoretical problem Brogan presents, however, and it is this sense that nostalgic thinking endorses conservative social systems rather than envisioning alternatives that motivates a strong critique from certain strands of feminism. Janice Doane and Devon Hodges, for example, assert that nostalgia supports patriarchy; within literary texts, the presence of nostalgia represents "a retreat to the past in the face of what a number of writers – most of them male – perceive to be the degeneracy of American culture brought about by the rise of feminist authority."[16] More directly challenging the claims of this study, Lynne Huffer asserts in *Maternal Pasts, Feminist Futures: Nostalgia, Ethics, and the Question of Difference* that the articulation of ethical models of human relationships demands the rejection of nostalgia. Nostalgia hinders ethics because it prevents individuals from exploring new kinds of relationships that are unburdened by the history of gender exploitation. "Because nostalgia is necessarily static and unchanging in its attempt to retrieve a lost utopian space," Huffer argues, "its structure upholds the status quo."[17] Huffer's argument suggests that even if nostalgic thinking does not necessarily endorse essentialism, it cannot help to envision genuine solutions to cultural crises because it presupposes that solutions can be found in existing or past societies. Since patriarchy is an undeniable historical reality, the longing to restore an idealized past will only reassert sexist social relations.

Arguments that nostalgia necessarily inculcates amnesia or reactionary politics will be countered by reading the novels this study discusses. Huffer, however, points to what may be the most serious critique of nostalgia in contemporary Anglophone literature: the possibility that nostalgia inhibits characters, authors, and readers from gaining greater knowledge about the worlds they inhabit. If this is the case, then the very utopian premise on which many forms of nostalgia are predicated becomes questionable. Most often, nostalgics are faulted for imagining a utopian world that never existed and that could never exist in the future. These critiques, in other words, do not necessarily question whether or not it would be preferable to live in such worlds; rather, they question their authenticity and the feasibility of achieving them. Huffer, in contrast, argues that nostalgia leads individuals to imagine worlds that are not, in fact, utopian. The worlds of nostalgia, on this understanding, are simply present ones dressed in slightly different terms. The fundamental social relations and the values associated with them are actually depressingly familiar. The real danger of nostalgic narratives is that they offer readers the illusion of utopian idealism without providing knowledge of legitimate alternatives to present circumstances.

This objection is particularly important to keep in mind because all the authors explored in subsequent chapters use nostalgia to articulate their disappointment with the present. One of the central claims of this study, however, is that more utopian visions of community in their literary texts are possible *only* through nostalgic evocations of lost or nonexistent communities. This issue is most explicitly addressed in Chapter 2, which explores how the nostalgia of Antoinette Mason, the Creole protagonist of Jean Rhys's *Wide Sargasso Sea*, provides the means for Rhys to explore and ultimately articulate a vision of community prohibited by colonial ideologies of racial difference. Antoinette can understand her own longing for intimacy with a black girl named Tia only retrospectively, many years later when she is herself the victim of Rochester's need for racial purity. The implication of Rhys's novel and the others in this study is that human longing can frequently be articulated in precise terms only after the fact and in the face of disappointment. And this claim points toward an answer to the first theoretical problem Brogan presents, how "inauthentic" experiences can serve as sources of knowledge. Nostalgia provides a mode of imagining more fully what has been and continues to be absent. To the extent that it enables individuals or literary characters to articulate in clearer and more precise terms unacknowledged disappointments and frustration with present circumstances, nostalgia does provide useful knowledge about the world.

The theoretical problems this study will face, as much as the resolutions I have begun to trace out here, help to situate the novels discussed in subsequent chapters within a larger literary history. If nostalgia is an historical phenomenon that arises out of and responds to different crises over time and space, its literary use and representation should also be seen as historically inflected. Indeed, the presence and perceived function of nostalgia in Anglophone novels shifts dramatically from Victorian to modern to contemporary eras. The nineteenth-century novel gives nostalgia a distinct cultural purpose for the first time, according to Nicholas Dames; within the fictional worlds of Jane Austen, Charles Dickens, and their contemporaries, nostalgia enables "the amelioration or cancellation of the past."[18] That is, Victorian literature anticipates the so-called "crisis of memory" that preoccupies literature throughout the twentieth century, but the threat memory represents is very different. Victorian novelists are concerned with an excess of memory, not its lack. Dames compellingly explores how Victorian novels work to eliminate excessive and chaotic reminiscences by promoting a certain kind of life: "a life no longer burdened by the past, a life lived as a coherent tale, summarizable, pointed, and finally moralizable."[19] This particular form of nostalgia arises in an environment in which amnesia is not a threat, as it will be with the authors in this study. All the authors examined here insist that the cultures in which they write are dominated by amnesia, and nostalgia in their literary texts refocuses attention on what has been forgotten. Indeed, it is emblematic of this shift that the word "amnesia" is not coined until late in the nineteenth century. Excessive remembrance represents a greater threat to Victorian novelists because it complicates efforts to isolate coherent moral lessons from the past and also because it encourages individuals to dwell excessively on the past rather than plan for the future. Nostalgia enables a kind of constructive forgetting and stabilization of the past that is particularly suitable for narratives whose focus is establishing readily recognizable models of moral behavior that can be imitated by readers and applied to future situations. Put more epigrammatically, nostalgia in Victorian fiction and culture does not represent an obsession with the past but, according to Dames, the means of liberating oneself from it.

While the differences between the uses of nostalgia in high modernist and contemporary literary texts will become more fully apparent in Chapter 4 comparison of Evelyn Waugh's *Brideshead Revisited* and Kazuo Ishiguro's *The Remains of the Day*, some key distinctions can be highlighted here with reference to a statement made by Ishiguro in an interview with Brian Shaffer:

I do understand why people are against nostalgia, particularly in places like Britain and France, because nostalgia is seen here as a bad political force to the extent that it's applied to a nation's memory. [. . .] And I would go along with that to a large extent; I accept why nostalgia has a bad name in general, at least on the political and historical level. But the pure emotion of nostalgia is actually quite a valuable thing that we all feel at times. [. . .] It's something that anchors us emotionally to a sense that things should and can be repaired. We can feel our way towards a better world because we've had an experience of it; we carry some sort of distant memory of that world somewhere even though it is a flawed memory, a flawed vision.[20]

The first and most obvious thing to note about this statement is the explicit endorsement of a kind of sentimentality from which high modernism sought to distinguish itself. This is not to say that nostalgia is absent from the works of high modernism; Robert Alter, Ian Baucom, and Jeffrey Perl have made compelling cases for discerning a profoundly nostalgic strain within modernist writings in Britain and continental Europe. Modernist nostalgia is nonetheless frequently concealed by the more obvious rhetoric of iconoclasm. Even that most tradition-obsessed of modernists, T. S. Eliot, describes an attitude toward the past very different from Ishiguro's. Over the course of his career, Eliot repeatedly critiques the "emotionalism" of his Victorian predecessors including, most notably, Thomas Hardy. The correct attitude toward the past demands "a continual extinction of personality," he famously writes.[21] Eliot would have been deeply uncomfortable with Ishiguro's sense that sentimental longings could guide individuals to envision "a better world." The useful past, tradition, is available only to the select few, and to obtain it requires "great labour" and knowledge of the entire "mind of Europe."[22]

Perhaps an even more striking difference between Ishiguro and high modernists is apparent in their attitudes toward the present. Ishiguro looks to nostalgia to help "repair" the present, but makes no claim that his work can or even should establish a radical break with it. His rhetoric suggests nothing like Ezra Pound's demand for radical transformation: "I want a new civilization."[23] Nor does he provide an equivalent to Virginia Woolf's insistence that she and her fellow writers stand across a great divide from their Edwardian predecessors, a divide that is cultural as much as literary: "in or about December, 1910, human character changed. [. . .A]nd when human relations change there is at the same time a change in religion, conduct, politics, and literature."[24] Nostalgia in modernist writing, in other words, is intimately connected to the movement's iconoclastic impulses. Nostalgia in these texts marks the partial or vestigial recovery of a past that has been betrayed and effaced by bourgeois modernization. Put another way, nostalgia enables the modern artist and reader to separate themselves from the more immediate past by establishing a mediated relationship to a distant past. This more distant past may be associated with ancient civilizations, for Eliot, or early nineteenth-century country Englishness, for E. M. Forster. But in all these cases, nostalgia promises at least a temporary respite from an industrialized and homogenizing modern world. To oversimplify, if nostalgia in Victorian literature functions to liberate readers from the past, it functions in modernist literature to liberate readers from the present.

Although it will take the entirety of this study to elaborate the distinctive features of nostalgia in contemporary Anglophone literature, Ishiguro's concession about the dangers of engaging in nostalgic reminiscences alerts readers to one key aspect: the self-conscious awareness that these narratives are engaging in a potentially compromised and ideologically questionable enterprise. What is so fascinating about Ishiguro and the other authors in this study is that they seem to be quite aware of the dangers of nostalgia *and yet nonetheless make it a central part of their narratives.* Each of the novels to be studied makes it abundantly clear to readers that the lost homelands for which characters nostalgically long are deeply flawed or never even existed. Yet the novels nonetheless assert the ethical value of articulating disappointment and frustration with the present by imagining a more satisfying past. In other words, nostalgia represents a necessary and often productive form of confronting loss and displacement. Indeed, the knowledge gained from nostalgic fantasies is crucial to the ethical visions of contemporary Anglophone novelists. The engagement with the past assumes its fullest ethical dimensions for these novels when they draw upon not only memory but also nostalgia, when they claim to recover not only what should have been remembered and preserved but also relationships and communities that *could have been.*

ETHICS

Such a claim demands some immediate clarification about both the usage of the term "ethics" and the potential contribution of literature to it. Following the lead of both narrative ethicists and theorists of postmodernism, my notion of ethics does not signify normative codes of behavior or depictions of virtue. As will become apparent in Chapters 1 and 2, contemporary literature largely fails to offer a significant contribution to these more traditional notions of ethics. To this extent, I am in substantial agreement with ethicists in the Levinasean tradition who understand ethics in terms of the interactive encounters between individuals. "'Ethics,' in this alternative sense," Adam Zachary Newton writes, "signifies recursive, contingent, and interactive dramas of encounter and recognition, the sort which fiction both crystallizes and recirculates in acts of interpretive engagement."[25] Rejecting a philosophical tradition that traces from Aristotle, Kant, and Hume through Habermas most recently, this newer movement abandons the idea that individuals can or should even try to arrive at uniform and universal criteria of moral behavior through a process of rational deliberation. The rejection of normative ethics here does not imply that people are unable to gain significant knowledge about the needs of others; rather, it suggests that such knowledge is always person-specific and cannot be universalized. As such, ethical relations are continually being redefined and negotiated based on with whom one interacts. Literary narratives are ethically significant, in this context, because they can cultivate within readers greater attentiveness to their interactions with others as "interpretive engagements" concerning potentially conflicting needs and values.

The novelists in this study themselves encourage explorations of their literary texts in ethical terms. While none of them attempts to formulate a consistent system of ethics, Chinua Achebe, N. Scott Momaday, and Toni Morrison explicitly speak of the moral and ethical functions of their narratives. The novel is "a form steeped in morality," according to Achebe, and it is the novelist's task to recollect instances of past injustice and to question authority.[26] The other authors in this study make at least implicit ethical claims in their novels, for all their narratives portray characters reconstructing experiences and events that have been effaced or actively forgotten by the cultures in which they reside. To the extent that Newton's argument is correct – that ethics depends on acquiring significant knowledge about the experiences of others – the fictional reconstructions of the past portrayed by the novels in this study imply that existing cultural narratives prevent individuals from gaining the knowledge necessary to discern their responsibilities to others.

Scholarship on ethnic American literatures, in particular, has drawn on these insights to argue that fiction is ethically significant because it challenges mainstream ideas of how and what individuals know about the world; put in more theoretical terms, the memories depicted in novels challenge the epistemologies underlying institutionally endorsed histories. David Palumbo-Liu, for example, argues that memory establishes the only epistemological foundation that can provide a discourse stable enough to constitute a legitimate critique of colonial and imperial histories: "All notions of ethnic writing as revision of history point to this term [memory], for it is through memory alone, as the repository of things left out of history, that the ethnic subject can challenge history."[27] Memory is so significant to ethnic writing because it implies a more direct rapport with the past than historical narratives can provide. In this way, memory is figured to be a more genuine and authentic experience of the past than history; the material it reports, which history suppresses, appears to be the "truth" of the past. The longing to reconnect with ancestral figures depicted in so many contemporary ethnic American novels can be read in this context as describing the longing among ethnic American communities to gain knowledge about their cultural traditions and experiences that mainstream histories do not provide. The ancestor figure becomes the crucial mediator between a late imperial or postcolonial present and a precolonial past, and the reconnection with the ancestor figure enables the recovery and transmission of memory to the next generation.

The implication of such readings, that the ethical potential of fiction resides primarily in its capacity to recover and disseminate lost memories, suffers from the concerns stated earlier about the difficulty of distinguishing between authentic and inauthentic experiences. The connection between ethics and epistemology suggested by Palumbo-Liu's work, however, will be crucial to this study. The exploration of literary nostalgia in subsequent chapters focuses on its tendency to encourage exploration of unacknowledged disappointment and frustration. Mr. Stevens' nostalgic fantasies for the lost glory of the English country house in Ishiguro's *The Remains of the Day*, for example, initiate an exploration that ultimately leads Stevens to recognize his own ethical failings. Stevens' internalization of the English class structure prevents him from tolerating direct criticisms of his employer's Nazi sympathies or recognizing his own tacit support for Nazism. Only after Stevens indulges in nostalgia for the lost past is he able to recognize Lord Darlington's and his own ideological blindness, for his nostalgia foregrounds the disparity between the world as it *is* and as it *could have been*. This disparity, throughout this study, represents a significant kind of knowledge that provides the basis for the novels and their characters to envision what more ethical social relations might be. And precisely because nostalgic fantasies so often take non-threatening or conventional forms initially, individuals like Stevens gain knowledge about themselves and their world that they would otherwise have repressed.

CONTEMPORARY ANGLOPHONE LITERATURE

Following the lead of thinkers such as Michael Valdez Moses, Simon Gikandi, and Edward Said, my project does not restrict itself exclusively to either "First World" or "Third World" literatures but explores the convergences and conversations among a variety of literary traditions. Moses, in particular, makes a strong case for a study of global Anglophone literature that still preserves cultural differences. Various postcolonialisms, on his understanding, are not simply alternatives to global modernity but also significant aspects of modernity's rise and diffusion: "But if my thesis has merit," Moses writes, "then the very existence of a single and hegemonic Eurocentric conception of literature is rendered obsolete, insofar as Western literature itself becomes part of a larger body of work that is truly global, hybrid, and cosmopolitan. [. . .] As I see it, contemporary postcolonial and Third World literatures are not radical alternatives to global modernity but distinctive and extremely significant reflections of its rise and diffusion."[28] The cumulative effects of industrial development, colonialism, and globalization have established a complex web of interrelations and influences among Anglophone cultures such that the fullest appreciation of individual works depends on understanding not only immediate cultural contexts but also international ones.

If the comparative approach Moses endorses offers much promise for literary studies, it presents a difficult set of theoretical problems as well. Any project that interconnects a wide range of literary traditions inevitably risks effacing cultural particularities. This risk becomes apparent even when addressing apparently simple questions of terminology – how should the literary convergences that Moses and others notice be labeled? Should scholars even risk a label at all? Strictly temporal labels like "twentieth-century literature" are so broadly inclusive and so arbitrary in terms of dating that they appear of limited value by themselves. Terms that characterize ideological or aesthetic commitments have their problems as well – this has been demonstrated most notably with respect to the term "postmodernism." Like other recent formulations such as "postcolonialism," "globalization," and "cosmopolitanism," the term "postmodernism" is used to describe a set of economic, social, and political forces that circulate across continents and national boundaries. But as the term has gained greater usage, it has lost so much specificity that by the 1990s it was no longer even clear whether the term marked an historical period or a transhistorical tendency. As a result, a range of scholars including Anthony Appiah, Homi Bhabha, Linda Hutcheon, and Helen Tiffin have made compelling cases for the dangers of applying the label "postmodern" to authors like Achebe and Morrison; such labels, the argument goes, threaten to appropriate these authors within a tradition of Western metaphysics that has historically silenced minority and non-Western populations.[29] As a result of this critical barrage, postmodernism is disappearing from the academic lexicon and has become too fraught a term to be useful for my own analysis.

Thus, although Ursula K. Heise offers a precedent for defining the texts in this study as postmodern, my study adopts with reservations the term "contemporary Anglophone literature."[30] This selection recognizes the concerns expressed by critics of broadly inclusive labels, but it also recognizes that trying to avoid terms altogether would be too awkward and disingenuous. This study includes ethnic American, Caribbean, British, and African authors because I believe they share important concerns that speak to each other. The term "contemporary Anglophone literature" identifies some fairly basic parameters of time and language for this analysis: it covers the period immediately after World War II and ends in the 1990s. It focuses on authors whose primary literary language is English, and it also emphasizes that the interconnections between different national and ethnic literary traditions are a defining trait or concern of this period as a whole. Put another way, my choice of terminology is meant to assert this study's commitment to exploring American, British, and various postcolonial literatures not only on their own terms but also with respect to each other. There is a very definite, if sometimes conflicting, sense of modernity or the "modern experience" among the authors in this study, and they are concerned with finding alternatives to it. Since the 1960s, there has arisen a cross-cultural collection of responses to this notion that bear strong resemblances to each other, responses which I will describe as a form of nostalgia. If the authors themselves do not always acknowledge a common strain, they nonetheless all live in cultures suffused by nostalgia. Each author, in turn, has struggled with the longing for lost or imagined homelands and the extent to which it should inform his or her vision. Taken together, their literary texts represent a "strand" of contemporary Anglophone literature that becomes increasingly significant in the latter part of the century.

Chapter 1 explores the ethical significance of nostalgic homelands in these literary texts in relation to the burgeoning philosophical and social science scholarship on place. Building on Doreen Massey's crucial insight that places are not simply physical locations but particular "articulations" of a network of social relations,[31] this chapter argues that the recollection or imagination of a lost home envisions an alternative set of social relations with which individuals can identify. The imagination of place, then, translates often amorphous feelings of disappointment with the present into a concrete image of a more satisfying community. Such efforts to "rearticulate" social relations, particularly with respect to race, have been a central task of ethnic American literature, and this chapter begins with an exploration of one of the most celebrated American authors since World War II, Toni Morrison. Morrison's novels envision a process of consolidating the various nostalgic longings of her fictional African-American communities into a shared idea of how social relations could have been organized differently, and this process provides a model for transforming race relations more generally in the contemporary United States. The chapter then proceeds to claim that similar efforts at rearticulation are apparent across a spectrum of contemporary Anglophone novelists from the British Ian McEwan to the Jamaican-born Joan Riley. Taken together, these novelists point to a broader shift away from modern Western philosophy's ethical preoccupations – individual autonomy, rational deliberation, and freedom from social mores – toward an understanding of ethics in terms of an ongoing process of negotiating among conflicting visions of community.

Chapter 2 explores more closely the potential contributions of nostalgic narratives to ethics. One of the central challenges ethics has faced since the Kantian era is to establish compelling moral claims for the victims of post-Enlightenment ideas of universal human "Progress." Jean Rhys' *Wide Sargasso Sea* intriguingly asserts that nostalgia addresses this problem by encouraging retrospective reflections on how colonial policies and narratives have failed to address human needs. Rhys is not alone in proposing such a solution; similar claims have been a central feature of Caribbean literature since the 1950s, and this chapter argues that nostalgic fantasies play an important role in overcoming internalized beliefs about the colonial project and its vision of progress. The characteristic tendency of nostalgia to interweave a disappointing present and a tantalizing, if unrealized and imaginary, past can foreground experiences of suffering effaced by colonial narratives. Rhys, V. S. Naipaul, Paule Marshall, and other Caribbean authors use nostalgia to create what Paul Ricoeur calls a "parallel history of victimisation," although the ethical focus of these novels differs significantly from his. Whereas Ricoeur focuses on "resuscitating and reanimating the unkept promises of the past," Rhys, Naipaul, and Marshall draw attention to unfulfilled promises associated with an imagined past.[32]

Chapter 3 explores the imagined pasts created by literary texts in relation to recent debates among historians over the significance of what has been called "counterfactual historical speculation" or, more prosaically, historical narratives based on hypothetical scenarios of what could have been. Native American novelists including N. Scott Momaday, James Welch, Leslie Marmon Silko, and Linda Hogan use literary narratives to interweave fragmentary memories, historical documents, and imagination in ways that resonate with the efforts of historians and literary scholars such as Edith Wyschogrod and Gary Saul Morson to recover a richer sense of the contingency of the past by discerning alternative paths that historical events could have taken. These efforts to "sideshadow" history or to recover the "negated possibles" of the past associate ethics with freedom from deterministic historical narratives. Momaday, Welch, Silko, and Hogan likewise challenge the determinism regarding the "decline" of Native American cultures posited by both mainstream American and certain tribal histories. Motivated by the sense that the last generation to have personally witnessed many tribal rituals is dying even as he is beginning his career as a novelist, Momaday seeks to build solidarity among diverse Native American populations by establishing within narrative a connection that never existed historically to tribal sacred sites. His redefinition of identity in terms of imagined rather than historical tribal affiliations has inspired two generations of Native American authors, even as later authors have increasingly defined ethnic identity in more explicitly politicized terms. This chapter concludes by arguing that Native American literature and poststructuralist historiography provide important correctives to each other: novels such as *House Made of Dawn* suggest that poststructuralist terminologies can occlude significant historical and cultural variations among minority groups; at the same time, Wyschogrod clarifies the risks of essentialistic identity categories employed by many Native American authors.

While the first three chapters focus on literary uses of nostalgia in relation to theoretical discourses on place, ethics, and historiography, Chapter 4 focuses on how contemporary Anglophone novels have used nostalgia to critique other nostalgic narratives circulating in culture and politics. This chapter reads the revival of the "estate novel" by Kazuo Ishiguro as a critical response to the nostalgia for past imperial glory that suffuses British postwar politics and culture. Since the seventeenth century, the English country house has served as metaphor for a good society; Ishiguro's revival of the estate novel genre critiques the nostalgic vision of Great Britain promoted by Thatcherism and earlier examples of this genre, such as Evelyn Waugh's *Brideshead Revisited*. This chapter argues that the depiction of the decline of the estate in both Waugh and Ishiguro challenges the thick ethical concepts associated with British national identity.[33] By appealing to a shared if imagined past, *Brideshead Revisited* and *The Remains of the Day* construct alternative visions of a shared national and ethical future – nostalgia, in other words, enables a "recovery" of the past that redefines the lost *ethos* of community. Ishiguro's sense of *ethos* contrasts with that presented by both Thatcherism and *Brideshead Revisited*, however; rejecting their essentialism, he emphasizes instead a spirit of accommodation and tolerance of difference.

The final chapter of this study takes up one of the central critiques of nostalgia: its tendency to encourage passivity and xenophobia. This critique is apparent, for example, in the "trauma theory" of Cathy Caruth, Dominick LaCapra, and Shoshana Felman which suggests that nostalgia represents a dangerous reaction to collective trauma, leading individuals to indulge in fantasies of the past rather than to confront crises facing them. This chapter argues that although the term "collective trauma" is particularly apropos in the postcolonial or late imperial context to describe the recurring cycle of violence and oppression produced by the colonial encounter, the works of Nigerian authors including Chinua Achebe, Wole Soyinka, and Ben Okri demonstrate a more positive attitude toward nostalgia and its role in resolving debates over national values and ideals. Struggling to confront the history of ethnic and religious violence since independence, these authors find the simultaneously concrete and vague character of nostalgia appealing. The articulation of the nation as it could have been provides an image of loss that can be shared across tribal, ethnic, and religious lines even if the conflicting parties cannot agree entirely on what the image itself signifies. The nostalgic image of nation provides the basis for establishing some shared goals for the future, and this chapter explores the extent to which the literary narratives of Achebe and Soyinka, in particular, might address the traumatic histories that have heretofore fragmented and divided their nation.

Ethics and Nostalgia in the Contemporary Novel, then, shifts the critical focus away from debates over the politics of literary texts engaged in reconstructing histories effaced by imperialism – debates that dominated literary studies in the 1990s. Instead, this study focuses on the ethics inspired by the most sentimental and "inauthentic" images produced by these texts. Despite their different origins, all the writers in this study use nostalgia to envision some degree of solidarity for communities struggling with displacement and cultural differences among their members, and this strategy requires closer examination. My own sense is that nostalgia can offer a definite though fraught contribution to ethics, and the preoccupation with roots, return, and lost pasts in contemporary Anglophone novels should neither be dismissed as reactionary nor be read in the idealized terms that ethnic studies sometimes encourages. The depictions of imagined homelands in these novels represent an effort less to recover a body of ancestral wisdom effaced by imperialism than to translate a community's various longings and aspirations into a set of common goals and ideals based on an image of the world as it could have been.

CHAPTER I

Narratives of return: locating ethics in the age of globalization

When it comes to being ethical, there is no escaping the imperative of place.

— Edward S. Casey, *Getting Back into Place*

Where I was before I came here, that place is real. It's never going away. Even if the whole farm — every tree and grass blade of it dies. The picture is still there and what's more, if you go there — you who never was there — if you go there and stand in the place where it was, it will happen again; it will be there for you, waiting for you. So, Denver, you can't never go there. Never. Because even though it's all over — over and done with — it's going to always be there waiting for you.

— Toni Morrison, *Beloved*

In the age of supersonic travel and virtual highways, place has reemerged as a central social and philosophical concern. Or one might at least get this impression from scanning the academic book lists in the humanities and social sciences since the early 1990s. A term previously dismissed as embodying stasis and conservative claims of authenticity now graces the titles of an impressive range of texts with widely varying politics and methodologies. Philosopher Edward S. Casey's *Getting Back into Place*, cultural geographer Doreen Massey's *Space, Place and Gender*, literary scholar Ian Baucom's *Out of Place*, and anthropologists Akhil Gupta and James Ferguson's edited volume *Culture, Power, Place* represent only a small sample of this phenomenon.

If these studies are taken at their word, the recent prominence of place in scholarly discourses does not represent simply another academic fad but a response to a global shift in how individuals relate to the locations they inhabit, traverse, and imagine. Indeed, place is cast as a period-defining concept by a range of studies that cannot otherwise agree even on a label for the period itself. Anthony Giddens identifies the recent interest in the spatial organization of social relations as a feature and consequence

20

of modernity; Fredric Jameson, in contrast, identifies it as a feature of postmodernity and its shift away from modernity's preoccupation with time; Massey associates it with neither modernity nor postmodernity but globalization.[1] All three concur, however, that the political, social, and economic forces that arise after World War II alter how places are perceived, making it increasingly difficult to define place in terms of "timeless identities" or a stable heritage. Developments in travel, electronic media, and capitalism now mean that locations are shaped more than ever by physically distant forces. As a result, space is increasingly defined as a web of overlapping networks of social relations spread across a broad range of locations, and places represent particular "articulations" of these networks, to use Massey's term (5). Challenging the consensus of modern philosophy and political theory, this more recent characterization highlights the dynamic rather than static qualities of places – their potential to take on multiple and even conflicting associations in people's minds.

The redefinition of space and place has been motivated largely by the desire to challenge dominant forms of social relations with respect to class, race, and gender. Massey, for example, argues that her work is, in political terms, anti-essentialist; her motivations for reconceptualizing space come from a desire to challenge how gender is typically defined and used to limit the power of women. According to Massey, all social relations are organized spatially, and gender exploitation is possible only because women have historically been relegated to a limited range of spaces, most of which are associated with domesticity. By highlighting how characterizations of the "woman's sphere" have normalized the uncompensated labor of childrearing and other domestic duties demanded of women, Massey hopes to encourage more egalitarian social reforms or at least to render problematic essentialistic conceptions of place. For claims that a place "belongs" for all time to a particular nationality, ethnicity, or gender can be sustained only by asserting that both the defining characteristics of a particular place and the identity categories of those who claim it (or who are bound to it) are stable and unchanging.

The political potential of the "spatial turn" in the post-World War II era, however, is tempered by a nagging question: to what extent is this paradigm shift an actual or idealized phenomenon? Massey herself has had to admit that her theory runs counter to political developments. "It is not being posited here that this is how places *are* currently seen (the kinds of defensive and exclusivist place-loyalties which currently abound immediately give the lie to this)," she writes. "But it is being argued that it is how places *could* be seen, and that were this to be the case then certain political arguments might be shifted" (121). The political reality, as Massey herself notes, is that the 1980s heralded in a reemergence of exclusivist claims to place across the globe. This same recognition has led less sanguine thinkers including Jameson and David Harvey to conclude that the political potential of space may be largely overstated. "Place-bound politics," Harvey contends, may be alluring but is ultimately counterproductive to progressive political movements.

While Harvey's concerns are valid, the promise of altering exploitative social relations by redefining how place is perceived remains compelling. Indeed, this promise helps to explain the images of idealized homes and imagined homelands that currently fill contemporary literature and cinema. Rather than dismissing them as kitsch or escapist fantasies, Massey's theory implies that such images can encourage a critical exploration of what form more egalitarian social relations might take. If places are social constructions that are continually in the process of being rearticulated, then even idealized or imagined articulations have the potential to redefine how places and the social relations that compose them can be understood. Even the most personal and intimate of places, the home, can function as a site for such explorations. "Home is that place [. . .] where one discovers new ways of seeing reality, frontiers of difference," bell hooks argues; as such, the process of envisioning a healthy "homeplace" invites individuals to reflect on how they perceive and interact with others.[2] Or, to put hooks' claim in somewhat different terms, every conception of place posits an ethics – an idea of how humans might interact with each other and their environment. And the identification with physically remote or imaginary places often implies the desire to redefine the ethics associated with the localities an individual inhabits.

This chapter, then, will explore the ethical significance of lost or imagined homelands in contemporary Anglophone literature, with particular reference to Toni Morrison's *Beloved* (1987), Ian McEwan's *Black Dogs* (1992), and Joan Riley's *The Unbelonging* (1985). Although these novels were written by authors from different cultural backgrounds – African-American, British, and Jamaican – they demonstrate a common interest in the relationship between place and ethics. The first two novels demonstrate even greater affinities, provocatively linking ethical insight to a process of retrospectively reflecting on places with which characters previously identified in the light of disappointing present conditions. Only in the face of disappointment can characters clearly articulate their needs and desires as they perceive the difference between the world as it *is* and as it *could have been*, and images of lost or even imagined places provide a means for individuals to express this difference. *Beloved, Black Dogs*, and, to a lesser extent, *The Unbelonging* ultimately call for a redefinition of ethics in terms of an ongoing communal process of negotiating among various and often conflicting needs – needs that are expressed through recalling or imagining past homeplaces.

THE REEMERGENCE OF PLACE AND ITS RELATION TO ETHICS

The etymological connection between place and ethics dates back to the initial coinage of the latter word. When Aristotle formed the term *ta ēthika*, "ethics," he derived it from Homer's word *ēthea*, which designated the "haunts" or "habitats" frequented by animals before their capture.[3] Homer was fascinated by the compulsion that horses felt to return to their old haunts despite efforts to domesticate them. Aristotle saw in this depiction a lesson about moral development: habits are formed at an early age and are very difficult to change thereafter. The effort to shape character and cultivate moral virtue, then, becomes the task of the science of ethics, and Aristotle perceived the perfection of virtue to depend on the cultivation of correct habits.

With his neologism, Aristotle cemented an idea that had been in circulation at least since Herodotus: namely, that an individual's place of birth shapes the way he or she will act; or, to use the more current understanding of the word *ēthos* (the singular form of *ēthea*), place molds an individual's "character." Herodotus previously appropriated the Homeric term *ēthea* in his effort to describe the places where particular barbarian communities belong – a description subsequently applied to all human communities.[4] The idea that individuals are profoundly influenced by their place of birth was apparent in not only ancient Greek but also Roman thinking. As Eugene Victor Walter notes, within the Latin tradition places were understood to be inhabited by spirits, *genius loci*, that act as guardians of particular localities and embody the distinctive characteristics of the people who live there.[5] These spirits had sufficient reality and independence that even as conquering Roman armies would absorb foreign lands, they would respect local divinities – often constructing votive tablets in their honor.

If the connection between place and ethics is no longer widely familiar, this is in large part because such a connection is incompatible with the economic, political, and philosophical ideals of modernity.[6] The economic incompatibility is probably most familiar to readers: the shift in the eighteenth century toward increasingly industrialized economies demanded that rural peasants be willing to move away from their places of birth toward urban centers, and the need to circulate capital in ever more efficient and profitable ways demanded, in Marx's famous phrase, "the annihilation of space by time." This explanation understands the ruptured connection between place and ethics primarily in exploitative terms. The rejection of place, however, is also crucial to efforts by philosophers since the Enlightenment to conceive of a universal ethics. To insist, as Immanuel Kant does, that the basic principle of ethics is to "act on a maxim which at the same time contains in itself its own universal validity for every rational being" requires an understanding of human nature that characterizes individuals as defined by a transcultural rationality, not by their place of origin or home.[7] The possibility that people from different regions or places might have very different characters, as Aristotle and ancient Greek philosophy suggested, presents an implicit challenge to Kant's criterion of universal validity. Kantian reason assumes not only that rationality itself is consistent across time and place but also that the basic ideals of human nature arrived at through reasoning will have universal appeal.[8] In this context, the habits inculcated by place do not contribute to moral reasoning and might even present an impediment: individuals might rely on habits rather than engaging their faculty of reason.

An attachment to place further conflicts with modern ideas of ethics because it limits the basic human capacity for emancipation. As Enlightenment thinkers increasingly valorized freedom as a universal and inalienable right, it was defined explicitly against a notion of social constraint associated with place. "From the Enlightenment on," Zygmunt Bauman argues, "it has been seen as a commonsensical truth that human emancipation, the releasing of genuine human potential, required that the bounds of communities be broken and individuals set free from the circumstances of their birth."[9] Place limits individuals by locating them within a community; freedom from place, on this understanding, implies the freedom to redefine oneself according to the pattern of one's own making. To realize one's fullest potential and "true" character demands separation from *ēthos* – the character imposed upon one by place.

Literary modernism largely concurred with this perception, suggesting that the courage to act ethically presupposes the rejection of habitat and habit. Dr. Aziz, in E. M. Forster's *A Passage to India*, for example, attributes Mr. Fielding's courage to his rootlessness, for men like him "had nothing to lose," while Aziz himself belongs to "a tradition which bound him."[10] Men like Aziz are depicted as examples of bad faith because they allow their habits and social conditioning to guide them rather than making conscious ethical decisions. The truly heroic modernist figure peels away whatever social or religious baggage might compromise the development of the self, uncovering individual authenticity beneath layers of habit and mores. James Joyce's Stephen Dedalus is the exemplary modern protagonist, then, in his choice of "silence, exile, and cunning" over "my home, my fatherland or my church."[11] Dedalus is heroic because he departs from tradition and the places that constrain or *characterize* him.

The modernist tendency to reject a connection between place and ethics persists to this day in much philosophy and cultural criticism. Many recent thinkers associate place with puerile sentimentality, mob loyalty, or fascist mythology. These discussions typically consider fascism to be the necessary end of an ethics of place, suggesting that place represents an "ominous utopia" that instills xenophobia.[12] Ethical thought is stifled by place, according to this line of thinking, because it fixes or calcifies individual identity. And so time rather than place is said to hold the possibility for ethics. "While place is dogmatic," Michel de Certeau asserts, "the coming back of time restores an ethics."[13] Because space is associated with stasis, individuals who define themselves in terms of particular places are perceived to lack the dynamism necessary to reject dogmatic beliefs and codes of behavior. Indeed, metaphorical and even literal dislocation is seen to be the necessary first step toward genuine ethical consciousness. For ethics is understood to depend on a rational and, above all, free individual will. Hence, dislocation becomes the necessary precondition for rational choice. In Ernesto Laclau's words, "dislocation is the very form of possibility. [. . .] Dislocation is the very form of freedom."[14]

Even among the theorists most responsible for the reemergence of place as a concept worthy of study, there is a sense that they are writing against an entrenched orthodoxy. Although the renewed interest in place can be traced back to Michel Foucault in the late 1960s – and to a lesser degree to Gaston Bachelard in the 1950s and Martin Heidegger some years earlier – as late as 1989 Edward Soja lamented the lack of serious academic attention to place: "Although others joined Foucault to urge a rebalancing of this prioritization of time over space," Soja writes, "no hegemonic shift has yet occurred to allow the critical eye – or the critical I – to see spatiality with the same acute depth of vision that comes with a focus on *durée*. [. . .] Space still tends to be treated as fixed, dead, undialectical; time as richness, life, dialectic, the revealing context for critical social theorization."[15] Soja's commentary reveals that the academic dismissal of place comes from the enduring perception that it cannot enable individuals or communities to redefine dominant social relations. This perception does not represent a fundamental shift away from the Greek and Roman perceptions of place; rather, it demonstrates a high degree of continuity of thinking. Place is still associated with habits, particularity, and fairly stable characteristics. What has changed is the attitude toward this understanding of place, away from seeing it as something to be respected and often admired to seeing it as something to be dismissed, rejected, or feared.

The reemerging interest in place, then, has been met with a certain dismay and resignation particularly among Marxian scholars, who sense that it connotes a flight from large-scale political movements. Laclau explicitly opposes space and politics: "Politics and space are antinomic terms."[16] Jameson paints a similar, if more nuanced, picture. He notes that the rise of postmodernism and its spatial preoccupation came in response to the failures of 1960s utopian politics.[17] While Harvey is more willing to recognize the existence of so-called "place-bound politics" than either Laclau or Jameson, he finds it to be sadly misguided and ineffectual.[18] Harvey argues that since the 1960s, oppositional movements have shifted away from organizing on the national or transnational scale and focused instead on much more local or regional support bases. The problem that he perceives in this shift is that it is far more appealing than effective. In *The Condition of Postmodernity* and subsequent work, Harvey claims that it is much easier for oppositional movements to dominate place than what he calls "universal fragmented space."[19] In other words, local or regional movements are much more likely to find causes that win support than national or international movements, but this focus on relatively easier gains tends to surrender larger political arenas to multinational corporations and other unsympathetic institutions. To concentrate political activism around a select number of places limits the possibility of mobilizing enough political power to make real change. Hence, Harvey concludes, "Place-bound politics appeals even though such a politics is doomed to failure."[20]

PRIMAL PLACES AND TONI MORRISON'S "BELOVED"

If the literary texts in this study call for a significant rethinking of the relationship between ethics and place, many concur with Harvey's assessment that place has limited political value, at least with respect to the large-scale terms that interest him. This is apparent in one of the most critically acclaimed works of contemporary Anglophone literature, Toni Morrison's *Beloved.* The closest thing to a large-scale political mobilization the novel presents would be the weekly gatherings of African Americans at the Clearing, where the entire community responds to Baby Suggs' "call." The gatherings blend elements of Christian revival, celebration, and group therapy through a mechanism that Maggie Sale describes in terms of traditional African-American "call-and-response" patterns.[21] It is significant to note, however, that whatever power the participants find in this ceremony, it is very much place-bound. The gatherings fail to mobilize individuals to act communally elsewhere or even to prevent outside forces from harming community members. When schoolteacher comes to claim the runaway Sethe, who is the daughter-in-law of Baby Suggs, no one in the community seeks to prevent him or to warn Sethe. The Clearing as a political unit breaks down shortly thereafter, when Baby Suggs refuses to continue the call. The social structure established by the "call-and-response" model proves, in this instance at least, to be fragile and dependent on the "caller" for perpetuation.[22]

Despite the apparent failure of the meetings at the Clearing to inspire political activism, Sethe recalls this place at three significant junctures in the novel as she deliberates over what course of action she should take:

Sethe wanted to be there now. At the least to listen to the spaces that the long-ago singing had left behind. At the most to get a clue from her husband's dead mother as to what she should do with her sword and shield now, dear Jesus, now nine years after Baby Suggs, holy, proved herself a liar, dismissed her great heart and lay in the keeping-room bed roused once in a while by a craving for color and not for another thing.[23]

"Too thick?" she said, thinking of the Clearing where Baby Suggs' commands knocked the pods off horse chestnuts. "Love is or it ain't. Thin love ain't love at all." (164)

For Sethe it was as though the Clearing had come to her with all its heat and simmering leaves, where the voices of women searched for the right combination, the key, the code, the sound that broke the back of words. Building voice upon voice until they found it, and when they did it was a wave of sound wide enough to sound deep water and knock the pods off chestnut trees. It broke over Sethe and she trembled like the baptized in its wash. (261)

The first quotation appears after Sethe physically returns to the Clearing, haunted by the recently gained knowledge that her missing husband Halle had gone insane decades before. Shortly after recalling the gatherings that once occurred there, she decides to commit herself to a new life with Paul D. Sethe recalls the Clearing again in the second quotation as she argues with Paul D over the legitimacy of murdering her child in order to prevent her from ever experiencing slavery; afterwards, Sethe decides to break all ties with the world outside of 124, including Paul D. Finally, Sethe recalls the Clearing again at the climax of the novel, as a group of thirty women come to 124 to exorcise Beloved; after recalling the Clearing this last time, she attacks the white abolitionist Mr. Bodwin in the false belief that he is schoolteacher coming back again to claim his former slaves. Each of these recollections occurs just before significant shifts in Sethe's behavior, and, as the first quotation suggests, the connection between Sethe's memories of place and her actions are not coincidental. Sethe's longing "to get a clue from her husband's dead mother as to what she should do" suggests a belief that the memories associated with the Clearing could somehow provide ethical guidance.

How such memories might provide guidance is by no means obvious. The memories associated with the Clearing have no direct bearing on Sethe's romantic life either in the past or present, so her memories would not provide explicit models for romantic relationships either to emulate or to avoid. bell hooks' argument regarding the political significance of "homeplaces" is partially helpful. "Whatever the shape and direction of black liberation struggle [. . .]," hooks argues, "domestic space has been a crucial site for organizing, for forming political solidarity."[24] But if the gatherings at the Clearing provided an environment in which community members could reclaim their subjectivities and the dignity denied them in other locations, which hooks sees as the basis of political solidarity, Sethe does not perceive the Clearing as an entirely safe environment. As the first quotation above suggests, her memories of the idyllic possibilities offered by the Clearing are inextricably linked to subsequent memories of Baby Suggs abandoning the very hope she promised to others. And when Sethe returns to the Clearing years after the gatherings have ended, she is attacked by a malignant spirit whom she associates initially with Baby Suggs. Yet Sethe continues to recall the Clearing even after this experience.

Sethe herself provides little indication about the ethical potential of the Clearing, for she offers conflicting versions of why she even goes. The first quotation suggests that Sethe initially feels that her physical return to this place will enable her to commune with Baby Suggs' spirit. If this were the consistent reason Sethe offers, then readers might conclude that place is ethically significant to the degree that it enables an individual to appeal to an external ethical authority for direct advice and guidance. But only two paragraphs later, Sethe sees herself on a very different mission: "Yet it was to the Clearing that Sethe determined to go – to pay tribute to Halle" (89). Ten pages later, Sethe will change her mind again about her rationale for returning to the Clearing: "she wanted Paul D. [. . .] More than commemorating Halle, that is what she had come to the Clearing to figure out, and now it *was* figured" (99). The fluidity of Sethe's rationales suggests that any account of an "ethics of place" needs to recognize that a particular place has multiple and shifting associations; the modernist account of place as static and homogeneous, in other words, provides little guidance for understanding the ethical vision of *Beloved*.

Edward S. Casey's work on the philosophical history of place provides an important clue for understanding Morrison's novel. Reflecting on the devastating consequences of modernity's rejection of place, he argues:

we rarely pause to consider how frequently people refer back to a certain place of origin as to an exemplar against which all subsequent places are implicitly to be measured. [. . .] To lack a primal place is to be "homeless" indeed, not only in the literal sense of having no permanently sheltering structure but also as being without any effective means of orientation in a complex and confusing world.[25]

According to this idea, the memories associated with a "primal place" establish a set of ideals or imply a model for social relationships against which subsequent life situations are measured. Sethe recalls her own primal place, the Clearing, when she recognizes that her current life situation is unsatisfactory. If the Clearing models very different kinds of relationships from the one she contemplates with Paul D, it nonetheless establishes what she hopes to gain from successful relationships. Sethe sees in a relationship with Paul D the possibility of restoring the freedom offered by the Clearing to express the whole range of human emotions, including sorrow and despair. For Paul D is described as a person with whom painful emotions might be shared: "he had become the kind of man who could walk into a house and make the women cry. Because with him, in his presence, they could" (17).

Although Casey himself recalls the Aristotelian connection between place and ethics, his conception departs significantly from classical Greek sources. The idea that "primal places" provide a model of a social network that guides individuals in their subsequent relationships differs considerably from the idea that an individual's place of birth establishes defining habits or character. Perhaps more radically, Casey's description of place as providing an "exemplar" suggests that individuals are not bound to return to their *ēthea*. Whereas Odysseus must leave Calypso's island and forsake immortality, security, and an eternally beautiful bride simply because it is not his homeland Ithaca, the individuals Casey describes would not necessarily feel compelled to make the same choice. Homer's Odysseus can only be "at home" in one location in the world because place is tied to physical locality; Casey's argument implies that a contemporary Odysseus might be "at home" in any number of localities because place now refers to networks of social relations that can be extended or reproduced in other locations.

Casey senses that efforts to recall or imagine "primal places" in adulthood do not necessarily imply a desire to restore lost childhood homes, and this helps to explain why Sethe might identify with the Clearing even after Baby Suggs gives up on the promise associated with it. The idea of primal places as exemplars suggests that such locations are models against which subsequent places are judged, but they do not necessarily represent a utopian "best of all possible worlds." The ideal of a community associated with a primal place can still provide an implicit model even if the ideal never materializes as a reality. This is evident in Sethe's attitude toward the Clearing. Neither the failure of the people who gather there to defend her against schoolteacher nor the failure of the gatherings themselves to provide a sustained and longlasting sense of solidarity is attributed to the Clearing itself, in Sethe's mind; not even Baby Suggs' recanting diminishes the ideal of community that orients Sethe's actions. Rather, these moments are seen as specific instances of people betraying an ideal. Baby Suggs proves herself "a liar," but the promise provided by the Clearing is not a lie.

Sethe begins to glimpse the possibility of redefining her most basic attitudes toward herself and others during the gatherings that occurred there; she later recalls, "Bit by bit, at 124 and in the Clearing, along with the others, she had claimed herself. Freeing yourself was one thing; claiming ownership of that freed self was another" (95). The gatherings themselves cannot ultimately provide the relationships for which Sethe is now able to long, however, evidenced by her obsessive attachment to the ghost of her dead child. But the Clearing does provide for her a concrete image of what "claiming ownership" of oneself might look like, and this enables her to enter into a more fulfilling relationship with Paul D, who helps her to discover finally that she and not Beloved is her "best thing" (272).

Sethe's growth over the novel emphasizes a point about place that is implicit in Casey's theory: individuals can shift which place becomes "primal" or even identify with multiple "primal places." This is most readily apparent in the case of Sethe. As noted earlier, one of the first places that influences Sethe's ethics is Sweet Home. Because Sweet Home is associated with a past that can always return at any given moment, Sethe chooses to remain in 124 despite its malignant attitude toward her. To move to a different place would risk precisely what she warns Denver against. Immediately before she warns Denver against going to Sweet Home, Sethe insists to her daughter that places contain memories that can be recalled by anyone who occupies them: "If a house burns down, it's gone, but the place – the picture of it – stays, and not just in my rememory, but out there, in the world" (36). Sethe's fear is that another place might have even more malignant memories than 124, and this attitude toward place shapes her attitudes toward relationships. Her initial reluctance to form a romantic relationship with Paul D is guided by her identification with Sweet Home as her primal place. For as long as Sweet Home rather than the Clearing serves as the place against which all her subsequent experiences are measured, Sethe will avoid relationships, believing that "the future was a matter of keeping the past at bay. The 'better life' she believed she and Denver were living was simply not that other one" (42). Only after she is able to identify more fully with the Clearing is she able to rethink her commitments and to pursue relationships outside of her nuclear family. Much of the struggle in *Beloved* and the other literary texts in this study is over precisely this: which place should function as an ethical orientation for individuals.

SITUATING ETHICS

The understanding of place presented here suggests that literary texts like *Beloved* qualify the Levinasean model of ethics described in this study's introduction by drawing attention to the ways in which "intersubjective encounters" are shaped by place. Various localities have distinct sets of associations and memories for individuals that inform how they see themselves and their relationships to others. As a result, the particular needs and longings of an individual cannot be understood except with reference to the places by which they define themselves or are defined. Baby Suggs, for example, cannot understand why her son would bother to take on the extra work to purchase her freedom until she crosses into free territory. This shift in defining place shifts her perception of self: "What for? What does a sixty-odd-year-old slavewoman who walks like a three-legged dog need freedom for? [But] when she stepped foot on free ground she could not believe that

Halle knew what she didn't [. . .] that there was nothing like it in this world" (141).

Likewise, the relationship between Sethe and Paul D cannot be understood without reference to the space they occupy, 124. As noted earlier, Sethe is initially very reluctant to enter into a romantic relationship with Paul D – a reluctance that can be overcome only after she shifts the primal place with which she identifies. But the place she currently occupies, 124, also needs to be transformed into an environment that is more accommodating to such a relationship. One of Paul D's first acts is to chase away temporarily the ghost that haunts 124. Before this act, the two are unable to share their feelings for each other; simply by reminding them of the presence of the ghost, Denver inhibits the potential intimacy between Sethe and Paul D: "'We have a ghost in here,' she said, and it worked. They were not a twosome any more" (13). Immediately after Paul D banishes the ghost from 124, he and Sethe walk up to her bedroom to consummate the beginning of their relationship.

Places shape intersubjective encounters in *Beloved* because each individual's attitude toward place shapes his or her values more generally. From his very first conversation in the novel, Paul D establishes an attitude toward place that suggests an unwillingness to be defined or restrained by a single location. "If a Negro got legs he ought to use them," Paul D reflects. "Sit down too long, somebody will figure out a way to tie them up" (10). This unwillingness to be associated with any single location reflects, of course, the anxiety of an ex-slave, someone who has had space defined for him. Wandering becomes associated with the ideal of freedom; remaining stationary is associated with captivity, even when Paul D is reflecting on the possibility of a romantic relationship. Hence, Paul D's unwillingness to risk captivity shapes the degree of emotional commitment he will make in his relationships. This is apparent in his nervous reflections about Sethe's commitment to Denver:

Risky, thought Paul D, very risky. For a used-to-be-slave woman to love anything that much was dangerous, especially if it was her children she had settled on to love. The best thing, he knew, was to love just a little bit; everything, just a little bit, so when they broke its back, or shoved it in a croaker sack, well, maybe you'd have a little love left over for the next one. (45)

The inability of Sethe and Paul D to resolve their differences stems in part from their conflicting attitudes toward place. This becomes most apparent during their argument over why Sethe murdered her child. In response to Paul D's assertion that her emotional commitment is too strong, that her love is "too thick," Sethe appeals to an ethical principle that reflects her identification with the Clearing: "'Too thick?' she said, thinking of the Clearing where Baby Suggs' commands knocked the pods off horse chestnuts. 'Love is or it ain't. Thin love ain't love at all.'" (164).

Sethe's association of her murderous act with memories of the Clearing is significant because it is a space with which Paul D has no familiarity. Hence, he is unable to draw upon it for guidance. Nor would he be likely to do so, given his unwillingness to identify himself with a single location. As a result, their ethics are very differently oriented, though both of them would assert that the ideal of freedom is a foundational value. Indeed, this shared value of freedom comes largely from having shared the same space in which freedom was denied, Sweet Home. Much of their intimacy early in the novel stems from having lived in and been defined by the same place. Because they associate freedom in their later lives with very different places, however, the ideal of freedom is achieved through very different kinds of acts: wandering for Paul D and remaining away from Sweet Home for Sethe.

Thus, the relationship between Sethe and Paul D fails not so much because they have conflicting values as because these values are shaped in very different ways by the places with which the characters identify. This qualification to the Levinasean ethical model finds a philosophical parallel with Casey's claim that place situates values. Extending his argument why orienting oneself with respect to place might be ethically useful, Casey asserts that "[p]laces embody values; better yet, they *situate* them."[26] Abstract values such as empathy, caring, freedom, and altruism take on very specific and unique valences as they are associated with particular places. Individuals perceive the significance of these values in their everyday lives because these values apply to their immediate surroundings and because the consequences of upholding or neglecting them have concrete, observable effects. Sethe saw in the gatherings that occurred at the Clearing a particular way in which freedom might be lived out, and this defines or "situates" for her what freedom should mean in other aspects of her life. Her infanticide, then, is seen as a means of fulfilling this ideal in a very tragic situation: when the choice is between seeing her child grow up at Sweet Home or die by her hand, death appears to offer more freedom.

Paul D's failure to articulate a viable alternative solution is a consequence of his general unwillingness to identify himself with place. According to Casey's argument, Paul D's attitude should cause him to experience difficulty in situating his values. This difficulty becomes apparent in his argument with Sethe. In response to Sethe's very concrete understanding of freedom, Paul D's claims become increasingly abstract. When Sethe demands that he provide an alternative solution to murdering her child, he founders. "There could have been a way. Some other way," he stammers (165). When she persists in making him apply his abstract values to create a specific solution, he retreats into making general pronouncements: "You got two feet, Sethe, not four." While the statement itself provides a distinct ethical criterion for a solution – something like "act in ways consistent with conventional human morality" – the statement itself is so absurdly abstract that it would be difficult to imagine how it should be applied.

This tendency toward abstraction on Paul D's part is reflected in his relationship to place. Immediately after he speaks these lines, the text notes that "and right then a forest sprang up between them; trackless and quiet" (165). Because Paul D's statement makes no attempt to reach out to Sethe or to understand "where she is coming from," to borrow the cliché, they are separated by the metaphorical "forest." The text does not suggest that Paul D is attempting to oppose the values associated with the forest against the values Sethe associates with the Clearing. The forest is described as "between them," signifying that it is an undefined space with which neither identifies.[27] In other words, Paul D's condemnation is not grounded in a deeply felt conception of place or belief system; as a result, Paul D himself does not identify with the ethical claims associated with the statement or even understand them. The text emphasizes this fact in the very next line: "Later he would wonder what made him say it. [. . .] How fast he had moved from his shame to hers" (165). Much of Paul D's subsequent ethical growth, as Satya Mohanty aptly suggests, depends on identifying more closely with Sethe and her perception of the world.[28]

Sethe does not represent an unqualified ethical role model in the novel either. While the argument between her and Paul D does suggest that the novel demonstrates a preference for an ethics situated in place and attentive to the needs of others, this does not mean that every identification with place is positive. Sethe's identification with 124 after Paul D leaves becomes unhealthy and ethically unsound. Seeing in Paul D's unwillingness to understand and condone her act a more general condemnation by the African-American community, Sethe attempts to isolate herself from the outside world. "The world is in this room," she insists. "This here's all there is and all there needs to be" (183). By refusing to leave the physical space of 124, Sethe hopes to create an autonomous and impermeable place for Beloved, Denver, and herself. But this effort only exacerbates Sethe's tendency to generalize her own beliefs to others. This was apparent earlier in her decision to murder her daughter, and reveals the flaw in her ethics. When schoolteacher came to recapture her, Sethe gathered her children as if they were not distinct beings but parts of herself: "She just flew. Collected every bit of life she had made, *all the parts of her* that were precious and fine and beautiful" (163, italics mine).

Because Sethe does not perceive her children as distinct and separate beings, she does not grant to them unique desires, values, and perceptions. She does not ask her children whether they would prefer death to slavery; Sethe simply assumes that their desires and her own are identical. Although her baby daughter is too young to answer such a question, Sethe does not even entertain the possibility that her children might have desires different from her own. Thus, she fails to answer Levinas' "call of the Other" even if she appears to have the benefit of the Other (in this case, her children) in mind. This becomes more and more apparent as she isolates herself. Without asking, Sethe assumes that her now-grown daughter Denver would desire similar isolation. But her assumptions actually lead her to neglect Denver, who must go out and forage for herself, her mother, and Beloved.[29] Simply situating values with respect to place, then, does not guarantee a healthy ethical framework, and the threat revealed by Sethe's attitude toward place closely resembles modernist concerns: stagnation and xenophobia.

A certain ambivalence about situating ethics is apparent throughout Morrison's fiction. In her most critically acclaimed and popular work prior to *Beloved, Song of Solomon* (1977), Morrison depicts the rural African-American community of Danville, Pennsylvania, as hampered by their memories of Old Macon Dead's farm. The old men of the town relate to Dead's visiting grandson, Milkman, their fond memories of the farm, and the penniless man who made it into one of the largest and most successful enterprises in the county. Their descriptions clearly indicate that these memories enable them to articulate their own values and aspirations in concrete form. The text notes that the farm "colored their lives like a paintbrush and spoke to them like a sermon. 'You see?' The farm said to them. 'See? See what you can do?'"[30] Yet, if it functions as a "primal place" for the community – providing a coherent model against which the farmers measure their own circumstances – the farmers nonetheless do not follow the model. Indeed, as Milkman discovers, they feel unable to improve their lives. The farm marks an ideal that cannot be replicated, and the old men look to Milkman for some "word from him that would rekindle the dream and stop the death they were dying."[31]

Morrison's more recent novel, *Paradise* (1998), demonstrates the potentially horrific results of individuals who do act on the model associated with their primal places. The memory of the town of Haven, Oklahoma, as it was before the Great Depression is carried by its inhabitants who served in World War II, and it provides an ideal that drives them to survive and to envision a future for themselves. "Loving what Haven had been – the idea of it and its reach – they carried that devotion, gentling and nursing it from Bataan to Guam, from Iwo Jima to Stuttgart, and they made up their minds to do it again."[32] Yet, it is this same memory that guides these men in 1976 to hunt down and murder the women who occupy a nearby mansion called the Convent. "That is why they are here in this Convent. To make sure that it never happens again. That nothing inside or out rots the one all-black town worth the pain."[33] Heroism and homicide spring from an individual's attachment to place, the novel suggests.

RETROSPECTION, MORAL AMBIVALENCE, AND IAN MCEWAN'S "BLACK DOGS"

The intense, if often ambivalent, preoccupation with place in Morrison's works is apparent in a broad range of contemporary Anglophone novels, and not only those written by postcolonial or ethnic minority authors. The globalization theses presented by Harvey, Jameson, Massey, and others account well for this interest among writers such as Chinua Achebe, Paule Marshall, and N. Scott Momaday, and Morrison. These authors are responding to systematic efforts by Western European and American colonial empires to dominate space and place, and the populations they describe have all suffered from physical dislocation and/ or cultural alienation. A similar preoccupation with lost or imagined places is also apparent, however, among some of the most celebrated American and British authors from "majority" populations. The relationship between place and ethics has figured, for example, in the work of Booker Prize-winning author Ian McEwan since his first novel, *The Cement Garden* (1978), and it becomes a central concern of later works, including *Black Dogs* (1992) and *Atonement* (2001). From the first lines of *Black Dogs*, the orphaned narrator Jeremy expresses a profound sense of alienation. Lamenting a childhood in which he never felt "rooted" and longed for the "hearths" that other children had the luxury of deserting, Jeremy asserts that his physical displacement had moral consequences:

I discovered that the emotional void, the feeling of belonging nowhere [. . .] had an important intellectual consequence: I had no attachments, I believed in nothing. [. . . T]here was simply no good cause, no enduring principle, no fundamental idea with which I could identify, no transcendent entity whose existence I could truthfully, passionately, or quietly assert.[34]

Because Jeremy lacks an attachment to place, he lacks moral attachments. He is obligated to nothing and no one. Only after his marriage to Jenny Tremaine does he begin to feel "rooted" (105), and the novel suggests that his familial attachments provide the basis for his subsequent ethical development.

The importance of "rootedness" in both Morrison's and McEwan's accounts of ethics is not merely an accident of language. Although they are writing within different literary traditions, the two authors similarly see themselves as engaged in a critique of modernity and the unqualified valorization of emancipation and individual authenticity characteristic of the period. This concern is particularly apparent in Morrison's nonfiction writings. In her essay "Rootedness," for example, she insists that the novel form has become important to African Americans because a sense of communal identity and ethics are increasingly attenuated: "We don't live in places where we can hear those stories anymore; parents don't sit around and tell their children those classical, mythological archetypal stories that we heard years ago. But new information has got to get out, and there are several ways to do it. One is in the novel."[35] The focus on individual success that she observes in white American culture is detrimental because it diminishes the importance of the wisdom of ancestral figures and the responsibilities of an individual to his or her community. Rootedness is all the more important for African Americans, in Morrison's account, because the benefits of individualism and mobility were seldom available to nonwhite populations; their defining experience of modernity has more frequently been displacement. "The overweening, defining event of the modern world is the mass movement of raced populations," she asserts in a piece entitled "Home," "beginning with the largest forced transfer of people in the history of the world: slavery."[36]

McEwan similarly conceives of forced migration and even genocide as the characteristic events of the modern age, and the protagonist of *Black Dogs* recognizes this after he visits the remains of the concentration camp at Majdanek. Witnessing the marvel of sinister ingenuity and horrific technical expertise, Jeremy perceives the camps to represent the culmination of Western visions of progress since the Enlightenment. But Jeremy is particularly unsettled by the realization that his sense of autonomy and freedom from attachments to church and state do not release him from culpability for the horrors he sees. "We were on the other side, we walked freely like the commandant once did," he notes (93). For McEwan, some identification with place or sense of "rootedness" is crucial to ethics because it encourages individuals to identify with others who inhabit or identify with similar locations, even if such identifications occur only briefly. At the concentration camp Jeremy discovers that he cannot identify with the Nazi's victims because he lacks any personal connection to the place. He is, in his own words, a "tourist" (93). While he feels a terrible nausea at what he sees, Jeremy has the luxury to leave and feel no responsibility to change his own actions afterwards.

McEwan is not, on the other hand, encouraging an unreflective attachment to place. Jeremy is quick to note the immature and even cruel behavior of classmates who took for granted the "hearths" that he envied. And while McEwan makes no explicit reference to the Nazi vision of *Heimat*, his decision to portray his protagonist visiting a concentration camp suggests at least some cognizance of the role played by evocations of place in legitimizing the Holocaust. The sense of rootlessness that Jeremy feels for the majority of his life is cast as a basic existential and ethical condition that is best addressed through a self-conscious and deliberate effort of retrospection. Jeremy's mother-in-law, June, states as much when she attributes Jeremy's rootlessness to his refusal to do what she has done, to "single out a certain event, find in something ordinary and explicable a means of expressing what otherwise might be lost to you" (39). June herself finds such a moment in her violent confrontation in France shortly after the war with two monstrous dogs rumored to have been trained by Nazis for purposes of torture. The story becomes an organizing principle for her life, enabling her to sense both the possibility and the necessity of confronting the lingering manifestations of the Nazi horror that the dogs represent.

By casting subsequent events of her life in relation to her "originary" experience, June defines for herself a basic criterion for how she should act – every act is measured by the extent to which it promotes a world in which no one else will ever experience the terror she felt. Like Casey, she believes that ethical development requires finding an orientation for oneself in an otherwise confusing world. And by redefining which events are central to her life story, June resituates herself with respect to place. On the day following the original incident, June purchases a house in the locale, and she moves there permanently five years later. The house provides a literal ground or foundation for her ethics, and her choice to live there emphasizes that her ethical commitments are inseparable from the experiences she associates with that place.

As Jeremy recasts his own life story in relation to his new family and their "primal places," he discovers that their ethical commitments begin to inform his own. At the Hôtel des Tilleuls, where June was staying forty years earlier when she was attacked by the black dogs, he witnesses a father abusing his child. Although Jeremy is initially very reluctant to become involved, he finds himself challenging the father and striking him despite the man's superior size and strength. Jeremy's action responds to memories of his own childhood: the abuse his niece Sally was subjected to by his brother-in-law and his own helplessness to stop it. But he is also responding to the physical violence visited upon June by the black dogs. The present moment becomes significant because Jeremy perceives it as an uncanny repetition of both June's and his own past. Despite the fact that he has never been in this physical location before, the restaurant has a specific set of associations for Jeremy because he identifies so closely with June's experience. At the same restaurant, June was told the history of the black dogs shortly after her confrontation with them; here, she began to recast her life story as a struggle against an evil that recurs in a variety of forms and guises. Hence, Jeremy is predisposed to perceive his own experience in similar terms, and he notes that the events in the restaurant appear to be an "embodiment" of his past (107). The restaurant becomes the site for revisiting his childhood and the unresolved guilt he feels for being unable to help his niece. Thus, despite a host of social codes and mores counseling against involvement, Jeremy confronts the father because he perceives himself to be personally responsible for the boy's wellbeing. In a way that recalls Massey's argument, Jeremy is able to alter the social relations governing the restaurant space because he has changed how he perceives the place itself, associating it with his own past and ideas of what constitutes a healthy environment.

The rather uncontroversial values that Jeremy expresses in this scene – that child abuse must not be tolerated – conceal the more radical claim McEwan is making about ethics. For McEwan, autonomy and rationality, the twin foundations of modern ethics, fail to promote a more just world. Jeremy's unwillingness to get involved in the scene of abuse playing out before him until the father strikes his child a second time does not result from the absence of rational reflection; Jeremy deliberates, but his deliberations concern not what is right but how he can avoid getting involved.[37] Rationalizing his inactivity, Jeremy tells himself, "Surely something is going to be said. Someone, not me, had to intervene" (112). His ultimate decision to confront the abusive father is not facilitated by freedom from social and cultural mores; rather, he acts because he cannot tolerate witnessing what he perceives to be a recurrence of the abuse he saw during his own childhood. More simply put, he acts because he is haunted by the past, not free from it. The experiences of child abuse that he associates with his sister's apartment establish a negative version of a "primal place" for Jeremy. That is, Jeremy perceives every place he occupies in relation to the apartment in which he was forced to spend his teenage years, and his ethical commitments are shaped by the desire to prevent such environments from existing again, for anyone.

The contrast between Jeremy's actions at Majdanek and at the hotel restaurant further illuminates the notion of ethics endorsed by *Black Dogs*. Jeremy can identify with the child at the restaurant because he associates the space with a set of experiences that are crucial to how he perceives himself. This identification has distinct ethical consequences: whereas Jeremy makes no commitment to act differently after his visit to the concentration camp, he commits himself in no uncertain terms at the restaurant. His attachment to the restaurant certainly compromises Jeremy's freedom; because he does not consider himself a "tourist" here, he cannot simply walk away when he observes the abusive father's violence. Or, to use McEwan's metaphor, Jeremy is "rooted" to this place because of the memories it evokes for him. In contrast to the modernist sensibilities discussed earlier in relation to *A Passage to India* and *A Portrait of the Artist As a Young Man*, in which freedom is the precondition of ethical agency, *Black Dogs* asserts that ethics depends on discerning one's responsibilities to others more than coming to terms with the exigencies of existential freedom. Indeed, to preserve the distinction that McEwan is drawing, it might be useful to describe what Jeremy feels as a moral rather than ethical responsibility. Jeremy is motivated not by rationally determined norms that constitute modern notions of ethics but by something more like the nonrational, nonnegotiable obligations an individual feels that Bernard Williams calls morality.[38] Before his identification with a family network, Jeremy was free to act, but he could find no reason to commit himself. After he identifies himself with it, particular localities become vitally important to him, and he feels compelled to preserve the ideals of community that he associates with them.

Jeremy's discovery of moral clarity, however, poses troubling ethical questions similar to those found in Morrison's works. Does a fistfight represent an ethical solution? Even if it is tempting to revisit the violence of the abuser on him, how does this act help the abused child? Jeremy may have had a moment of epiphany, but his narrative never speculates about what goes through the child's mind as he witnesses a stranger beating up his father. And if Jeremy discovers a sense of moral clarity by redefining the present moment in terms of past incidents, to what extent can his discovery be generalized? The novel certainly invites readers to see his struggle in terms of larger geopolitical events. Shortly before traveling to the French restaurant, Jeremy flies to Berlin to witness the destruction of the Berlin Wall; there, Jeremy comes face to face with literal manifestations of the lingering horrors of Nazism metaphorically represented by the black dogs. Amid the celebrations of freedom and reunions among families separated by the Cold War, he sees a group of skinheads attacking a Turkish worker. Yet, while there is a symbolic affinity between the two scenes, the restaurant scene provides little insight into the political problems of building solidarity in post-Cold War Europe. Jeremy's relative lack of sympathy for the worker emphasizes the limits of an identification with place to eliminate moral ambivalence and uncertainty.

The ambivalence Jeremy struggles with throughout his narrative is emblematic of moral and ethical debates more generally after World War II. "Irreparable and irredeemable ambivalence" are inescapable features of "postmodern moral life," according to Zygmunt Bauman.[39] This sensibility is shared by a wide spectrum of philosophers from Bernard Williams to Alasdair MacIntyre. The reasons for this state of affairs differ considerably among these thinkers: Williams attributes moral ambivalence to the limits of philosophy in providing answers to difficult dilemmas; MacIntyre speaks of a "catastrophe" that occurs during the early modern era as thinkers increasingly turn away from a coherent theory of morality.[40] But the basic result is the same either way – moral debates have an "interminable character" because of the absence of a clear means of evaluating competing claims.[41] The large political debates of the moment over abortion, capital punishment, and other nagging issues provide testimony to this situation, as proponents on all sides base their claims on normative concepts and invoke the language of morality.

Thus, McEwan's apparent reluctance to praise or to condemn unambiguously Jeremy's violence – like Morrison's unwillingness to praise or to condemn Sethe's infanticide – does not represent either hesitancy to apply moral terms to a narrative or moral relativism. Rather, both novels convey a sense that moral goods are often in conflict. In *Beloved* the preservation of freedom and the preservation of life are both compelling ideals, and yet they appear to come at the expense of each other on the day when schoolteacher comes to 124. In *Black Dogs* Jeremy is torn between principles of pacifism and preventing abuse, principles rendered incompatible as he witnesses the child's suffering in the French restaurant.

The Levinasean tradition sees the irresolvable character of such dilemmas to be the result of the nature of morality itself. Because an individual's responsibilities are defined in terms of answering the unique needs of others, it becomes essentially impossible to generalize or to codify them. Moreover, the Levinasean understanding of morality suggests that each intersubjective encounter establishes a set of demands on an individual that are not only unique but also incommensurable. Thus, any effort to compare the various needs of others would threaten to efface their distinctiveness. The assumption that there might be a universal, rational calculus that could prioritize responsibilities sufficiently to establish uniform ethical norms or rules has been a central error of Western philosophy, according to Levinas. He writes, "Western philosophy has most often been an ontology: a reduction of the other to the same by interposition of a middle and neutral term that ensures the comprehension of being."[42] Resisting the idea that rationality might provide the "middle and neutral term" by which to comprehend others and their needs, Levinas rejects the possibility of arriving at certainty or closure on difficult dilemmas. Even the most sophisticated philosophical reasoning cannot eliminate the ambivalence of moral life because it makes certain assumptions about human nature, interests, and needs that are not equally true of all individuals.

From the Levinasean perspective, a personal connection to a "primal place" fails to resolve this problem because moral responsibility precedes any cognizance of location. Individuals are defined by an *a priori* responsibility to care for others; following Levinas, Bauman asserts that existence is defined not by "being *with* others" but "being *for* others."[43] In contrast to the impulse of Western ontology to define human existence in terms of separation from others, Bauman and Levinas insist that moral responsibility is the essence of a being – in the very moment of coming into existence, an individual is defined by his or her responsibility for others.

However, this characterization of *a priori* morality does not imply either inherent goodness or even the ability to understand how to fulfill one's responsibilities. Rather, Bauman argues:

To say that human beings are "essentially moral beings" does not mean to say that we are basically good [. . .] To say that the human condition is moral before it is or may be anything else means: well before we are told authoritatively what is "good" and what "evil" (and, sometimes, what is neither) we face the choice between good and evil; we face it already at the very first, inescapable moment of encounter with the Other. This means in its turn that, whether we choose it or not, we confront our situation as a moral problem and our life choices as moral dilemmas.[44]

In other words, the *a priori* nature of morality means that an individual's responsibilities to others begin before he or she is capable of rational deliberation. A person's earliest interactions with others, Bauman suggests, involve moral choices. As a result, no one can legitimately claim moral certainty. Nor does this situation alter fundamentally after individuals reach adulthood and develop greater rational faculties, for they still remain unable to eliminate the basic uncertainties that arise from the "inescapable moment of encounter with the Other." Bauman's point is that rational deliberation even under the most ideal circumstances cannot lead to certainty about the precise needs of others. The child in the French restaurant establishes a moral claim on that fateful day without ever saying a word, a claim that demands Jeremy's immediate and concrete response. Yet no amount of deliberation can definitively ascertain whether he arrived at the best conclusion, or whether he could have done more. Nor can his identification with place resolve these questions, according to Bauman, because the child's claim has nothing to do with his resemblance to others Jeremy has known; the location or place of their encounter is likewise irrelevant to any sense of responsibility Jeremy should feel. Indeed, attention to place might occlude the broad metaphorical connections the novel draws between Jeremy's situation, Nazism, and enduring racial tensions in European nations. The radical reading that Levinas might encourage would suggest that Jeremy should be responsible for not just one child but many; likewise, his responsibility for the boy perhaps should not end at the restaurant but continue indefinitely. For moral life is inescapably haunting. Or, as Bauman puts it, "*The moral self is a self always haunted by the suspicion that it is not moral enough.*"[45]

Black Dogs also describes its characters as "haunted," though the novel attributes a somewhat more positive connotation to this term. The term haunting, as it is first used by June, refers to her recasting of present events with reference to her "primal experience" of confronting the black dogs. Thus, whereas haunting is an inescapable and confusing circumstance of life for Bauman, it is chosen to a large degree in *Black Dogs*; this is evident in June's decision to make the locale of her confrontation her new home, guaranteeing that she will repeatedly recall or be haunted by her first experience there. June chooses to be haunted because it provides the means for her to translate vague, *a priori* moral impulses into more specific ethical commitments. Her decision to resist the dogs attacking her was not initially motivated by any particular set of values or principles, simply terror and the longing to survive. Any insight June gains from this experience comes afterwards, as she reflects on the social circumstances that could have led to the creation of the dogs and on what commitments might be necessary for her to make in order to prevent others from having to suffer a similar experience. Put another way, the significance of a "primal experience" or the place with which it is associated is frequently not self-evident, but needs to be continually clarified in the light of retrospection and subsequent life experiences. As such, the threat of recurrence apparent in Jeremy's assertion that "they will return to haunt us, somewhere in Europe, in another time" is not altogether ominous (160); by identifying other instances of injustice as subsequent manifestations of the black dogs, June and Jeremy are more able to identify their responsibilities than they were before they were haunted. Paradoxically, then, ethics in *Black Dogs* depends on conceiving present events as repetitions to ensure that past injustices will not be repeated.

Jeremy's recognition that the black dogs continually threaten to return suggests that haunting, as it has been defined here, is characterized by a duality – a sense of both longing and terror. Casting his own story as "haunted" by June's may fulfill Jeremy's longing to associate himself with place and a network of social relationships, but it leaves him and his readers with a rather terrifying possibility: ethical dilemmas are irresolvable. McEwan's novel cannot conceive of a way of finally eliminating the black dogs. The particular injustices associated with them will endlessly return in a variety of guises and permutations such as the skinheads present at the tearing down of the Berlin Wall. The longing and terror associated with haunting are inseparable because they both result from the same narrative process of identifying the present in terms of past dilemmas; Jeremy cannot use his mother-in-law's memories of the black dogs to provide an ethical orientation for himself without at the same time confirming that the threat embodied by the dogs continues to exist.

The very means of clarifying moral responsibilities instills a sense that moral "success" will ever be elusive and fleeting.

While this state of affairs represents a catastrophe to thinkers such as MacIntyre, it represents a more honest recognition of the complexity of moral life for Bauman. Bauman considers efforts to eliminate ambivalence to be a betrayal of moral responsibility. The distinction between ethics and morals that Bauman creates is crucial to his point here. Like Williams, Bauman casts morality in terms of nonrational, *a priori* responsibilities that individuals have to care for others; ethics, in contrast, represents a much more narrow enterprise for Bauman, characterized as a rational effort to establish uniform normative codes of behavior. Bauman insists that the process of determining such codes inevitably threatens to arrive at general principles by ignoring or effacing variations in human needs. Indeed, on his reading, efforts by modern thinkers to conceive of a universal ethics seek to avoid the terrifying aspects of morality. The valorization of reason associated with modernity "axiomatically assumed that feelings, much as acting out of affections, have no moral significance – only choice, the rational faculty, and the decisions it dictates can reflect upon the actor as a moral person."[46] This line of thinking would not tolerate something as vague and nonrational as the *a priori* impulses Bauman describes to guide human relationships. But Bauman insists that morality is "endemically and irredeemably *non-rational*" in how it establishes very particular and personal responsibilities for others that cannot be generalized into universal principles; ethics represents a betrayal of morality because it seeks to establish such principles.[47] The postmodern era's rejection of universalizing narratives, from this perspective, enables the return of morality and a more realistic sense of the inescapable challenges that moral life presents.

While the novels in this study share affinities with Bauman's characterization of modernity and his sense that moral life is incurably haunting, they suggest a somewhat different reason for this situation. The key to understanding the difference is to focus on the putatively *a priori* character of moral responsibility. *Black Dogs, Beloved,* and the other novels in subsequent chapters would not contradict Bauman's assertion that individuals are faced with choices between good and evil long before the concepts are given names, but they suggest that any specific feelings of moral responsibility arise only retrospectively, after the fact, and in response to the development of a social network associated with a particular place. The teenage Jeremy may feel guilty when he leaves his niece with her abusive parents in order to attend university; however, he has no prior moment to measure his feelings against and is thus unable to ascertain what a more appropriate response might be than simply abandoning her. Put another way, because he has no serious attachment to place, he can leave his sister's apartment and the relationships associated with it. Twenty years later at the restaurant, in contrast, he can translate a similar feeling of guilt into a specific imperative to defend the abused child because he has been haunted by memories of Sally and because he is now "rooted" in a familial network that has enabled him to define for himself a coherent idea of what a healthy environment might be. Haunting is irresolvable in the novel, then, less because Jeremy never knows if he is moral enough than because he can never fulfill his responsibilities in the moment, only belatedly.

The belatedness of insight will be apparent in most of the texts covered in this study, and will profoundly shape the visions of ethics they propose. In *Beloved* this becomes most apparent in its conclusion. At the climax of Morrison's novel, a group of thirty women return to the place where Sethe murdered her daughter. Having heard that the ghost of the murdered child has returned to 124 to haunt Sethe, the women are determined to stop this invasion from the other world. Upon arriving, however, the first thing the women see is a vision of themselves shortly before Sethe's murderous act: "When they caught up with each other, all thirty, and arrived at 124, the first thing they saw was not Denver sitting on the steps, but themselves. Younger, stronger, even as little girls lying in the grass asleep [. . .] there they were, young and happy, playing in Baby Suggs' yard, not feeling the envy that surfaced the next day" (258). On that day, they did nothing to warn Sethe or to prevent schoolteacher from recapturing her and her children. Confronted by their own past actions, the women are haunted – the present moment becomes refigured as a repetition of their prior experience. Perceiving this repetition, the women feel a sense of shame that clarifies their responsibility to protect the community despite their animosity toward Sethe.[48] As a result, both Sethe and the women act differently from how they did years earlier: Sethe directs her violence against the perceived threat to the community rather than toward her children; the women act in concert to prevent violence by restraining Sethe.[49]

What is particularly important to note is that the text gives no indication that the women should have or even could have acted differently the first time around. As was the case in *Black Dogs*, only retrospectively can the members of the African-American community in *Beloved* perceive their moral responsibilities because responsibility itself arises from a discrepancy between what *is* and what *could have been*. Indeed, this discrepancy establishes a concrete and inescapable moral responsibility for the community members to Sethe and each other. This responsibility is terrifying because it can never be fully acted upon in the moment, only after the fact. The final pages of the novel reassert this idea by presenting the "disremembered" presence of Beloved, who remains an ongoing source of shame: "Although she has claim, she is not claimed. In the place where long grass opens, the girl who waited to be loved and cry shame erupts into her separate parts" (274). But retrospection does enable individuals to act upon their recognized obligations, if only belatedly. By perceiving the present in terms of earlier events, individuals can react to their initial responsibility on subsequent occasions. Neither the women of *Beloved* nor Jeremy of *Black Dogs* can return to the past and ameliorate suffering where they failed to before; they can, however, redirect the shame they experienced to guide them in subsequent interactions.

The central implication here is that moral responsibility can be understood only through a process of *ethical* deliberation. *Beloved* and *Black Dogs* retain Bauman's suspicion of ethics in the sense of legislated and uniform codes of normative behavior. But they insist on a process of discerning and negotiating moral responsibilities among individuals who identify with a particular place. It is ethics in this sense that the novels of Morrison and McEwan endorse. Sethe's actions demonstrate the threat of morality unguided by ethics. Her decision to murder her children is profoundly a moral one, and it requires the entirety of the novel before she can entertain suggestions made by those around her that the attempt to answer one's moral responsibilities (to prevent the suffering her children would face under slavery) can lead to profoundly unethical actions (infanticide). Likewise, Jeremy's violence against the father of the abused child is guided by a moral principle, yet Jeremy himself needs to be warned by another diner at the hotel restaurant not to take his violence too far.[50]

While an identification with place does not eliminate moral ambivalence in McEwan's or Morrison's novels, it plays a crucial role in the negotiation of shared ethical commitments. As Morrison notes, the women who return to 124 initially do so for a variety of reasons. Some come out of altruistic concern for Sethe; others come out of curiosity; still others, like Ella, come because they perceive in Beloved a threat to themselves – that their own ghosts might return to haunt them. After coming together in place, however, they are united by a set of memories about the last gathering at 124 and their common sense of guilt over not acting on Sethe's behalf. The memories associated with 124 thereby provide a kind of shared narrative that enables them to express their responsibilities to each other and to ghosts of their various individual pasts. In other words, 124 becomes a communal "primal place" much as the French restaurant does in *Black Dogs*; these shared places, which are products of memory, longing, and fantasy, provide the basis for a kind of solidarity. This is not to claim that either novel envisions a homogeneity of identity or beliefs. The struggle to restrain Sethe from attacking Mr. Bodwin gives the lie to this. But the debate over how to act now has a shared set of images and memories. Sethe attacks because she links this moment to her earlier experience; the other women restrain her because they, too, recall the last murder to occur at 124. The decision by the women to return to this place, then, minimally points to an implicit desire to revisit their earlier choice – not out of a false hope to undo that incident but to use it to guide their future decisions.

IMAGINED HOMELANDS AND JOAN RILEY'S "THE UNBELONGING"

This chapter began with an exploration of the promise that Doreen Massey attributes to place – the promise of achieving more egalitarian and just social relations by redefining how space and place are perceived. My subsequent analysis suggested that literary texts including *Beloved* and *Black Dogs* work to fulfill this promise through their articulation of imagined "homeplaces." By recasting the defining memories and experiences associated with particular places, the novels in this study present alternatives to the models of racial and other social relations that exist in the societies in which the authors write. The retrospective character of these novels might compromise such efforts, however. The nostalgia implicit in the portrayals of primal places such as the Clearing and the "hearths" that Jeremy envies could well limit their potential to challenge prevailing ideas about social relations and ethics. Massey herself demonstrates great anxiety about nostalgia, and repeatedly distinguishes her interest in place from it. She insists that "[t]he anti-essentialist construction of this alternative concept of place immediately problematizes, for instance, any automatic associations with nostalgia and timeless stasis" (121; see also 5, 119). Because nostalgia is equated with stasis, she suggests, it inhibits efforts to rearticulate social relations.

Massey's concern must be kept in mind as subsequent chapters explore the significance of nostalgia more directly. Similar concerns are apparent among all the literary texts discussed in this study, and greater attention to them will complicate the thesis presented so far. Of the literary texts to be discussed in subsequent chapters, Salman Rushdie's *Shame* (1983) is perhaps the most critical of an attachment to place. For Rushdie, all such attachments are based on nostalgic myths that encourage intolerance and fundamentalism. A more intimate portrayal of the dangers of a nostalgic attachment to place comes in Joan Riley's *The Unbelonging*. Riley's novel describes the struggles of a teenage Jamaican immigrant, Hyacinth Williams, to find a sense of place within British society. Faced with an abusive father and a vindictive stepmother, as well as insults and injury from all levels of white society around her, Hyacinth finds herself increasingly longing to return to her childhood home. The novel makes it clear, however, that her "memories" are idealized fantasies recast in reaction to her intolerable present:

How much she longed for the sun-bleached cheerfulness of the grey wood shack that had been her home for the first eleven years of her life. How different it had been from this peeling, black-painted house full of fear and hate. [. . .] It had been so nice with Aunt Joyce, who always understood, had never treated her badly. She had been popular, with lots of friends. No one had teased her, taunted her. Now her only happiness was sleep, for that was when she could go home again and take up her interrupted life.[51]

The narrative provides readers and Hyacinth herself with numerous clues that her recollections are false, and the idyllic picture is shattered in the novel's final chapter. Here, an adult Hyacinth finally manages to return to Jamaica and is terrified by the slums and poverty she sees. She is unable even to recognize her childhood friend Florence, who now considers her a foreigner. The dream of returning to place that sustained and drove Hyacinth throughout her teenage years, the novel implies, was built on self-deception.

In ethical terms, the novel suggests that Hyacinth's "primal place" prevents her from acting in ways that address the needs of others or even herself. Because she identifies herself exclusively in terms of it, she spurns the advances of friends and potential lovers who are not from Jamaica. She refuses to tolerate any criticisms of Jamaican society, insisting that no racism exists in her home country. Even when faced with reports of violence and abuse there from more recent immigrants like Perlene, she insists with willful ignorance that such reports arise from American and Communist propaganda. Perhaps the most damning indication of her ethical failure comes in her brief conversation with Florence at the end of the novel. Florence describes the despair and alcoholism that overcame

Aunt Joyce after Hyacinth's departure, and she asks Hyacinth why she never sent money to help care for her aunt or even bothered to write. Hyacinth cannot provide an answer because she cannot countenance the reality that her childhood home has changed. Precisely because Jamaica exists in her imagination as a place frozen in time, it never occurs to her that her aunt might grow old, ill, and need her help. Hyacinth's fantasies of return invariably cast Aunt Joyce attired in the same dress and hat in which she had last seen her; indeed, "everything was the same" in her daydreams (32). Because she disregards the realities of Jamaica in the construction of her imagined homeland, Hyacinth is unaware of and unwilling to deal with her responsibilities to others.

Hyacinth's nostalgic fantasies are not entirely without ethical value, however. This becomes apparent shortly after Hyacinth is finally removed from the household of her abusive father and placed in a reception centre. Feeling lonelier than ever, she "vow[s]" to return to Jamaica one day (77). For the first time in the novel, her passive fantasy becomes a concrete goal toward which she will labor. Hyacinth takes another vow only two pages later, after receiving the news that she has failed six out of nine subjects at her 'O' levels. Here, she "vow[s]" to get a university education despite her failures (79), and much of the rest of the novel describes her relentless pursuit of academic success, culminating with her winning a postgraduate position at a university in Jamaica. Lacking family, friends, and support network, Hyacinth manages nonetheless to address her own basic needs for subsistence because of her nostalgic longing to return to place. And while this modest success does not outweigh her profound neglect of Aunt Joyce, it enables her to return to Jamaica and to discover the consequences of her failure.

Hyacinth differs from Sethe and Jeremy, then, in her desire to inhabit physically the imagined homeland she has conceived for herself. As demonstrated earlier, Sethe recalls the Clearing when faced with crucial decisions of what sort of life she wishes to have, with whom she hopes to share it, and where she would like to be, yet she demonstrates no desire to recreate her primal place. Likewise, Jeremy longs for the "hearths" other children took for granted, but his actions demonstrate a desire to create a safe environment for himself and others in the present. Hyacinth's attitude toward place is problematic because it leads her to believe that she can be happy only if she inhabits a world that in reality never existed, and this is particularly apparent in the passage quoted above where she describes her present existence simply as an "interruption" of her life. Riley has underlined in interviews the dangers of valuing memory over daily life. The past is often a "handicap" for Jamaican immigrants like herself, she asserts: "It's something that stops [people] from going forward because they've never actually come to terms with exile."[52] In other words, recollections of lost or longed-for places often conceal the real conditions that are the source of disappointment, and thereby limit individuals' ability to confront the situations that have led them to indulge in nostalgia.

The consequences of Hyacinth's nostalgia clarify the common ethical ground of *Beloved*, *Black Dogs*, and *The Unbelonging*. All three of these texts deny the idea of ethical self-sufficiency. None of the characters in these novels appears able to arrive at ethically sound decisions without the input of others. Almost invariably, when they claim self-sufficiency, characters find themselves performing actions harmful to others and themselves. Both Sethe's decision to murder her children and Jeremy's decision to confront the abusive father represent moments when they act on moral impulses but fail to ask the advice of even those they seek to aid. The tragedy of *Beloved* is not replayed in *Black Dogs* only because another diner halts Jeremy and helps him to see where his violence might lead if left unrestrained. In a similar vein, *The Unbelonging* attributes Hyacinth's failure neither to her attachment to place nor to her nostalgia. The most politically active character in the novel, the Zimbabwean immigrant Charles, defends her sentimentalization of Jamaica. In response to Perlene's criticism, he notes: "I too romanticise aspects of my country when I feel homesick. There is no harm in it, so long as I know the reality" (121). Hyacinth's real failure, Charles' response implies, is her unwillingness to seek out knowledge of the truth. Her insistence that she does not need to – that she has sufficient knowledge and wisdom to make her decisions – prevents her from using her primal place as an ethical orientation to the degree that Sethe and Jeremy do. Had she engaged in constructive dialogue with Perlene and the other immigrants, the novel suggests, Hyacinth would have been able to make more sound decisions and to identify herself with an activist community. *Beloved* provides numerous examples of growth through dialogue, including the argument between Paul D and Sethe and the exorcism of Beloved discussed earlier. Perhaps the greatest sign of the novel's optimism in this regard is that Paul D, despite his earlier ethical failings, is cast as the one who in the final pages helps Sethe to redefine her emotional commitments after losing Beloved, to find a reason to live and to cultivate new relationships.

The denial of ethical self-sufficiency in the novels of Morrison, McEwan, and Riley points to at least one reason for the broader reemergence of place as a concept of interest in an age of globalization. The emphasis in these novels on the radical differences among individuals in terms of their needs and longings means that conceptions of ethics as either a personal code or a set of universal norms are insufficient to address the complexities of moral life highlighted by Bauman and others. Massey's conception of place as a particular articulation of a network of social relations that are continually in flux provides a way of thinking about ethics as a communal process of negotiating needs. The images of place that individuals conceive for themselves express their own particular needs, not abstractly or in a vacuum but in relation to those others with whom they interact. Such conceptions can be taken up and debated by these others, and the often conflicting images of 124, the French restaurant, and Jamaica in the texts explored in this chapter point to a process by which characters struggle to reconcile their notions of the good life. The fact that such struggles remain unresolved in the literary narratives discussed here does not represent a failure of ethics but a recognition that the forms that social relations take at any given time and locality are not equally satisfying to all individuals and are subject to change. While Massey herself does not discuss place in terms of ethics, her observation that places contain and are often constituted by conflict suggests precisely this point. And her critique of definitions of place as a bounded site of authenticity is motivated by the same concern raised in this chapter: the possibility that individuals might impose very narrow and exclusive ideas of social relations on others.

This possibility will be a recurring concern in subsequent chapters as novels return again and again to fantasies of lost or imagined homelands, exploring the extent to which such fantasies might contribute to ethical deliberations. If nostalgia becomes crucial to efforts to envision more inclusive communities and the responsibilities of community members to each other, it inevitably threatens to promote exclusivity and insensitivity to difference. But these texts seem willing to take that risk.

CHAPTER 2

Nostalgia and narrative ethics in Caribbean literature

We need, therefore, a kind of parallel history of, let us say, victimisation, which would counter the history of success and victory. To memorize the victims of history – the sufferers, the humiliated, the forgotten – should be a task for all of us at the end of this century.
　　　　　　　　　　　　– Paul Ricoeur, "Memory and Forgetting"

One of the most disturbing consequences of colonization could well be this notion of a single History, and therefore of power, which has been imposed on others by the West. [. . .] Because the Caribbean notion of time was fixed in the void of an imposed nonhistory, the writer must contribute to reconstituting its tormented chronology[.]
　　　　　　　　　– Edouard Glissant, *Caribbean Discourse: Selected Essays*

The last chapter concluded with a rather ambivalent claim. If the longing for lost or imagined "homeplaces" is crucial to ethical insight in *Beloved, Black Dogs,* and *The Unbelonging,* it also threatens to promote essentialistic visions of community. Sethe's longing for the community once associated with the Clearing enables her to recommit herself to a new relationship with Paul D, but it previously led her to isolate herself from the outside world in an effort to create a homogeneous community for Denver, Beloved, and herself. The ambivalence of nostalgia in Morrison's text points to a more general theoretical problem facing the authors in this study: how to critique imperialist narratives without reinforcing their philosophical categories or biases. Nostalgia figures prominently in such narratives produced throughout Europe and the United States long before it was used in discourses of resistance, and thus there is a very real possibility that the alternative histories presented in *Beloved* and elsewhere might reaffirm essentialistic notions of nonwhite populations. "Imperialist nostalgia," to recall Renato Rosaldo's term, played a prominent role in the rationalization of colonial policies across the globe, promoting the notion that the disappearance or acculturation of non-Western groups was a lamentable but inevitable consequence of their inability to adapt to a globalized environment.

This is not to deny that appeals to nostalgic essentialism have also been used to critique various forms of imperialism. Perhaps the best-known instance emerges in the 1930s among a group of French African and Caribbean writers identified with the *négritude* movement. The evocation of a black spiritual essence by Aimé Césaire of Martinique, Léopold Senghor of Senegal, and Léon Damas of French Guyana was cast as a means of constructing a philosophical basis for challenging colonial racism. As Patrick Taylor points out, however, the movement failed to challenge the basic philosophical categories of racial difference on which the colonial system was based. *Négritude* as an ideology posits an unchanging black essence that effaces the immense cultural diversity among African and Caribbean communities. "Negritude expresses [. . .] a romantic longing for a one-dimensional, utopian society," Taylor writes; rather than destroying colonial myths, it effects a "restoration of oppressive mythical structures" that inhibits political activism.[1] The nostalgia for a golden age of Africa on which the *négritude* movement is based, according to this critique, fails to provide the basis for liberatory narratives because the characterization of black essence reinforces Western stereotypes of colonized populations.

The eclipse of *négritude* in recent decades does not mark the disappearance of nostalgia in Anglophone literature. Nor should the critique of *négritude* represent the final word on the function of nostalgia in literary texts responding to enduring legacies of colonization and modernity. The longing for lost or imagined homelands has been and continues to be a central feature of the various literary traditions that constitute contemporary Anglophone literature. The case of Caribbean literature is illustrative in this regard: as George Lamming writes in his seminal work *The Pleasures of Exile* (1960), the emergence of a generation of writers in the 1950s able to write about the colonial situation in the British West Indies was possible only because the authors themselves had left the Caribbean and were reflecting retrospectively on their experiences. "[N]o islander from the West Indies sees himself as a West Indian until he encounters another islander in foreign territory," Lamming asserts. "In this sense, most West Indians of my generation were born in England. The category West Indian, formerly understood as a geographical term, now assumes cultural significance."[2] By implication, the rise of Caribbean literature required identification with a land whose very existence as a conceptual category is constituted nostalgically. Kamau Brathwaite,

Jan Carew, Wilson Harris, V. S. Naipaul, Vic Reid, Sam Selvon, and Lamming himself produced literary works about their birthplaces only after having moved away from them.

The imagined returns to the Caribbean and to ancestral homes associated with Africa that fill the pages of Caribbean literature since Lamming are nostalgic, then, but they rarely demonstrate the sentimentality associated with nostalgia. Naipaul's harsh portrayals of ignorance, lawlessness, and cultural sterility among colonized populations in *A House for Mr. Biswas* (1961), *The Mimic Men* (1967), and *A Bend in the River* (1979), as well as in his nonfictional work, represent the extreme on the continuum. But even in more generous portrayals, such as Derek Walcott's *Omeros* (1990), the nostalgic return is highly qualified. The protagonist of the epic poem, Achille, undertakes an imagined journey to Africa to meet his father. Yet the narrator's characterization of Achille's fantasy, "It was like the African movies / he had yelped at in childhood," undermines the idea of a return to a precolonial cultural purity.[3] If the image of Africa serves Caribbean discourses of resistance, Walcott's poem implies, it does not do so in the ways understood by proponents of *négritude*. Evocations of Africa cannot, in Walcott's account, enable the creation of a discursive space that stands outside of the history of the colonial encounter; his own poem, no less than Achille's Hollywood-inspired vision of Africa, is complicit with Western representations.

The insistent question these literary texts inspire is why so many Caribbean authors describe nostalgic fantasies that are recognizably ideologically compromised. Although Walcott, like many of his contemporaries, rejects the nostalgia of *négritude*, he does not reject nostalgia. Achille's Africa is not culturally authentic or historically accurate, but it is a fantasy of an ancestral space that nonetheless occupies a central location in *Omeros*. The presence of such fantasies is particularly interesting, given that Caribbean literature since Lamming's *The Pleasures of Exile* has been identified in terms of an ethical charge to counteract the internalization of colonial values among the colonized peoples of the British West Indies and beyond. "Colonialism is the very basis and structure of the West Indian's cultural awareness," Lamming asserts. "In order to change this way of seeing, the West Indian must change the very structure, the very basis of his values."[4] To the extent that Caribbean literary texts have responded to this challenge in subsequent decades, nostalgic language and imagery have been central features of the response.

Naipaul provides an intriguing clue regarding nostalgia's potential contribution to ethics in *Finding the Center* (1984). Describing his progress and growth as a writer, he notes that "[t]o become a writer, that noble thing, I had thought it necessary to leave. Actually to write, it was necessary to go back. It was the beginning of self-knowledge."[5] Here, Naipaul rejects modernist tropes of displacement and psychic exile as the basis for literary production. Rather, his shifting attitudes toward the Trinidad of his childhood are themselves the source for his writing. Conditioned by his youthful longing to escape from the colonial periphery to the metropole and his subsequent disappointment with England, Naipaul conceives of writing as a recursive process in which the writer explores his or her past from multiple vantage points in time. As did many of his contemporaries, Naipaul found England far less inviting in actuality than in fantasy – and his experiences there redefined his attitudes toward both England and Trinidad. While Naipaul has never recast the Caribbean in terms as positive as Lamming or Walcott have, he shares with them a tendency in his literary texts toward a certain selective retrospection. The novel form provides the space for a series of redescriptions of the past that, for Naipaul, represent a process of acquiring knowledge not altogether determined by colonial ideology and rhetoric.

My broader claim here builds on what has become a central tenet of narrative ethics: that literature can contribute to ethics by virtue of acquainting readers with different worlds and providing alternative ways of perceiving familiar ones. Narratives of "inauthentic" experiences like nostalgia can offer a unique contribution in this regard, encouraging readers to perceive present social arrangements with respect to idealized images of what could have been. This strategy is apparent in what has arguably become the most canonical postcolonial Caribbean novel, Jean Rhys' *Wide Sargasso Sea* (1966). Rhys uses nostalgia in *Wide Sargasso Sea* to critique the vision of time endorsed by *Jane Eyre* and colonial narratives more generally: one that is linear, progressive, and looks to the future for the consolation of suffering. Such narratives must conceal victims whose suffering will not find future consolation, victims like Bertha Mason. In contrast, *Wide Sargasso Sea* establishes a past-oriented or nostalgic vision of narrative time. By defining the present in terms of its failure to satisfy past longings, Rhys' novel continually evokes images of loss – actual and imagined. In this way, the interweaving of a disappointing present and a tantalizing, if unrealized and imaginary, past creates something like Paul Ricoeur's vision of a "parallel history of [. . .] victimisation," foregrounding memories of suffering, alternative histories, lost possibilities, and uncertainty. Or, to put it in Martha Nussbaum's terms, nostalgia in *Wide Sargasso Sea* plays a crucial role in Rhys' effort to establish a different set of "evaluative commitments" from those associated with *Jane Eyre* and colonial discourses during the Victorian era.

Wide Sargasso Sea differs from Ricoeur, however, in its insistent focus on worlds that never were. The suffering of Rhys' protagonist, Antoinette, comes less from specific acts of cruelty than from lost opportunities to form genuine and satisfying relationships – opportunities that were prohibited by her own internalization of colonial ideologies and racist stereotypes. In this context, Antoinette's nostalgia not only counters the narrative temporality associated with *Jane Eyre*, and thereby draws attention to and empathy for Antoinette's suffering, it also helps her to envision more equitable forms of community. The longing to return to lost and nonexistent places apparent in *Wide Sargasso Sea* and the novels of other Caribbean authors such as V. S. Naipaul and Paule Marshall enable a critical retelling of the past in ways that reduce prior dependence on colonial modes of interpretation.

This chapter's analysis of nostalgia in the works of three of the most prominent postwar Caribbean writers – Rhys, Naipaul, and Marshall – seeks to contribute to current discourses on narrative ethics as well as literary theory.[6] For all three novelists speak to one of the challenges taken up by post-Kantian ethics: how to establish ethical claims without invoking normative codes or categorical imperatives. The contemporary philosophers Alasdair MacIntyre, Martha Nussbaum, Paul Ricoeur, Richard Rorty, Charles Taylor, and Bernard Williams have been preoccupied by this question, and notably all of them have looked to narrative to provide a means of sharing, debating, and negotiating communal ethical values. Literary studies have drawn upon these thinkers to suggest three central ways in which narratives can assist ethical deliberations: 1) they provide an opportunity to identify with potentially unfamiliar descriptions of the world, thus encouraging readers or listeners to empathize with the values and needs of others; 2) they challenge the truth claims of existing histories and beliefs by redescribing reality from alternative perspectives; 3) they expose the ambiguities and aporias of any ethical project.[7] The second model particularly sees in narrative the possibility for minority or marginalized groups to tell history in their own terms.

Not surprisingly, postcolonial literatures have provided some of the most dynamic examples of what Ricoeur terms "telling otherwise."[8] Their use of intertextuality, mimicry, and catachresis has challenged endorsed histories of empire and Enlightenment metaphysics. Chinua Achebe, N. Scott Momaday, Toni Morrison, Salman Rushdie, and Ngugi wa Thiong'o all make implicit or explicit ethical claims about literary forms and the necessity to retell the past in ways that do not simply validate existing institutions of power. However, postcolonial literatures – and *Wide Sargasso Sea* especially – also explore how narrative can refigure which claims of suffering readers tend to validate; in this way, such texts also resemble the third model of how literature assists ethics. These literatures suggest that simply invoking notions of justice and ethics will not address the suffering that figures like Bertha Mason feel. Colonial missionaries everywhere considered themselves bringers of justice, light, and emancipation, not suffering; *Jane Eyre* and other novels of its era likewise explicitly endorse these ideals. Hence, the challenge for Rhys, Naipaul, and Marshall is not only to "tell otherwise" but also to provide a persuasive alternative to the ways of reading and interpretive biases associated with British literature during the colonial era.[9]

EMPATHY AND NARRATIVE TIME

Jean Rhys' *Wide Sargasso Sea* provides a particularly useful starting point because, on the one hand, it has become one of the canonical texts of postcolonial studies for its critique of *Jane Eyre* and colonialism more generally; on the other hand, it has itself been subject to critique for its simplified and essentialistic portrayals of the black populations in the West Indies. Scholars have explored how the novel's intertextuality succeeds in "breaking the master narrative" of *Jane Eyre* specifically and the British imperial project more generally by giving the suppressed Bertha Mason a voice;[10] giving her a different name, Antoinette;[11] relocating the action to the West Indies; and changing the frame of reference. Yet, an opposing line of analysis argues that the novel reproduces the racism it critiques through what Veronica Gregg calls a "racialist usurpation of the voices, acts, and identities of 'black people.'"[12] What is intriguing about this debate is that both lines of scholarship seem so correct.[13] The novel's rewriting of Bertha Mason's fate depends on repeated nostalgic evocations of a past that never was. Like Anna Morgan in Rhys' earlier novel, *Voyage in the Dark* (1934), Antoinette expresses a profound longing for the West Indies of her youth; both women contrast their lifeless and lonely present among the white English with a vibrant past among the black West Indians. Their retrospective identifications with romanticized black communities to which neither belonged seem to confirm Gregg's claim of "racialist usurpation." To explore the ethical implications of *Wide Sargasso Sea*, then, requires confronting a disconcerting fact: Antoinette's own search for moral purpose depends on a nostalgic fantasy of return to a community that no longer exists and may never have existed. She can claim, "Now at last I know why I was brought here and what I have to do," only after she dreams of a reunion across the Sargasso Sea with her childhood playmate Tia (who attempted to kill Antoinette at their last actual meeting).[14]

Nostalgia might seem like a peculiar tone for a novel that seeks to rewrite a canonical Victorian novel and depict Bertha Mason's effaced suffering. Yet, throughout her narrative, Antoinette opposes a disappointing present with a comforting and inaccessible past. Early in the novel, she describes a time in her life when she could have sought comfort from her mother: "Once I would have gone back [. . .] to be near her when she brushed her hair, a soft black cloak to cover me, hide me, keep me safe. But not any longer. Not any more" (22). This same attitude remains with Antoinette throughout her narrative, even as she seemingly lives out the fate of Bertha Mason by burning Thornfield Hall in the novel's penultimate scene (this scene is revealed afterwards to have been a dream that Antoinette might or might not choose to fulfill). Even in these final moments, she cherishes hope for a nostalgic return to a lost past and lost community: as she stands atop the burning Thornfield Hall, she looks down into a pool and sees the image of her black childhood playmate, Tia. Poignantly, her apparent suicide leap is an effort to establish a communion with her sometime friend and her past.

If Antoinette longs to return to a world and a relationship that never were, her nostalgia nonetheless identifies Rhys' basic ethical problem with *Jane Eyre*: the absence of empathy for Bertha Mason. Addressing this absence is at the heart of Rhys' and Ricoeur's vision of rewriting history. For Ricoeur, the focus on "success and victory" in traditional historical narratives discourages empathy for the victims and losers they depict, thereby eliminating any moral ambiguity about the course events have taken. Rhys depicts a similar denial of empathy from the first page of *Wide Sargasso Sea*. "They say when trouble comes close ranks," Antoinette notes in the opening paragraph, "and so the white people did. But we were not in their ranks" (17). The refusal by the "white people" to identify with the Creole population represents a refusal to empathize with or even to acknowledge Antoinette's suffering. The particular biases inculcated by the colonial system in the West Indies prevent such moments of recognition; likewise, they prevent Creole identification with the black communities on the island. Even Antoinette's final dream of a reunion with Tia points to the tension created by colonial categories of racial difference. When Antoinette dreams of finding herself on the roof of Thornfield Hall, peering over the edge and seeing her childhood home, Tia exudes derision as much as empathy: "But when I looked over the edge I saw the pool at Coulibri. Tia was there. She beckoned to me and when I hesitated, she laughed. I heard her say, You frightened?" (190). Her language evokes a childhood incident in which Tia had previously challenged Antoinette, provoking her with the epithet "white nigger" (24). If empathy or sensibility is privileged in Rhys' earlier fiction, as Andrew Gibson argues, "intensely valued as an ethical mode of attending to the world, valued above other such modes," it is almost absent in *Wide Sargasso Sea*.[15]

By depicting Antoinette's fantasy of reunion with Tia, the novel uses her nostalgia to identify the absence of empathy as a product of the colonial system implemented in the West Indies. Antoinette's fantasy alludes to the fact that her last actual meeting with Tia ended in violence; when the Coulibri estate is burning and Antoinette flees to Tia, the other girl attacks her. Only retrospectively do the two girls feel an empathy that is born of identification: "I looked at her and I saw her face crumple up as she began to cry," Antoinette says. "We stared at each other, blood on my face, tears on hers. It was as if I saw myself. Like in a looking glass" (45). Before this moment, Tia perceives her relationship with Antoinette in terms of the colonial economy – she is a black child striking against the white child of former slaveholders. The consequences of her violence create an awareness of what the two young women could have shared in a world without racial categories of difference. But this awareness can only be experienced nostalgically, after the fact. It is nonetheless so powerful that it guides Antoinette to envision in her final dream a reunion with Tia, not with her mother or her caretaker, Christophine. Her dream, then, imagines a restoration that is not possible within her life and expresses regret for intimacy felt too late.

Antoinette's nostalgia, however, does not itself erase her colonialist attitudes. Antoinette reproduces the tendency of the former slaveholders to deny blacks independent subjectivities. She reduces Tia to the embodiment of her idealized past: "I ran to her, for she was all that was left of my life as it had been" (45). Within her imagination, Tia does not exist as an independent entity but as the remnant of something Antoinette herself has lost. Nor does Antoinette's nostalgia lead her to challenge, in the first part of her narrative at least, her own position within either the colonial system or the narrative of *Jane Eyre*. This becomes particularly apparent when she describes a series of dreams that anticipate her fate in

Brontë's novel: imprisonment in Thornfield Hall and the annihilation of her identity as Antoinette, leaving only Rochester's Bertha. Indeed, she resigns herself to the inevitability, even desirability, of playing the role assigned her by her husband: "I follow him [Rochester], sick with fear but I make no effort to save myself; if anyone were to save me, I would refuse. This must happen" (59–60).[16]

The sense of inevitability Antoinette feels is a product of her internalization of the narrative temporality guiding *Jane Eyre*. As will become more apparent later, *Wide Sargasso Sea* critiques Brontë's novel in large part because the latter structures its events in ways that shift empathy away from Bertha to Jane. The story begins with Jane's imprisonment in the red-room and proceeds to follow *her* struggle for emancipation and salvation. The intertwined narratives of individual enlightenment, colonial expansion, and Christian eschatology that *Jane Eyre* aligns itself with draw significance from a vision of progress that necessitates Bertha's disappearance. There can be no place for her within the world that Brontë's novel envisions, if only for the reason that Rochester cannot marry Jane until he "divorces" himself from obvious signs of his colonial past, including his Creole wife. Jane herself feels little empathy for Bertha, and this is striking because from the first pages she demonstrates a hatred of cruelty, repeatedly evokes metaphors of emancipation, and chooses principle over personal gain.[17] Although Jane notices Bertha's plight and laments her suffering, she neither dwells on it nor identifies a perpetrator – madness provides her with a category with which to identify suffering without implicating Rochester.[18] Bertha becomes not a victim but an impediment.

Antoinette's nostalgic fantasies of community and place seem to guarantee her progression toward Thornfield Hall and madness – her progression toward becoming Bertha Mason. Antoinette's reunion with Tia in her final dream requires that she leap from the roof of Thornfield Hall, thereby reproducing in action if not intent Bertha Mason's suicide in *Jane Eyre*. In other words, her own attempt to escape from the social and physical constraints placed on her leads her to fulfill her role within Jane's narrative. Her earliest nostalgic construction of the past similarly implies a sense of inevitability regarding her fate. Antoinette describes how as a child she sought shelter within the garden at Coulibri, a shelter she longs for retrospectively from within Thornfield Hall. Yet her description draws upon the Judaeo-Christian image of Eden: "Our garden was large and beautiful as that garden in the Bible – the tree of life grew there. But it had gone wild" (19). Antoinette's metaphor here not only foreshadows the loss of place but also limits the likelihood of her eliciting readers' empathy. The Edenic story exists within a larger narrative in which the loss of the idealized place is a foregone conclusion; indeed, for many Christians, the Fall is only the first step along a divinely ordained history toward a more full and eternal union with God. If Antoinette's goal is to present to herself and her readers the basis for an alternative narrative of the life she could have enjoyed if not for Rochester, she undermines this effort by casting her life in the West Indies in prelapsarian terms. Far from providing an alternative to her fate in *Jane Eyre*, then, her nostalgic reflections appear to imply its inescapability.

Antoinette's description of the Coulibri garden provides an important caveat to Paul Ricoeur's notion of "telling otherwise." Narratives that purport to challenge endorsed histories often confirm rather than destabilize existing modes of interpretation. Because Antoinette has internalized a notion of linear progressive time, her own fantasies sustain an ideology that not only demands her demise but also denies her suffering. More precisely, the suffering she experiences cannot be interpreted as caused either by a colonial policy that demands rigid racial separation or by a beneficiary of the policy, like Rochester. Rather, it is the sad but causeless result of her own madness. On this point, Gayatri Spivak's critique of *Wide Sargasso Sea* is most acute. Spivak concludes that Antoinette does not and cannot represent a perspective critical of imperialism: "No perspective *critical* of imperialism can turn the Other into a self, because the project of imperialism has always already refracted what might have been the absolutely Other into a domesticated Other that consolidates the imperial self."[19]

From Spivak's perspective, "telling otherwise" fails because even well-intentioned narratives reproduce imperialist ways of reading. While Rhys seems far more self-conscious of this point than Spivak credits, the problem nonetheless remains. Providing the "lost history" of Bertha Mason does not necessarily change how readers view her or make them more likely to empathize with her suffering. The problem, in other words, is not primarily the result of insufficient information on the part of readers but a tendency to interpret new information in terms of existing paradigms. If Antoinette's nostalgia is to aid the process of recounting suffering – if nostalgia is to aid ethics – then it must enable her to reformulate the ways in which her experiences are perceived.

TELLING OTHERWISE, TELLING AGAIN

Wide Sargasso Sea reformulates readings of Bertha Mason and *Jane Eyre* by using nostalgia to establish a very different sense of narrative time, one that is past-directed and preoccupied with regret. I observed in the last section that Bertha is an unsympathetic figure in large part because she is defined within a narrative whose trajectory effaces her suffering. *Jane Eyre* does not efface all suffering, of course, simply instances in which no future consolation can be promised.[20] Indeed, *Jane Eyre* celebrates the Christian model of suffering as sacrifice; Jane ends her narrative by quoting the final letter of St. John Rivers, colonial missionary to India, before his death: "Daily He announces more distinctly, 'surely I come quickly!' and hourly I more eagerly respond, 'Amen; even so, come, Lord Jesus!'"[21] St. John's personal suffering is mitigated, even valorized, by the promise of the continuing development of the colonial missionary project – a sentiment that Jane herself takes as a model. Antoinette explicitly rejects this sentiment. She recounts how in her convent school: "I learnt to say very quickly as the others did, 'offer up all the prayers, works and sufferings of this day.' But what about happiness, I thought at first, is there no happiness? There must be" (56).

Antoinette rejects the narrative of Christian consolation, rejects a "masterplot" that would subsume suffering. Not only does she refuse to "offer up" her suffering but she dwells on these moments, insisting that they have caused irreparable harm. She asserts, for example, that the scar on her forehead from the stone Tia threw at her not only marks the loss of their relationship but also threatens the formation of future relationships: "Aunt Cora told me that [the wound] was healing up and that it wouldn't spoil me on my wedding day," Antoinette remarks to Rochester. "But I think it did spoil me for my wedding day and all the other days and nights" (133). Indeed, even from the first pages, Antoinette is preoccupied with regret: "My father, visitors, horses, feeling safe in bed – all belonged to the past" (17). The contrast in tone with Jane's narrative is stark – not only does Antoinette refuse consolation, she denies the future any promise. Antoinette perceives all safety and beauty to lie in a nostalgic and inaccessible past, and her narrative repeatedly establishes this point. Her regret, then, is not simply a passive longing but a mode of prioritizing a lost, even nonexistent, past over an intolerable present.

The nostalgic tone of *Wide Sargasso Sea* represents the final development in Rhys' longstanding preoccupation with time. Time is perhaps the central concern of her strongest previous novel, *Voyage in the Dark*. In a letter to Evelyn Scott, Rhys writes that the "big idea" of the novel has something "to do with time being an illusion I think. I mean that the past exists – side by side with the present, not behind it, that what was – is."[22] Rhys imagines a model for describing the past that insists upon its continuing presence in daily life. This understanding is essential to *Wide Sargasso Sea*'s critique of *Jane Eyre*. As demonstrated earlier, little empathy for Bertha Mason is possible within a narrative scheme guided by its progress toward Jane's marriage and insertion into bourgeois British society. This is true not only because Bertha is relegated to a minor role but also because the narrative is profoundly forward-looking. Even the concluding image of the novel points to the future – the promise of St. John's (and Jane's) union with God. The past functions only as the record of trials on the pilgrimage toward salvation. In Rhys' terms, the past in *Jane Eyre* exists "behind" the present, not "side by side" with it. As a consequence, its narrative cannot establish even an injunction to remember Bertha Mason. Antoinette's nostalgia, in contrast, impedes any linear progress in her narrative: the moment of longing remains to be viewed again and again. Progressive time proposes a moral order that in *Jane Eyre* exonerates Rochester and Jane of any culpability. The past is conceived as a record of progress, the march from ignorance to enlightenment, and so there is literally nothing to atone *for*.

Reconfiguring narrative can change how events are evaluated, then, by changing the way readers experience the relationship between events and their contexts; in other words, refiguring narrative time can alter the meaning of experience and thereby transform how figures such as Bertha Mason are read. As Ricoeur writes, the making of narrative "resignifies the world in its temporal dimension, to the extent that narrating, telling, reciting is to remake action following the [work's] invitation."[23] This implies that the significance of a given event derives from its place within the narratives describing it. More specifically, this argument suggests that the configuration of time posited by a narrative shapes how readers or listeners interpret its events. Bertha's arson appears meaningless, an act of madness, because the dominant narrative temporality of *Jane Eyre* is linear and progressive. Such an act might be pitied for its "self-destructive" character but otherwise makes little sense within a narrative preoccupied with how present actions enable individuals to achieve desired future outcomes. By proposing alternative temporalities, however, *Wide Sargasso Sea* constructs other modes of interpreting the significance of events. The insistent focus on the past in Rhys' novel leads readers to perceive the arson less in terms of the literal elimination of Bertha's access to the future than in terms of a response to intolerable loss.

Thus, the madwoman in the attic appears more like a feminist subject rebelling against patriarchal institutions or an anticolonial hero revisiting the violence of colonialism back upon its own centers. The physical act has not changed – the burning of Thornfield Hall – but how readers can relate to it has. Even to the extent that *Wide Sargasso Sea* reenacts what Laura Ciolkowski calls the "commonsense structures of Englishness," its emphasis on regret, repetition, and the coexistence of past and present challenges the "commonsense" structure of time that underlies colonial history.[24] Minimally, Antoinette's narrative invites readers to return to and linger on the scant details of Bertha Mason's life in Jane's narrative; in so doing, it delays and thereby questions Jane's conception of progress.[25] The act of "telling otherwise" – even when it is ideologically compromised – points to the contingency and constructedness of a vision of progress that depends on the appearance of inevitability and divine sanction.

On this point, *Wide Sargasso Sea* intersects with the larger aspirations of postcolonial studies. Its theorists have struggled not only to challenge narratives of colonial progress but also to envision a counterhistory whose central focus is the victims of various colonial enterprises. Toward this end, Homi Bhabha, Edward Said, and others have sought to articulate "temporalities of other marginal 'minority' histories" or to locate postcolonial subjects in terms of "the history of *all* subjugated men and women."[26] Such histories are concerned less with progress than with justice. This becomes possible by proposing that history is composed of multiple and often incompatible stories. If temporality involves a particular conception of how time functions in the world (for example, linearly progressive, cyclical, linearly degenerative, monadic, etc.), and if every history posits a particular temporality, then the postcolonial strategy of creating alternative temporalities opposes time itself to colonial history, arguing that no single historical narrative can encompass or represent time faithfully. While Said and Bhabha do not depend on nostalgia to achieve their ends, as *Wide Sargasso Sea* does, they do depend on narrative's ability to provide an interpretive description of events in order to refigure existing histories. Indeed, Said's call for contrapuntal readings of colonial history, like Bhabha's notion of "time lag," grants narrative the task of providing connections and convergences among colonial experiences in Africa, India, and Latin America – a task that draws upon the aesthetic capacities of narrative to refigure how the relationship between the past and present is perceived so that the present can never be divorced from the past but exists "side by side" with it, to reinvoke Rhys' phrase. Ricoeur becomes most useful on this point. His notion of "telling otherwise" can be read to suggest that the ethical aspect of narrative resides not in the events it describes but in the implication that *any* event can be narrated again and therefore described otherwise.

The emphasis on regret rather than progress in *Wide Sargasso Sea* makes an even stronger claim than either Ricoeur or Said might accept: nostalgia can change history without claiming to depict historical realities.[27] If Said's history utilizes narrative to reinterpret events, its truth claims still depend on evoking actual historical occurrences. In contrast, history in *Wide Sargasso Sea* is defined by images of communities never formed, empathy never felt, suffering never shared – in other words, history is defined by what *never* occurred. Antoinette, Tia, Rochester, and Jane are all submitted to cruelty on the basis of race, gender, and/or primogeniture but only Rochester and Jane form anything resembling a satisfying relationship. The awareness of lost opportunity becomes clearer only because of Rhys' poignant depictions of communities that never were. And the novel takes pains to make evident that the nostalgic fantasies Antoinette creates are never depicted as historical realities. *Wide Sargasso Sea* refuses the temptation to portray an idealized organic community destroyed by colonialism. Antoinette's fantasy of reunion does not belie the fact that there never was an original *union* between her and Tia. Antoinette's own internalization of racial stereotypes, if nothing else, prevents this possibility. But for precisely this reason, nostalgia is valuable: minimally, it enables her to describe her experiences and relationships in ways she had previously been unable to do.

SUCCESSIVE REDESCRIPTION: V. S. NAIPAUL

The foregoing claims argue against the predominant tendency in academic discourses to associate nostalgia with passivity, self-deception, and reactionary ideals – certainly not with ethics. As noted in the introductory chapter of this study, nostalgia is described as a "social disease," to use Susan Stewart's term, that evokes "necessarily insatiable demands" for a nonexistent origin.[28] Yet, although Rhys challenges this notion by casting the longing for nonexistent origins as crucial to the rewriting of colonial narratives and ethical ideals, *Wide Sargasso Sea* does not dismiss altogether Stewart's concerns. Antoinette's insistent focus on regret leads her to create a narrative whose events are oddly predetermined.

Until the final paragraph, the suicide leap from Thornfield Hall that *Jane Eyre* describes appears almost fated. This is in large part because Rhys' novel repeatedly foreshadows these events in Antoinette's earlier experiences: her mother is locked up in a secluded home by a husband who describes her as insane; Antoinette's childhood home, Coulibri, burns to the ground and a parrot falls to its death from the roof; even Antoinette's time in the convent school suggests the imprisonment she will face in Thornfield Hall. Such prefigurations would seem to imply that Antoinette is characterized by a sense of passivity that, for Stewart, is an inevitable product of the insatiable demands of the nostalgic.

An even greater sense of determinism haunts the writings of V. S. Naipaul. "Fate. There is nothing we can do about it," Biswas' grandfather asserts in Naipaul's early epic novel, *A House for Mr. Biswas*.[29] The grandfather's characterization of the inevitability of present circumstances and the inability of individuals to change their lives echoes throughout this novel and Naipaul's work as a whole. From the first sentence of the novel, Naipaul describes Biswas as being acted upon by circumstances outside of his control: he is fired from his job as a journalist owing to illness, an illness that will kill him ten weeks later. *The Mimic Men* similarly presents a protagonist, Ralph Singh, whose present is determined long before the action of the novel begins. Removed from political office and exiled from the fictional Caribbean island Isabella, Singh spends his days in a London flat writing his memoirs. Indeed, his fate follows a pattern that in turn prefigures the careers of the politicians who follow him. Yet neither Naipaul nor his characters demonstrate empathy toward others who have suffered or are victims of a seemingly deterministic cycle of violence in postcolonial nations. "The world is what it is; men who are nothing, who allow themselves to become nothing, have no place in it," the narrator Salim states almost matter of factly in the opening passage of *A Bend in the River*.[30]

The apparent lack of empathy for colonized populations demonstrated by Naipaul in these passages is crucial to understanding the debates surrounding his work and the critique of nostalgia more generally. Almost no other living author has been subject to such vicious *ad hominem* criticisms. Phrases such as "the Naipaul fallacy," coined by Anthony Appiah, and "Naipaulicity," coined by Chris Searle, indicate the furious reaction that Naipaul's work provokes.[31] According to his critics, Naipaul's work demonstrates colonialist sympathies and endorses Western bourgeois ideologies. By failing to demonstrate any empathy for the suffering he describes, Naipaul reinscribes "received colonial assumptions" about postcolonial populations and exonerates his elite Western readership from any sense of responsibility for the political, social, and economic strife occurring in newly independent nations.[32] In one of the most sensitive critiques of his work, Sara Suleri argues that Naipaul's preoccupation with formalist issues and his own place within the Western literary canon leads him to reconstruct India, Africa, and the Caribbean as purely literary territories divorced from colonial histories that have shaped current circumstances. This separation of territory from history is possible, according to Suleri, through Naipaul's strategic use of nostalgia. Declarations such as those found in his essay "Conrad's Darkness," that the colonial era represented "the time of great peace," suggest to Suleri "a nostalgic will both to conceive of the past in purely literary terms and, furthermore, to stake out the idea of unramified time: only in relation to such a canonical clock can Naipaul then map out his idiom of perpetual arrival."[33] On this reading, Naipaul shares with Rhys a preoccupation with constructing alternative narrative temporalities, but his interest is not similarly motivated by a desire to establish an ethical critique of colonial narratives.

An exploration of the relationship between ethics and nostalgia in Naipaul's work is all the more crucial because both his supporters and his detractors employ the language of morality and ethics to support their case. This becomes particularly apparent in an exchange between Edward Said and John Lukacs that has subsequently been transcribed in the journal *Salmagundi*. Speaking in the context of a discussion about intellectuals in the postcolonial world, Said argues, "The most attractive and immoral move, however, has been Naipaul's, who has allowed himself quite consciously to be turned into a witness for the Western prosecution."[34] For Said, the postcolonial intellectual has a moral responsibility to indict imperialism; Naipaul fails in this regard because he uses his status as a Third World immigrant to gain literary authority, yet ignores the historical actualities of Africa, India, the Caribbean, and Latin America in his writings. Lukacs responds by arguing that the intellectual has a primary responsibility to tell the truth, and that indictments of the colonial powers are a secondary concern. "[Naipaul's] principal concern is not with injustice, or justice, but with truth," he asserts. "[. . .] He is deeply concerned with the rhetoric of those who address public issues. And he wishes that not only more Easterners but also more Westerners were concerned with the ethics of rhetoric."[35] In other words, Naipaul's critiques of the political truisms and simplifications employed by postcolonial regimes and political groups demonstrate his ethical commitment to interrogating how language is employed for ideological ends.

Naipaul himself claims that literary texts are distinctive forms of art because of their engagement with moral questions, but understanding how this sensibility relates to the nostalgia in his work is more complicated than was the case with Rhys because of his conflicting attitudes toward the longing for lost or idealized homes.[36] A profound longing for place is apparent in Naipaul's works, particularly *The Mimic Men* and his most autobiographical novel, *The Enigma of Arrival* (1987). The narrator of the latter repeatedly demonstrates a longing for an England he never personally experienced: "So I grew to feel that the grandeur belonged to the past; that I had come to England at the wrong time; that I had come too late to find England, the heart of empire, which (like a provincial, from a far corner of the empire) I had created in my fantasy."[37]

Yet the narrator demonstrates no sympathy for the nostalgia of a neighbor who laments the poor treatment that a former champion race-horse is receiving. "His sentimentality frightened me," the narrator comments (39). Naipaul himself has highlighted on several occasions the dangers of nostalgia, criticizing African writers who seek "to write nostalgically about tribal life"; and despite portrayals of him to the contrary, Naipaul insists that he feels no longing for the colonial era. "I feel no nostalgia for the miserable security of the old ways," he states in a 1979 interview.[38]

This last statement provides a useful clue for understanding Naipaul's attitude toward nostalgia: while his characters' nostalgia tends to be associated with England, their longing to return undermines the authenticity of Englishness. As is apparent from the passage quoted from *The Enigma of Arrival,* in the very act of articulating regret the narrator comes to recognize that he longs for an ideal that is a product of his own fantasy, not an historical reality. Indulging in such fantasies does not lead the narrator to reassert the endurance of Englishness but to recognize that it never existed in the way that he heretofore believed. To this extent, Naipaul shares the attitude of postcolonial critics such as Homi Bhabha and Simon Gikandi that Englishness as a concept is not a stable essence that is reproduced across the globe in its colonies; rather, it is produced belatedly in response to the rise of the empire and cultural contacts with other societies across the globe. Although this idea is more fully articulated in *The Enigma of Arrival,* it is already apparent in *The Mimic Men.* Singh repeatedly describes his longing to return to the island of Isabella to live out his retirement, yet he recognizes the impossibility of fulfilling this wish. And this recognition, within the same paragraph, leads him to the insight that his fantasies correspond with "patterns" inculcated by the colonial education system in which Singh and his fellow political leaders spent their formative years. "My career is by no means unusual. It falls into the pattern," Singh recognizes. "[W]e lack power, and we do not understand that we lack power."[39]

While *The Mimic Men* shares the sense of determinism that defines *A House for Mr. Biswas*, it maintains some degree of hope that the recognition of the ways in which fantasies are structured by colonial discourse can lead to some positive change. More precisely, the ethical function of nostalgia at this point in Naipaul's career arises from its capacity to unsettle internalized colonial ideals. This becomes particularly apparent in the third chapter, where in a series of three passages the narrator describes first his longing to return to Isabella and to retire to a rundown cocoa estate; second, the drab London hotel in which he currently resides; and third, his altered perception of his initial fantasy based on the recognition of his present situation. As Singh finds himself returning to his fantasy in the third scene of this series, he discovers contradictions that were not previously apparent to him. He notes, "It was a dream of the past, and it came at a time when, by creating drama and insecurity, we had destroyed the past. [. . .] It was a yearning, from the peak of power, for withdrawal; it was a wistful desire to undo" (43).

Singh's passionate effort to fulfill the "pattern" laid out for him by his colonial education leads him to recognize that his longing to return to a "pure" and authentic past is itself a colonial fantasy to conceal the exploitation of the island and its inhabitants. His internalization of imperialist nostalgia, to recall Rosaldo's term, leads him to perpetuate this exploitation when he himself is in power, reproducing many of the policies of his colonial predecessors. Indeed, the estate to which he longs to retire stands as a literal marker of the remnants of the colonial order and his desire to find himself occupying a central position within it. The impossibility of achieving this desire, however, leads Singh to recognize the extent to which the colonial education system instilled in him a false sense of exclusivity, that he and the other elite of Isabella shared more with the British occupiers than with the other islanders. This recognition suggests that if nostalgia represents a central tool of colonial power and knowledge, it also has a tendency to destabilize such knowledge precisely because it encourages individuals like Singh to imagine themselves fulfilling fantasies that the colonial system never intended them to fulfill.

The idea that nostalgia can destabilize colonial knowledge suggests that the broader project of *The Mimic Men* might be read as the articulation of a different kind of colonial history. Singh points in this direction as he begins to discuss why he is writing his memoirs. Although he claims that his writing is personal rather than political, he asserts categorically that there has been no accurate colonial history to date: "For there is no such thing as history nowadays; there are only manifestos and antiquarian research; and on the subject of empire there is only the pamphleteering of churls" (38). Over the course of the novel, Singh repeatedly criticizes existing historical narratives for being efforts to impose patterns on events after the fact. This becomes most explicitly apparent when Singh discusses the political movement his father began: "In the history books, as I say, my father's movement is now made to appear just another part of a recognizable pattern of events in one region of the world" (168).

The imposition of an interpretive pattern threatens to limit the unique features and circumstances that brought about his father's movement. On this point, Naipaul seems in accord with Said. Histories of the colonial era need to attend to particularities and avoid generalizations in order to understand how moments of resistance became possible. By foregrounding his uncertainty about why his father began his grassroots movement, Singh resists any easy reading of his own narrative as providing an alternative interpretive pattern. Read optimistically, the novel's repeated focus on the personal events and circumstances of Singh's life and its reluctance to describe mass movements in any detail point to an effort to think about history without reference to broader metanarratives, colonial or otherwise.

The obvious problem with this optimistic reading is that the focus on the personal tends to make Singh a synecdoche for the nation as a whole. The events of Isabella's history seem to be inseparable from the details of the narrator's life; his personal neuroses come to signify a gloss for the nation, reading political turmoil in terms of individual psychological issues. Nana Wilson-Tagoe is particularly critical of Naipaul on this point, asserting that his decision to retain Singh as the sole point of view in the novel despite Singh's inability to overcome personal crises limits the novel's ability to provide useful social critique.[40] This argument discounts the possibility that Singh's neuroses are foregrounded in the novel precisely to make readers cautious about identifying with his interpretation of events, which might simply impose one more interpretive pattern on to colonial history. But Wilson-Tagoe's basic concern still stands, that

Naipaul's narratives risk effacing or even reproducing the very critique they present.

To explore the extent to which Naipaul's broader project of rewriting colonial history from a personal perspective is compromised, I return to *The Enigma of Arrival.* This novel is particularly important in any analysis of Naipaul's work not only because it is identified as his most personal and autobiographical novel but also because it has been perceived as representing a departure from his previous writings. Here, as nowhere else, Naipaul interrogates ideas of Englishness and articulates his disappointment with the colonial center that occupied a prominent place in his youthful fantasies. Yet, the majority of Naipaul scholarship does not read the novel as a critique of imperialism but as a subtle effort to repress newly acquired knowledge of the fictive character of England that had been so crucial to the constitution of Naipaul's own identity. Ian Baucom argues that when confronted with the disparity between his childhood fantasies of England and its reality for a Caribbean immigrant, Naipaul refuses to relinquish his nostalgia for the England that had never been, and instead preserves the idea of a genuine, "authentic" national identity by displacing Englishness into the nostalgic past. "In the place of an England that survives as its own counterfeit," Baucom argues, "he will locate an England that fails to exist, not because it never was but because it has been lost. He will find that England in the very fact of his belatedness and in the resonant stones of ruin."[41]

In this regard, Naipaul joins a longstanding English discourse of national melancholy tracing back to John Ruskin and Thomas Carlyle, a discourse that refuses to define national identity in terms of future goals but turns instead toward an idealized past as the basis for genuine Englishness. Naipaul cannot fit comfortably within this tradition, of course, given his status as an immigrant. And Baucom recognizes that Naipaul differs from contemporaries also positioning themselves within this tradition, such as Prince Charles. Unlike many of them, however, Naipaul recognizes that no literal return to the nostalgic past is possible; such returns can exist only within the realm of fantasies and the artistic representations they inspire. Yet, what both troubles and fascinates Baucom is the sense that Naipaul endorses an ideal of national authenticity despite his self-consciousness about the contingency and artifice underlying constructions of Englishness.

The idea that nostalgia leads to the repression of knowledge about the nature of Englishness, however, overlooks the fact that *The Enigma of*

Arrival repeatedly demonstrates a pining for Trinidad, not just England. Perhaps the first time the narrator recognizes his nostalgia is just before his eighteenth birthday as he leaves Trinidad. Looking back on his island home from the airplane, the narrator confronts a physical and metaphorical landscape of which he had been previously unaware. The narrator notes that "the landscape of my childhood was like something which I had missed, something I had never seen. [. . .] The world in which I had lived all my life so far was a world I had never seen" (105). His sudden longing to return, while certainly not yet as strong as his desire to depart, nonetheless leads to a reevaluation of his childhood and of Trinidad more generally. His new attitude does not represent a radical shift at this point, but marks a sense that his previous knowledge was inaccurate and limited. Much later, as the narrator finds the England of his fantasies to be a disappointing reality, he will be more cognizant of the ways in which his prior knowledge was shaped by colonial ideologies and more able to articulate this fact explicitly. Even his ideas about writing, he realizes, were "ideas bred essentially out of empire, wealth and imperial security, [. . .] transmitted to me in Trinidad" (146). And the pages that follow this recognition describe the narrator accepting a commission to write a book about Port of Spain, Trinidad, and his subsequent discovery of the island's precolonial history, a history concealed by imperial conquest. Indeed, the narrator comes to feel in these passages "a deep romance" not for England but for the Trinidad concealed by Spanish and British occupation (158).

The reevaluation of Trinidad and its history points to a broader epistemological claim in the novel: knowledge arises out of a process of successive redescription. One of the most intriguing features of *The Enigma of Arrival* is that the narrator's initial descriptions of Trinidad, England, the lives of his neighbors, and even the physical appearance of his landlord are all inaccurate. Only after the narrator witnesses these scenes or people a second time is he able to describe them with some degree of accuracy. Yet the narrator attributes his inaccuracies to neither personal ineptitude nor youthfulness solely but to something about the nature of knowledge itself. One of the most explicit statements to this effect occurs just after he recognizes that his ideas of what defines a writer are shaped by colonial ideology. Recognizing that such ideology has damaged both his writing and himself, the narrator states:

it was necessary for me to make a pattern of the knowledge I already possessed. That kind of pattern was beyond me in 1950. Because of my ideas about the writer, I took everything I saw for granted. I thought I knew it all already, like a bright student. I thought that as a writer I had only to find out what I had read about and already knew. (146)

Reinvoking the term "pattern," which figured so significantly in *The Mimic Men*, the narrator of *The Enigma of Arrival* asserts that knowledge is not produced simply by acquiring a set of discrete facts but through an interpretive process shaped by a person's particular ideological biases. That he was unable to make sense of his experience as a young immigrant in 1950 is the result of his own internalization of colonial ideology, his perception that "I knew it all already." Only in the face of a sufficient number of discrepancies is he able later in life to rethink and revise his modes of interpreting his experience. The challenge the narrator describes, then, is not arriving at new facts that counter existing historical documents but finding new ways of perceiving the world and processing it. Or, more simply put, the challenge is to "make a pattern" rather than simply accepting those inculcated by the British colonial education system.

Hence, Naipaul's emphasis on personal rather than national narratives can be read not so much as a retreat from the moral responsibilities of the postcolonial intellectual, as Said suggests, but rather as an effort to work through the epistemological problem presented by colonial ideology – establishing new interpretive patterns for understanding his own experience. The failure to undertake this task, for Naipaul, has led to the political disasters apparent throughout the postcolonial world. Politicians and revolutionaries alike are simply repeating the errors of their predecessors. Naipaul asserts:

revolutions can come about very easily in undeveloped societies, precisely because there is so little understanding of the society even as it is; so little intellectual base. And of course for that reason, the result of the revolution is nothing. Nothing has changed; the deficiencies remain, they remain un-analyzed; and the response is the same; the march, the borrowed ideas, the refusal to understand what makes a whole society – or a whole world.[42]

By focusing on his personal experience specifically, Naipaul is better able (at least on his own account) to analyze his actions when he begins to repeat or reproduce destructive ideologies. Here, then, *The Enigma of Arrival* goes a step beyond *The Mimic Men* and its efforts to rewrite colonial history. The narrator is more capable of creating his own patterns for interpreting his experience than Singh was, and nostalgia becomes crucial to this process by encouraging him to return to previous moments and to redescribe them in the light of present knowledge.

The function of nostalgia in *The Enigma of Arrival* finds an analog in Slavoj Žižek's theory of revolution. For Žižek, revolutions always come "too soon" because they need to create their own prefigurative narratives in order to reach fruition, a process that can be accomplished only through enacting their own failure. "The first seizures of power *are necessarily premature*," according to this argument, because the appropriate moment comes when the working class achieves a maturity that "can arrive only after a series of 'premature', failed attempts."[43] The "appropriate moment" for revolution always comes after the first seizure of power because it is only in retrospect that individuals recognize where they failed and thereby understand what a better model could have been. In terms of *The Enigma of Arrival*, Žižek's argument implies that the narrator's successive redescription of his childhood, of the history of Trinidad, and of England enables a more precise description of how previous perceptions have failed to correspond to reality. The novel's insistent return to moments of failed insight, moments when the narrator's expectations or beliefs were disappointed, recasts the defining metanarrative or ideological pattern that guides his narrative. This becomes particularly apparent with respect to the narrator's experience of time. Whereas the dominant metaphor of the early narrative is decay, the more prominent metaphor as the novel progresses is flux. In the latter half of the novel, the narrator notes that now "I lived not with the idea of decay [. . .] so much as with the idea of change. I lived with the idea of change, of flux, and learned, profoundly, not to grieve for it" (210). This transformation of the dominant metaphor is apparent in the narrative structure, which moves from a tragic linearity to a more redemptive cyclicity. While each of the novel's five sections portrays a death, the ending of each section points to some degree of rebirth or at least modestly positive change. The repetition of the pattern across the novel's sections implies that by the end of the novel the narrator operates with a different set of ideological biases associated with flux rather than imperial decline, biases that no longer incline the narrator to identify England as the central symbol of civilization.

The emphasis on flux does not imply an endorsement of relativism, however, as Evelyn O'Callaghan suggests. For O'Callaghan, the epistemological significance of the shift in narrative temporality lies in the deconstruction of certainty: "Above all, the text insists on a pattern of repetitive revision of perceptions and judgments so that certainties collapse and the only constant proves to be flux. [. . .] Perception is revealed as misperception, followed by adjustment of perception, only to be revealed as further misperception, and so on ad infinitum."[44] The critique of certainty, for O'Callaghan, applies not only to colonial narratives but *The Enigma of Arrival* itself. Its narrator may learn that his previous accounts of the world are erroneous, constructed on the basis of a set of interpretive biases inculcated by his education in Trinidad and England; however, he is unable to provide a more accurate account of his circumstances. This reading of Naipaul identifies his work in terms of the broader "postmodern turn" arising in the aftermath of World War II, a turn away from ideas of objective knowledge, epistemological certainty, and universal progress. Yet, this reading suggests a rather impoverished account of knowledge, one that overlooks the potential for more and less accurate characterizations. Naipaul is no relativist. If absolute objectivity is belied by the very subjective perspective the narrator provides, the narrator never suggests that all accounts of the world are *equally* inaccurate. During a scene describing the funeral of his sister, for example, the narrator laments his inability to believe in the Hindu rites he witnesses:

Those earth rites went back far. They would always have been partly mysterious. But we couldn't surrender to them now. We had become self-aware. Forty years before, we would not have been so self-aware. We would have accepted; we would have felt ourselves to be more whole, more in tune with the land and the spirit of the earth. (351)

While the narrator laments a lost wholeness he might have felt once, he insists that he has gained more accurate knowledge of the world. "Self-aware[ness]" is opposed to "whole[ness]." In other words, the narrator does not insist that both ages had equivalent though different knowledge systems. His present knowledge is more accurate, though less comforting, than what he used to possess. This does not deny O'Callahan's point that even this knowledge would, if the narrative continued, presumably also be in need of correction. But this recognition suggests that the inquiry engaged in by the narrator is an ongoing process of refinement rather than a blanket rejection of all truth claims.

The potential limits of Naipaul's knowledge even at the conclusion of the novel point to what Satya Mohanty has termed the epistemological significance of error. For Mohanty, the existence of error in all accounts of the world does not preclude a kind of objective knowledge. If the positivist ideal of objectivity as transparent, unmediated knowledge is unfeasible, a recognition that certain theories or interpretive patterns enable more accurate descriptions of human experience than others remains possible. Within this more nuanced account of objectivity, error plays a crucial role in human inquiry. The inevitable existence of error in any account does not represent the basis for an *a priori* skepticism of all truth claims, as certain strands of postmodern theory contend. Rather, Mohanty asserts that careful analysis of error can produce "an analysis of the differences between different kinds of subjective or theoretical bias or interest, an analysis that distinguishes those biases that are limiting or counterproductive from those that are in fact necessary for knowledge, that are epistemically productive and useful."[45] For Naipaul, then, this suggests that the series of perceptions and misperceptions his narrator experiences enable a more sophisticated and accurate historical knowledge distinct from a notion of transparent or "absolute truth." The limits of the narrator's knowledge even at the end serve as a reminder that the process of identifying error is interminable, and any ethical deliberation is likewise subject to constant reevaluation and revision based on the best available knowledge at any given moment.

The idea of successive redescription provides a different way for readers to perceive the apparent determinism in both Naipaul and Rhys. The tendency of Naipaul's narrator and Antoinette to prefigure present events in relation to their childhood need not imply passivity but an effort to redescribe their experiences in terms of a narrative pattern that enables a rethinking of internalized colonial ideological biases. Indeed, the refiguration of time and prioritization of regret over progress in *Wide Sargasso Sea* explored in the last section depend on these prefigurative moments. Antoinette's repeated attempts to envision a place for herself – from the Coulibri garden to the rooftop of Thornfield Hall – suggest that she engages in an iterative process of identifying more fully and compellingly alternatives to present conditions of life. That is, the vision of a "reunion" with Tia – as problematic as it is – is impossible at the beginning of Antoinette's narrative; her own racism prevents explicit longing for her black playmate.

If Antoinette's earliest attempts to envision place and community only confirm the inevitability of lost place, exile, and death, these stories clarify what a more successful narrative would need to account for. The combination of unself-conscious use of the Edenic metaphor, failure to recognize her own racial prejudice, and inability to assert her own subjectivity guarantee that Antoinette's story of the garden at Coulibri reproduces the plot of *Jane Eyre*. Her subsequent attempts to envision a childhood place, however, suggest at least an implicit recognition of this failure. When she proceeds to recall her time in the convent school, Antoinette retrospectively recasts her depiction: "Quickly, while I can, I must remember the hot classroom. [. . .] We are cross-stitching silk roses on a pale background. [. . .] Underneath, I will write my name in fire red, Antoinette Mason, née Cosway, Mount Calvary Convent, Spanish Town, Jamaica, 1839" (53).

The linking of name and location asserts Antoinette's sense of belonging *to* a place and *with* her fellow schoolgirls. This effort to redefine herself and her relationship to the past will be interrupted only a few pages later by Rochester, who will claim the narratorial voice for the majority of the novel. Yet, the admittedly fragile and attenuated conception of community presented here begins a process of envisioning the reunion with Tia that occurs in her final dream. The metaphor of "fire red" thread with which she writes her name prefigures the fire she will set alight at Thornfield Hall – the act by which she will mark her name in Jane's narrative. She is capable here, as she was not earlier, of articulating her unique subjectivity with respect to a particular place and time – a place and time effaced by *Jane Eyre*.

Prefiguring the present in her childhood memories employs narrative repetition in ways different from the more familiar model of "colonial mimicry" as articulated by Homi Bhabha. Repetition, for Bhabha, points to the ambivalence of colonial discourse – its longing for "a subject of a difference that is almost the same, but not quite."[46] Through mimicry, postcolonial narratives destabilize the authority of colonial discourses by foregrounding this ambivalence. Graham Huggan's excellent essay on *Wide Sargasso Sea* demonstrates the implications of this notion of repetition. Focusing on images of parrots and parroting in the novel, Huggan argues that mimicry in Rhys' text resists incorporation within patriarchal and colonial discourse by appearing to submit to it, a submission marked by literal and metaphorical parroting. Ultimately this provides "a mode for the destabilization of a set of binary constructs (white/black, insider/ outsider, and so forth) which provide a spurious rationalization in *Wide Sargasso Sea* for the self-privileging practices of colonial power."[47] In contrast, the narrative repetitions produced by nostalgia are potentially disruptive to colonial narratives because they allow Antoinette to reformulate the way she perceives her own past. This iterative process of describing the lost places of the garden and the convent progressively diminishes her internalization of patriarchal and colonial biases by focusing on the losses they produced in her life.

Nostalgia allows a recovery, if only in the imagination, of the past that *Jane Eyre* erases. This becomes most apparent in her final dream as Antoinette stands on the rooftop of Thornfield Hall: "Then I turned round and saw the sky. It was red and all my life was in it" (189). Her narrative quest has finally arrived at the point where she can *locate* her memories in a place: "all my life was in it." She experiences the moment in terms of her own past and not that written by *Jane Eyre.* The redness of the sky, coming from the flames that are consuming Thornfield Hall, recalls the imagery of fire associated with earlier places: the fire at Coulibri and the "fire red" thread with which she stitches her name while at the convent school. These aesthetic connections between moments configure her life story as a coherent whole with particular longings and exigencies. This in turn grants significance to her actions, for they now appear – as Bertha's did not – to respond to her ongoing concerns. When she sets fire to Thornfield Hall in order to "write [her] name in fire red," continuing the process begun at the convent (53), the arson becomes her "writing" – not an act of madness, as *Jane Eyre* casts it, but an act of resistance against the history of colonial violence.

This last point distinguishes Rhys from Naipaul, and suggests why the former and not the latter might have become a canonical postcolonial author. While Naipaul also ends *The Enigma of Arrival* with a recognition of colonial violence and a call to action, the action he calls for does not obviously change the circumstances he observes. Although the narrator "was to learn that the ground was bloody, that there had been aboriginal people there once, who had been killed or made to die away," his very next words are strangely elegiac and empty of any claim about ongoing consequences: "our sacred world had vanished" (354). Indeed, the action the narrator finds most appropriate to his recognition is to begin writing the very novel he has now concluded, a novel which opens with a description of an English gardener and his garden. This conclusion is maddeningly serene to many postcolonial scholars because the discipline of postcolonial studies has arisen from a felt need to establish an institutional space for cultural expressions that challenge the values, epistemologies, and actions of colonial powers. Rhys presents more clearly a model for translating increased knowledge about colonial exploitation into determined acts of resistance. Whether or not Antoinette chooses to act out her dream of burning Thornfield Hall, the novel indicates that she will defy her captors in some recognizable way. Readers must search much harder in the final pages of *The Enigma of Arrival* to find in the image of the narrator retreating to his cottage some sense of resistance and hope for the future, and Naipaul's unwillingness to model his vision of ethics more straightforwardly has led to the tendency to read him as an apologist of empire.

REVERSING HISTORY: PAULE MARSHALL

Although the nostalgia apparent in Rhys and Naipaul has been a central feature of Caribbean writings since Lamming – and has played a crucial role in the critique of colonial values and philosophical biases – it is nonetheless viewed with suspicion by a number of Caribbean authors. Particularly within Caribbean women's fiction since the late 1980s, nostalgia often represents a "dangerous element," according to Mary Condé.[48] The longing for lost origins risks endorsing patriarchal traditions that link women to domestic spaces, and Caribbean women's fiction is particularly attuned to the ways in which writings of the 1950s to the 1970s so often recast imagined homelands as essentialistic maternal figures.

Jamaica Kincaid has been most outspoken in rejecting the metaphorical equation of home and mother. The harsh portrayals of mothers in *Lucy* (1990) and elsewhere have become particularly notorious, leading to unflattering reviews of Kincaid as being motivated by personal resentment. However, her depictions of maternal figures can be read as part of a sustained critique of earlier Caribbean writings that claim to recover lost communal histories and traditions. "I am very much against those new attempts to bind people of colour to traditional things," Kincaid asserts in an interview with Gerhard Dilger. "One of the reasons I left home was that I was a victim of tradition."[49] Reestablishing connections to ancestral sources and cultural practices disrupted by colonialism and the slave trade does not provide the basis for a universally liberatory narrative, according to Kincaid. Such a strategy risks reinstating patriarchal ethical norms that preexist the influences of colonialism and discourses of Western modernity, norms that restrict women to fairly conservative and limited social roles.

While Paule Marshall does not share Kincaid's outright rejection of a connection to African traditions, she does demonstrate similar reservations about nostalgia. Her first novel, *Brown Girl, Brownstones* (1959), culminates with its protagonist Selina Boyce preparing to reverse the journey undertaken by her parents from Barbados to Brooklyn. Frustrated with her life in a racist United States, Selina rejects the opportunity to go to college and the faint promise of bourgeois assimilation it implies, choosing instead to leave the country. Yet Marshall refuses to portray this trip as an unambiguous return to Afro-Caribbean cultural traditions. Selina leaves behind her mother and the Brooklyn Association of Barbadians, her most immediate and personal connection with the Caribbean; the ambivalence of her return is marked in the final paragraph as she removes one of two silver bangles "she had always worn" as her ship leaves harbor – a move that identifies both her physical and her psychic journey as a departure more than homecoming.[50]

More substantial reservations about nostalgia are present in Marshall's *The Chosen Place, The Timeless People* (1969). The members of the development team sent by the Center for Applied Social Research to Bourne Island all find themselves projecting their fantasies and memories on to the Bournehills community, a group of poor Afro-Caribbean farmers and laborers isolated geographically and culturally from the rest of the island. The Bournehills area is cast as somehow outside of time, and the development team perceive their journey there as a "return" to a premodern existence. Harriet, the wife of project manager Saul Amron, notes that during the airplane ride to the island "she had the sensation of being borne backward in time rather than forward in space."[51] The Bournehills residents are alternately characterized as uncanny reminders of people whom various team members have met before and as timeless people living lives synchronized with natural rhythms. Even Saul, an experienced anthropologist and perhaps the most altruistic member of the team, attributes a kind of agelessness and spiritualism to the community (137).

Caren Kaplan's analysis of Western travel writing clarifies the dangers of such identifications. Kaplan notes that the themes of nostalgia and exile apparent throughout European and American travel writing do not undermine but ultimately endorse a kind of colonial ideology that casts the Caribbean and elsewhere as remnants of a premodern era. That is, colonized spaces are defined vis-à-vis Western ones, denying thereby the originality and validity of indigenous cultures.[52] The same mentality leads the development team in *The Chosen Place, The Timeless People* to characterize the Bournehills community in terms of their own preoccupations, desires, and frustrations – characterizations that necessarily diminish their attentiveness to the worldviews of community members. Read in terms of the epistemological questions raised in the last section with respect to Naipaul, Marshall suggests that the development team are limited in their ability to gain accurate knowledge about the Bournehills community by their tendency to read the Afro-Caribbean population in terms of their own cultural biases or interpretive "patterns."

In ethical terms, then, Marshall's novel suggests that the danger of nostalgia lies in that it encourages a universalizing ethics. Marshall certainly never denies that Saul is guided by an impulse to help the people of Bournehills; if the Center for Applied Social Research has economic self-interest in mind, Saul is guided by a commitment to bring health and prosperity to the exploited. He fantasizes about Bournehills "reborn" and works tirelessly toward that end (23). Marshall also does not depict Saul as insensitive to cultural difference; to the contrary, he is quite critical of Harriet for assuming that the Bournehills residents would have similar desires to her own. "Everybody doesn't live by your standards. Your values aren't necessarily the world's," he insists (181).

Yet Saul himself holds a more subtle form of universalism. While he accepts that development will take different forms in different areas of the world, he retains the belief that development itself is a universal goal. And he appears to believe that accomplishing such development will redeem his own sense of guilt. This becomes most apparent in his relationship with one of the island's inhabitants, Merle Kinbona. Late in the novel, he recognizes "that perhaps in Merle he was being offered a chance to make good that old failure [to his first wife]. Perhaps this, more than anything else, was what bound him to her" (399). In this moment, Saul is guided by an ethical imperative to care for others, but his desire to find in the process appeasement for his own past means that his relationship with Merle is defined to no small degree by needs that are not hers but his own. The risk of using nostalgia to guide ethics, then, is that it identifies the present too simply as a permutation of a past experience. Marshall provides a cautionary tale about the model of successive redescription apparent in both Rhys and Naipaul, suggesting that such redescriptions do not necessarily provide more accurate knowledge or ethical insight about the present.

It would be a mistake to read Marshall and Kincaid as entirely rejecting nostalgia, however. As Katherine Sugg recognizes, if Kincaid refuses to present narrative trajectories common to romantic plots about women and the domestic sphere, she ultimately embraces a kind of nostalgic affect.[53] And Marshall demonstrates nostalgia much more explicitly in her writing. She notes:

I'm trying to trace history . . . to take, for example, the infamous triangle route of slavery and to reverse it so that we make the journey back from America to the West Indies, to Africa . . . to make that trip back. I'm not talking about in actual terms. I'm talking about a psychological and spiritual journey back in order to move forward. You have to psychologically go through chaos in order to overcome it.[54]

The longing to "reverse" the route back to Africa is motivated by an epistemological claim that overcoming "chaos" requires a radical rethinking of Afro-Caribbean historical knowledge. While Marshall does not define specifically what she means by chaos, it appears to refer to the historical experiences of enslaved Africans and their descendants. On this understanding, Marshall shares with Naipaul the idea that knowledge concerns not only the reconstruction of specific historical facts but also the creation of interpretive structures or narrative "patterns" by which individuals can make sense of their experiences. "Chaos" results from an inability to make sense of the horrific and inconceivable policies of colonial governments, and the islanders' longing for the homeland of their African ancestors invites an imaginative exploration of these experiences in terms of a coherent narrative of loss and return. Marshall's insistence that the return to Africa does not require a physical journey emphasizes that a recovery of a lost precolonial "purity" is neither possible nor even entirely desirable. The Afro-Caribbean populations she describes may have come into existence because of Western efforts to sunder African peoples from their historical backgrounds, but such populations have subsequently established unique identities that diverge from African cultural traditions.

From the perspective of *The Chosen Place, The Timeless People*, the most successful instance of imagined return is associated with the carnival masque replayed every year by the Bournehills community. Hortense Spillers suggests that the yearly depiction of Cuffee Ned's temporarily successful slave revolt against colonial authorities enables the community to construct a "redemptive historical scheme" that enables renewal by removing individuals from their discrete time and place.[55] The yearly reenactments mythologize Cuffee Ned so that he is not associated solely with a particular historical moment but comes to represent a kind of transhistorical messianic figure. The messianism associated with Cuffee Ned takes on a distinctly nostalgic tone as the marchers in the masque sing "*They had worked together!* [. . .] *They had been a people!*" (287). The story of Cuffee Ned provides the opportunity for the present community to imagine its own precursor, to envision a political solidarity that is currently threatened by the vicissitudes of economic deprivation and false promises of economic development. The success of the masque becomes apparent in a utopian moment in which islanders from all races and cultural backgrounds come together and join the Bournehills parade.

The novel's messianism does not claim that an actual return represents a viable possibility; the novel does not even claim that the solidarity achieved during carnival has an enduring quality. On the contrary, the various groups break up immediately after the celebrations. This recognition is crucial because it complicates Marshall's own commentary on the significance of the masque. During the ritual reenactment, according to Marshall, the Bournehills community "seem[s] apart from the Western notion of time altogether and as much a part of the past as the present. They might have been the rebel slaves who had refused to die. They might have been the original Africans who survived the crossing."[56] The dispersal of the crowd immediately after the masque, however, belies any idea that the community achieves or even seeks long-term identification with the "original Africans." Rather, the ceremony provides the basis for new Afro-Caribbean discourses capable of asserting the limits of Western versions of history and their emphasis on linear time.[57] The refiguration of narrative time in terms of cyclical repetition counters the implicit logic of progress that continues to inform imperialist discourses including Saul's narrative of Third World development.

Nostalgia becomes essential to the process of redescription here. Only because the Bournehills residents actively indulge in their fantasies of return to the moment of the Cuffee Ned slave revolt are they able to endow their present cultural practices with broader significance. These fantasies enable them to recast their masque not as an anachronistic holdover by individuals who have lost fluency with traditional cultural practices but rather as a part of a cyclical process of return and rejuvenation. By recasting their nostalgia in narrative form, community members redefine the present so that it evokes the presence of a past largely forgotten, providing a means of infusing meaning to fragmentary rituals whose original wholeness and reference has been effaced. Thus, the refiguration of narrative temporality in Marshall, as was also the case with Rhys and Naipaul, does not propose to recover a static ideal. Rather, the emphasis on return and cyclicity works against the tendency within linear narratives to dismiss loss as an inevitable byproduct of progress. Marshall never idealizes the poverty and rural agrarian life of the Bournehills community, and she clearly recognizes the value of certain forms of modernization and economic development. The repeated invocations of ancestral sources in her novels, however, caution against embracing modernization in solely Western terms. In this sense, Marshall's writings might be seen as redefining what constitutes a more genuinely progressive narrative, one more attentive to the victims of previous discourses of progress.

This idea is apparent even in Marshall's later works, such as *Praisesong for the Widow* (1983), in which she makes increasingly bolder claims about collective memory and memories passed along bloodlines. Like *The Chosen Place, The Timeless People*, *Praisesong for the Widow* describes a yearly pilgrimage by Afro-Caribbean populations to the island of Carriacou for a ritual reenactment of past events. The Carriacou Excursion, as it is called, attracts the attention of Avey Johnson, a middle-aged African-American widow who is fleeing from her affluent but shallow life in the United States. The music and dancing she observes, however, contradict notions that she has somehow returned to a mystical source of Afro-Caribbean culture and identity:

It was the essence of something rather than the thing itself she was witnessing. [. . .] All that was left were a few names of what they called nations which they could no longer even pronounce properly, the fragments of a dozen or so songs, the shadowy forms of long-ago dances and rum kegs for drums. The bare-bones. The burnt-out ends.[58]

Yet her initial frustration with what she witnesses is gradually replaced by a respect and love for the determination the participants demonstrate. As this passage indicates, Avey Johnson's nostalgia for a place of origin untouched by Western modernity enables her to describe the events she sees in very different terms than she would otherwise have been able to do. Although "separation and loss" are the dominant themes of the music she hears (244), Avey nonetheless reads the moment with respect to an idealized past "essence" rather than the encroachment of the tourist industry occurring around them. The essentialism of this text does not, however, endorse an either/or scenario for descendants of the black diaspora, that Afro-Caribbeans must either embrace modernity or reclaim a lost African cultural purity. Neither Avey nor the other participants in the Excursion seriously entertain the idea of living in Carriacou year-round. The basic economic realities of Caribbean life render such a notion unfeasible. But the recollection of the past at periodic intervals has crucial ethical value in offering alternative ideals to those promoted by Western imperial powers; by positing a common nostalgic past, the participants are capable of creating a basis for solidarity in the present despite current cultural differences and a high degree of acculturation.

Because the novel insists that a cultural essence endures, the ethics promoted by *Praisesong for the Widow* is more explicitly linked to the restoration of the past than was the case for either Rhys or Naipaul. Indeed, Avey's nostalgia inspires within her a quasi-evangelical impulse to spread the news about the Carriacou Excursion:

Nor would she stop with the taxi driver, but would take it upon herself to speak of the excursion to others elsewhere. Her territory would be the street corners and front lawns in their small section of North White Plains. And the shopping mall and train station. As well the canyon streets and office buildings of Manhattan. She would haunt the entranceways of skyscrapers. And whenever she spotted one of them [young African-Americans] amid the crowd, she would stop them. (255)

The sense of self-assurance that Avey displays here arises from her sense that the nostalgic past can be reconstructed in the present. In the final page of the novel, she decides to rebuild the house her great-aunt left her, to live out her retirement there, and to bring her grandchildren there to hear stories of their Igbo ancestors.

The convergence here between the fictional works of Rhys, Naipaul, and Marshall recalls the broader theoretical claim this chapter has staked out: the nostalgia in the works of these three authors represents salient examples of a phenomenon central to the genesis and production of Caribbean literature since the 1950s. The selective recollection of a lost or idealized past has served as a crucial strategy employed by Caribbean authors to redescribe the struggles facing postcolonial communities and the ongoing legacy of colonization. As cited in the epigraph to this chapter, the Martinique-born artist and intellectual Edouard Glissant writes, "One of the most disturbing consequences of colonization could well be this notion of a single History, and therefore of power, which has been imposed on others by the West."[59] In somewhat different ways, Rhys, Naipaul, and Marshall all answer Glissant's call for writers to challenge the idea of linear, universal historical time projected by the West, and to struggle to "contribute to reconstituting [the Caribbean's] tormented chronology."[60]

The longing to return that these authors describe, then, arises not from a sense of passive frustration or helplessness but from a recognition that Western epistemologies and ethics are intimately tied to specific ideas about time and progress. By casting the dominant experience of time within their fictional works in terms of repetition rather than the linear development projected by colonial histories and texts, Rhys, Naipaul, and Marshall reexamine colonial values and assumptions that continue to be prevalent even among postcolonial communities. Put in more general terms, the ethical value of nostalgia resides in its potential to open up epistemological investigations foreclosed by dominant cultural narratives.

The literary works of Rhys, Naipaul, and Marshall suggest that nostalgia is frequently far from comforting; it disturbs readers with images of what could have been. The haunting irony of nostalgia is particularly acute in *Wide Sargasso Sea*: nostalgia enables Antoinette to envision a more life-sustaining form of community than she could have otherwise done but at the expense of casting it as an irretrievably lost possibility. As a consequence, the moral demands placed on readers are both definite and uncertain – definite, in the sense that Antoinette's narrative establishes her as a compelling victim; uncertain, in the sense that the text provides no clear sense of what readers are supposed to do with this image of her. This uncertainty is only accentuated by Rhys' insistence that no action can ameliorate Antoinette's suffering – the final image of her is not the one of bitter defiance presented in *Jane Eyre* but rather one of a woman waking from a dream in which she recognizes for the first time the magnitude of her loss: the friendship and home she never experienced. If the final image of Bertha Mason offers at least the possibility of reading in the destruction of Thornfield Hall some sense of resistance to the history of colonial violence, the ultimate fate of Antoinette remains unresolved within the minds of readers.

On this point, Rhys speaks usefully to both Ricoeur's vision of a parallel history of victimization and the aspirations of this study. The strength of the ethical critique in *Wide Sargasso Sea* does not come from an explicit polemic against either *Jane Eyre* or colonialism. Antoinette herself, as demonstrated earlier, reproduces racist attitudes and colonial stereotypes. Indeed, she does so more than Jane. However, the novel acquaints readers with Antoinette's struggle to overcome her own internalization of these modes of thinking regarding race and time. In Ricoeur's terms, what Rhys accomplishes through Antoinette's narrative is nothing less than a redescription of reality. And since writing *Time and Narrative*, Ricoeur has increasingly claimed such a utopian function for narrative, envisioning the possibility of challenging "positions of power" through it. Narrative achieves this not only by describing past events but also by taking "the risk of resuscitating and reanimating the unkept promises of the past."[61] Rhys, however, draws attention less to unkept promises than to promises of empathy and solidarity that were never made. For Rhys, Naipaul, and Marshall, no originary moment of promise exists as such but it is constituted retrospectively through narrative, through repeated efforts to retell the past. And herein lies the irony: nostalgia does not provide a false, idyllic past but the impetus to struggle for a more utopian future. As Antoinette puts it, "Now at last I know why I was brought here and what I have to do" (190).

CHAPTER 3

"Loss was in the order of things": recalling loss, reclaiming place in Native American fiction

I followed their ancient way to my grandmother's grave. Though she lived out her long life in the shadow of Rainy Mountain, the immense landscape of the continental interior – all of its seasons and its sounds – lay like memory in her blood. She could tell of the Crows, whom she had never seen, and of the Black Hills, where she had never been. I wanted to see in reality what she had seen more perfectly in the mind's eye.
– N. Scott Momaday, *House Made of Dawn*

Is it possible to shape a community of shared experience in the wake of the cataclysm? What role does the heterological historian play in refiguring social existence always already disfigured by the cataclysm?
– Edith Wyschogrod, *An Ethics of Remembering*

Reading the last lines of *Wide Sargasso Sea* highlights one of the most intriguing claims made by the novels in this study: a nostalgic attitude toward the past can enable characters and readers alike to acquire, in certain instances, a kind of historical knowledge that recasts past events in the light of unfulfilled possibilities. Although Antoinette's nostalgia leads her to fantasize about events that never occurred, it nonetheless provides the basis for her new awareness at the end of the novel. Antoinette has gained knowledge about her internalization of colonial narratives and how it prohibited her from forming a more genuine relationship with Tia. By the same token, the "true history" of Bertha Mason is not meant to provide readers with a plausibly accurate reconstruction of hypothetical events "left out" of *Jane Eyre*. Rhys not only refuses to say whether Antoinette will burn Thornfield Hall but also changes the chronology of Brontë's novel, even moving the date of the marriage between Rochester and Bertha. The knowledge readers gain by reading *Wide Sargasso Sea* comes instead from greater awareness of how the internalization of colonial narratives has prevented certain relationships and communities from ever coming into being. And this is a form of knowledge that nostalgic narratives are uniquely able to offer; precisely because such narratives focus on what could have been, readers can perceive more clearly what circumstances or forces prevent individuals from realizing the relationships for which they long.

The argument that nostalgic fantasies provide useful historical knowledge stands in uneasy relation to conventional ideas about the study of history and the function of historical reconstructions. This chapter explores the implications of this argument with respect to the burgeoning scholarly interest in so-called "alternative histories" or "counterfactual historical speculation." Edith Wyschogrod represents one of the most interesting thinkers in this regard, arguing that the historian's "promise to the dead to tell the truth about the past" is fulfilled by depicting events that never occurred as much as by chronicling those that have.[1] For Wyschogrod, the imperative to tell the truth demands that historians not only chronicle events but also seek a complexity and phenomenological richness that demands the depiction of a range of historical possibilities – both events that occurred and alternative scenarios that might have occurred under slightly different circumstances. These latter events Wyschogrod terms the "negated possibles" of history (167). Within literary studies, a similar impulse has led Michael André Bernstein and Gary Saul Morson to insist upon the importance of what they call *sideshadowing*. Through sideshadowing, Holocaust writers and others portray not only historical actualities and impossibilities but also a "*middle realm* of possibilities that could have happened even if they did not."[2] In so doing, these writers reject the temptation to establish simple causal relationships between events, which for Morson and Bernstein tend to endorse historical determinism; instead, these writers are concerned with recovering the contingency of events – the sense that at any given historical juncture a range of outcomes are possible. As will become more apparent later, Wyschogrod, Bernstein, and Morson agree that such recoveries are useful forms of historical knowledge and that the possibility of ethics itself depends on them.

A preoccupation with alternative history has been a central feature of the Native American novel ever since the publication of N. Scott Momaday's Pulitzer Prize-winning *House Made of Dawn* (1968). This first novel of what has been termed the "Native American literary renaissance" depicts a struggle closely resembling that described by Wyschogrod: to negotiate between the responsibility to recount the past truthfully and the longing to draw selectively upon and even to refigure the past for the needs of the present. Simply to record a chronicle of suffering and oppression risks implying a kind of historical determinism that would deny Native American populations any sense of agency. At the same time, Momaday and subsequent Native American authors have all felt a moral responsibility to record the victimization of these same populations, who suffer from the loss of cultural continuity and physical proximity to sacred sites that historically have been the bases of tribal identities. Momaday balances these competing claims by depicting two intertwined narrative plotlines: one in which characters undertake a journey to sacred sites associated with ancestor figures, and a second in which the ancestral figures themselves confront a parallel crisis in their own era that they subsequently overcome. The intertwining of plotlines enables the description of both the enduring consequences of the European invasion of the Americas and the enduring possibilities of recovering a connection to tribal pasts through the mediation of literary forms.

In one of the several sets of these paired narratives in *House Made of Dawn*, John "Big Bluff" Tosamah, self-styled Priest of the Sun, describes his journey to Rainy Mountain to visit the gravesite of his grandmother, Aho.[3] Before 1887 Rainy Mountain was the site of the Kiowa Sun Dance – what Tosamah refers to as the "essential act of their faith" (133). His story not only relates the experience of loss after the United States Army bans the ritual but also reclaims a connection to Aho, who witnessed the final Sun Dance and yet learned to endure cultural displacement without abandoning tribal traditions. Tosamah's identification with her enables him to imagine an alternative to those histories describing the decline and disappearance of Native Americans by refiguring his life story in terms of a larger cyclical, though not predetermined, history. Because the experience of loss that Tosamah faces was previously felt and endured by Aho, her story implies the possibility that he, too, can endure and keep tribal traditions alive for future generations.

The potential for creating alternative histories that Momaday identifies in fiction has proved to be a central impetus for the Native American literary renaissance over the past three decades. Leslie Marmon Silko, James Welch, Linda Hogan, Louise Erdrich, Gerald Vizenor and others have all responded to and elaborated on the idea of history articulated in *House Made of Dawn*. As Louis Owens notes in his excellent study of Native American literature, there are striking similarities in worldview reflected in novels by authors from very diverse tribal and cultural backgrounds. Again and again, novels written by Native Americans have returned to the question of what constitutes a viable identity within an American society that commodifies tribal beliefs and disregards political and economic rights guaranteed by treaties. As Owens puts it, the question that defines Native American literature is: "What does it mean to be Indian – or mixedblood – in contemporary America?"[4] Neither Euro-American nor traditional tribal histories provide sufficient knowledge to answer this question because, as Owens' phrasing makes apparent, the very terms of tribal identities are now inextricably linked to social relationships with other groups that compose the conglomerate, if often contested, notion of Americanness. Native American novels provide a crucial intervention in this regard, and their articulation of alternative histories represents a response to the challenge of constructing a Pan-Indian identity that manages to preserve unique tribal cultures and to establish broad political solidarity. An analysis of Momaday and subsequent Native American authors, then, can provide an important contribution to the analysis of nostalgia in this study, clarifying how the historical knowledge produced by nostalgic narratives might help to build solidarity among groups not historically aligned.

Understanding the idea of alternative history articulated by Native American novels requires addressing rather than avoiding one of their most provocative claims: that narrative reconstructions can provide know-ledge of the past with a degree of intimacy matching, even exceeding, that provided by direct witness. Indeed, the intimacy claimed by characters – and frequently by the authors themselves in their nonfiction writings – goes far beyond that claimed by Rhys, Naipaul, or even Marshall explored in the last chapter, and would be deeply troubling to historians like Wyschogrod. Momaday repeatedly depicts characters claiming not simply to provide hypothetical alternative scenarios of the past but to "recover" the memories of ancestors. Characters describe visitations by long-dead ancestral figures; Momaday even projects himself into the past in his memoir, *The Names* (1976). My contention is that such claims must be read in terms of widespread anxieties among Native American thinkers and writers since the 1960s about cultural assimilation and acculturation. As Momaday makes clear in *House Made of Dawn*, the inescapable reality of cultural and physical displacement in the "late imperial" era means that figures like Tosamah and the novel's protagonist, Abel, no longer live as their ancestors did, in close physical proximity to places associated with tribal traditions, memory, and values.[5] Yet, restoring some connection to place is absolutely essential for the wellbeing of tribal members, according to Momaday: "the Indian conceives of himself in terms of the land . . . it is the only dimension in which his life is possible."[6]

Focusing particularly on the works of the two most prominent Native American authors, Momaday and Silko, this chapter explores the possibility of experiencing such a connection to sacred sites through the mediation of narrative. The interweaving of memory, imagination, and longing characteristic of nostalgia becomes crucial in this context, creating the possibility for characters, and readers by implication, to draw upon the experiences and stories of others to guide them in the imaginative "recollection" of events they never personally experienced. This is not to say that nostalgia restores an unproblematic connection to the past. Neither Momaday's nor Silko's narratives suggest that nostalgic fantasies replace the need for preserving personal memories, though characters use such fantasies to claim an intimacy with the past that resembles memory. *House Made of Dawn* and *Ceremony* refuse to deny the realities of acculturation and cultural alienation but rather draw attention to them; the use of nostalgia in Native American novels, in other words, does not abandon Wyschogrod's insistence on the writer's responsibility to fulfill the promise to "tell the truth about the past." Rather, such reconstructions of the past rely on individuals who retain at least fragmentary memories to recall them on behalf of the larger tribal community.[7] Indeed, such recollection becomes a basic moral responsibility.

REMEMBERING WHERE SHE HAD NEVER BEEN

Although Momaday has repeatedly demonstrated nostalgia for precolonial tribal life in his work, he resists the temptation to define the present in terms of absence and the past in terms of "authentic" memory. As the first epigraph to this chapter indicates, *House Made of Dawn* ironically associates Tosamah with personal experience and his grandmother with imagination or even nostalgia. He goes to Rainy Mountain to see "in reality" what she had seen "in the mind's eye."[8] Indeed, Tosamah reveals in a sermon to his Pan-Indian congregation in Los Angeles that his grandmother was only seven when the final Sun Dance occurred. For the vast majority of her life, she was prevented from going to Rainy Mountain; only in death is she reunited with this sacred space. Defying expectation, Tosamah's sermon reveals that the ancestor figure is not a personal witness to cultural traditions from which younger Native Americans feel separated: "she could tell of Crows, whom she had never seen," Tosamah states, "and of the Black Hills, where she had never been" (129). Yet, Tosamah insists that her imagination provides the most treasured source of cultural memory; she "had seen more perfectly in the mind's eye" what he personally witnesses.

Understanding why Tosamah privileges his grandmother's nostalgia requires a recognition of the historical context of the 1960s. Tosamah's experience reflects that of thousands of Native Americans in the Southwest who were relocated to urban areas of California during the 1950s as part of government relocation plans. Such policies had the effect of diminishing the political power of numerous tribes, and further removing large segments of a generation of Native Americans from the sacred spaces associated with their ancestors. The potential acculturation and cultural assimilation facing the relocated by the end of the decade was exacerbated by the death of the last generation to have witnessed certain rituals such as the Kiowa Sun Dance.[9] Aho and other members of her generation retained personal memories of the time before the experience of physical and cultural displacement caused by the United States government's banning of the ritual. With the passing of this generation comes the recognition that the tribal past is no longer preserved even in the memory of individuals, but only in stories and places like Rainy Mountain. Tosamah, like Momaday himself, experienced the Sun Dance only through stories told to him by his grandmother. The challenge Momaday faced in writing *House Made of Dawn* and *The Way to Rainy Mountain* at the end of the 1960s, then, was to construct narratives that could both account for the sense of lost tradition and recreate an intimacy with this lost past, to "remember" what he and his readers never personally experienced.

This challenge resembles that facing the contemporary historian, as defined by Wyschogrod. To resurrect the past "just as it was," the historian "must, *per impossibile*, be there (*Da*), to somehow inhabit the past she wishes to recover" (146). This impossibility becomes the defining condition of writing history because all contemporary history, for Wyschogrod, must proceed out of an awareness of "cataclysm" (xiii). The postwar era is defined by the perception of a metaphysical void in the wake of the series of mass exterminations that litter the twentieth century, and cataclysm becomes a term to evoke this sense of cultural rupture.[10] In this context, the historian must no longer perceive history as an *object* of study; an ethical representation of the past demands that the historian "utter the promise [to name the dead] from out of the cataclysm" (xiii). This promise, in other words, demands a reconstruction of the past as it was perceived by those living in the moment, not as a set of events to be viewed retrospectively. Failure to do so risks reducing the experiences of suffering that the historian describes into a data set that may be treated with detachment and even disregard. By restoring the "presentness" of the past, Wyschogrod's historian can attune readers to the contingency of any given moment and resist the tendency to perceive past events as foregone conclusions. Otherwise, the historian tends to *foreshadow* the present, to use Morson's term, thereby granting a sense of inevitability, even determinism, to history.

Aho provides a model for achieving Wyschogrod's dream of inhabiting the past; as noted earlier, Tosamah claims that "she could tell of the Crows, whom she had never seen, and of the Black Hills, where she had never been" (129). She achieves this by drawing upon tribal stories of individuals who have seen the Crows and the Black Hills. Using the historical details within these stories as a guide, she imagines herself "experiencing" these events as if she had been there. This blurring of the distinction between memory and imagination makes it possible for Aho not only to retain childhood experiences like the Sun Dance but also to claim a larger set of tribal memories. Hence, she is capable of bearing "a vision of deicide" after the United States Army banned the Sun Dance, for she continues to experience the ritual within her imagination. "She had learned that in words and in language, and there only," according to Tosamah, "she could have whole and consummate being" (94). By valuing imagination over personal witness, she both asserts the endurance of her culture despite relocation by the United States government and opens up the possibility of defining herself with respect to the stories of others as well as her own. For her comments do not specify that her "consummate being" is defined by her *own* words and stories; she retells tribal stories with the same attitude that she retells her own personal life. A two-century-old story about the origins of Devils Tower, for example, is told as if it were personally witnessed (131).

The merging of memory and imagination here and in Momaday's later work claims an intimacy with the past that goes far beyond what Wyschogrod would understand as responsible history. Her assertion that history writing is an inevitably fraught enterprise in which the past "can never be recovered in face-to-face encounter but only as image" stands in stark contrast to Aho's "memories" of the ancestral past in *House Made of Dawn* and Momaday's projection of himself into the ancestral past in his memoir *The Names* (112).[11] In this respect anyway, Momaday appears to share far more with theorists of postmodernism such as Arjun Appadurai and Charles Jencks. Appadurai argues that cultural displacement can be a positive condition, offering the opportunity for reinvention through imagination. "The imagination is now central to all forms of agency," Appadurai writes, "is itself a social fact, and is the key component of the new global order."[12] Individuals and communities all over the world, according to Appadurai, enact a process similar to Aho's in which they draw upon other cultures for ideas for remaking their own lives. From this perspective, Aho's efforts to recover and rearticulate Native American identity depend on a certain lost immediacy with her Kiowa identity. The banning of the Sun Dance makes it possible for Aho to "recollect" a much wider realm of tribal culture and history because her connection is established by an act of imagination. Jencks makes a similar argument, suggesting that cultural displacement enables individuals to assemble and select a history from any number of cultures. "We now have the luxury of inhabiting successive worlds as we tire of each one's qualities," Jencks writes, "a luxury previous ages, with their lack of opportunity, did not have."[13]

In contrast to Appadurai and Jencks, however, Momaday insists that the task of imagination is not only to envision "successive worlds" but also to recreate an intimacy with lost worlds. Indeed, Momaday resembles Wyschogrod in his insistence on commemorating experiences of loss and making such experiences essential to a community's identity. Particularly in his subsequent works, loss becomes the defining trope of history. In the prologue to *The Names*, for example, Momaday relates the history of the Kiowa, declaring that loss "was in the order of things, then, from the beginning."[14] The Kiowa come into being as a people, according to the story, by emerging from a hollow log; for Momaday, this emergence marks the loss of both the collective womb of "some primordial darkness" and the other Kiowa who were prevented from entering this world: "They were many more than now, but not all of them got out."[15] Loss thus becomes a defining feature of Kiowa identity; the tribal name *Kwuda*, or "coming out," evokes memories of those left behind. To associate the genesis and identity of the people with loss insists on commemorating the past and also represents a strategy for making subsequent losses meaningful. This strategy rereads the conquest of North America and the subjugation of Native American tribes in terms of an historical cycle in which such losses are undeniable but not apocalyptic. Even the loss of Rainy Mountain does not represent the destruction of the people but an integral part of their tribal history.

Momaday's efforts to retain Rainy Mountain as a central tribal site long after physical access is prohibited suggests that the function of imagination in *House Made of Dawn* differs from its function in Appadurai's and Jencks' theories. Imagination, for the latter, serves to discover new forms of agency. Within this context, preservation of the past as such is not a vital goal; indeed, Appadurai refers to the past as "a synchronic warehouse of cultural scenarios" for individuals to draw upon and discard as necessary.[16] Jencks likewise perceives cultural memories to be interchangeable and malleable. For Momaday, however, preserving a connection to the past is essential, even if this means that the connection is sustained by memory tinged with nostalgia. To the extent that imagination establishes agency in Momaday, it does so by reestablishing some presence of the past in daily life. This becomes more explicit in Momaday's most famous essay, "The Man Made of Words." In this essay, Momaday imagines himself being visited by the spirit of a tribal elder named Ko-sahn while he was writing *The Way to Rainy Mountain*. She insists that his fictional description of her is true simply because he imagines it so: "you have imagined me well, and so I am. You have imagined that I dream, and so I do." More importantly, however, she also insists that such imagination is necessary for Momaday's own being: "You see, I have existence, whole being, in your imagination. It is but one kind of being, to be sure, but it is perhaps the best of all kinds. If I am not here in this room, grandson, then surely neither are you."[17]

This last point suggests why nostalgia might be a privileged rather than compromised form of recollection for Momaday. Nostalgia opens up the possibility of "recalling" individuals and places that would otherwise be lost even as it foregrounds their loss. Ko-sahn's comments suggest the importance of her presence to Momaday's own life even as they remind him of his tenuous link to her and the Kiowa traditions he associates with her. This recollection does not deny the reality of what has been lost. Indeed, Momaday's efforts to recreate in this fictionalized reunion the day he actually did spend with Ko-sahn accentuate rather than deny her physical absence. The story underlines the fact that she continues to exist only within the recollections of others. Yet, in the context of the 1960s and 1970s, this notion of imaginative recollection addresses precisely the anxieties faced by Native Americans who felt an increasingly attenuated link to the past. By suggesting that his most intimate experiences are the product of imagination as much as memory, Momaday provocatively insists on the possibility for readers to experience Rainy Mountain with an intimacy resembling his own. If the identification with place, in other words, does not require physical proximity but an act of imagination, individuals can identify with mediated representations of place as well as the places themselves.

RELOCATING HISTORY

Momaday himself appears to challenge or at least qualify this claim elsewhere in *House Made of Dawn* through the depiction of the novel's protagonist, Abel. If Rainy Mountain is the central site of commemoration in *House Made of Dawn*, it is nonetheless inaccessible to him physically and figuratively. Abel is not Kiowa – in fact, he is a mixedblood of uncertain origins – though Tosamah definitely envisions Rainy Mountain to have become a Pan-Indian site of memory. From the first pages of the novel, however, Abel is described as alienated, drunken, displaced, and frustrated to such a degree that he cannot restore or even recall a connection to place. Momaday accentuates Abel's sense of displacement by counterpointing Tosamah's sermon with a sequence of bitter and frustrated memories that float through Abel's mind as he lies half-delirious from a vicious police beating on the beach in the Los Angeles area. Tosamah's story gives nothing to Abel. Rather than creating "harmony out of alienation and chaos, linking the world into one fluid working system," as Linda Hogan argues, the stark contrasts between Tosamah and Abel in the enmeshed storylines underline their very different relations to tribal places.[18] Indeed, the contrast suggests a rather troubling question: if recalling place is necessary for the recovery of Native American traditions, as Momaday asserts, what hope is there for a dislocated, diasporic subject like Abel to find a sense of community when he cannot remember place except in terms of being denied it?

The implications of this question incline me to be less optimistic than scholars who take *House Made of Dawn* to be a "narrative of healing."[19] Healing presupposes an original state of wholeness that is never apparent in the novel. Abel cannot *restore* himself to physical and psychic health by reestablishing a sense of place and tribal identity because he was never integrated within the reservation community in the first place. From birth, Abel is alienated: his father is absent and dismissed as "an outsider anyway" (11); Abel himself almost never interacts with anyone besides his brother and his grandfather, Francisco. Nor does the narrative structure promise much progress – its cyclicity suggests the likelihood of Abel's failure to establish a sense of belonging to place and community by foreshadowing the final chronological moments in the prologue.[20] From the first page to the last, Abel is isolated: from "He was alone and running" (1) to "He was alone and running on" (212). Retrospectively, readers discover why he is running, but this recognition does not alter the reality of his alienation.[21] Indeed, Morson's theory of foreshadowing would suggest that Momaday's prologue diminishes the significance of the efforts undertaken by various characters to help Abel because it depicts his alienation as a foregone conclusion.

Wyschogrod can be read to provide a somewhat different answer to the problem Abel embodies. Her theory of "negated possibles" asserts that any given moment has a set of possible future outcomes that are progressively negated as the moment moves from the present to the past (167). These alternative possibilities were viable at the time, even though they were subsequently annihilated. Indeed, Wyschogrod argues that they are essential for understanding the past and retaining a sense that the future continues to hold the promise of multiple possibilities. Hence, the historian has a responsibility to recover these alternative pasts. "It is this double disclosiveness of historical narrative," Wyschogrod writes, "the inclusion of paths not taken, that places possibility within the conspectus of the past" (167). In this light, Momaday's prologue foreshadows Abel's failure not in order to deny any hope to his quest but quite the opposite – it draws attention to the hope that exists at every moment in his life but which is never realized. The numerous ceremonies, memories, and stories in the novel function like "negated possibles." Tosamah's sermon, in particular, provides a model for responding to cultural displacement that Abel could have followed. In this way, Momaday clarifies for readers more precisely why Abel fails and why his failure need not have happened.

The contrast between Tosamah and Abel helps to establish why the latter's nostalgia only increases his sense of alienation. Unlike Tosamah and Aho, Abel denies rather than accepts the loss of culture and place. After returning from military service to the reservation, Abel insists that "he could remember whole and in detail" his life before leaving; only subsequent experiences are remembered as fragments (23). But when he tries to pray and sing, he finds he cannot. His insistence that the words remain "like memory, in the reach of his hearing" only underlines the fact that he cannot remember (58).[22] Indeed, there are strong hints that he never really understood the prayers in the first place; when Abel recalls the funeral prayers spoken over his dead brother, he insists that "he knew what it meant – not the words, which he never really heard, but the low sound itself" (13). But it is precisely the words that Abel lacks when he wishes later to "make a song out of the colored canyon [. . .] a creation song" to heal himself (59).

Abel's nostalgia leaves no possibility for his restoration because he insists on an idealized version of the past that stands in absolute contrast to his present alienation. Hence, from Abel's perspective, the ability to form a creation song is irrevocably lost. He never considers the possibility of "re-learning" these songs or seeking aid from the tribal elders because to do so would force him to recognize that he never knew them in the first place. Whereas Tosamah learns to value his grandmother's stories and draws upon her example of reclaiming place through remembering loss, Abel dismisses his grandfather, Francisco, as a man who "had not under-stood, would not understand, only wept" (23). Abel's insistence that he retains cultural experiences and traditions of which he was never a part leads to frustration and a metaphorical aphasia: "but he was dumb. Not dumb – silence was the older and better part of custom still – but *inarticulate*," the narrator notes (58).[23]

Aphasia has such profoundly negative consequences in the novel be-cause, for Momaday, imagination and language are inseparable. Indeed, this inseparability is a basic assumption in Momaday's thinking, and crucial to his conceptualization of Native American identity. In his essay "The Man Made of Words," Momaday asserts that an American Indian is "an idea which a given man has of himself"; however, he immediately adds that such an idea takes form only after it has been articulated: "And that idea [of what an Indian is], in order to be realized completely, has to be expressed."[24] Abel's aphasia means that he loses the ability to refigure his identity. Language was essential for Tosamah's and Aho's efforts – only after they expressed their fantasies in language could they reclaim an association with place and tribe. The contrast with Abel's situation is accentuated in the scenes that counterpoint Tosamah's sermon and Abel's fragmented memories as he lies on the beach after being beaten by the police. In these scenes Abel becomes identified with small silversided fish that hurl themselves on to the beaches by the hundreds (89). He himself cannot understand this identification: "Why should Abel think of the fishes? He could not understand the sea; it was not of his world" (98). While Tosamah uses the experience of loss to imagine a new attachment to place, Abel passively allows himself to be defined by a metaphor that emphasizes his helplessness and displacement. The metaphor is perni-cious, for it emphasizes the fish's – and Abel's, by extension – inability either to return to place or to survive in their displaced environment.

The novel offers little hope for Abel to address his cultural and physical displacement, for Abel remains aphasic from beginning to end. When he does attempt to speak to Francisco, the text notes that "he could not say the things he wanted" (58); after being relocated to Los Angeles, Abel refuses to talk to anyone for a long time (153). Even in the final scene of the novel, Abel has not regained his voice: "he began to sing. There was no sound, and he had no voice" (212). As a consequence, he cannot establish a connection to place through imagination, as Tosamah does. On the contrary, Abel's displacement becomes more pronounced over the course of the novel. He is taken from the reservation and put in prison for murdering the albino Fragua; later, he is relocated to Los Angeles, where he ultimately becomes identified with the beached silversided fish. And when he returns to the reservation, it appears that he returns too late. His grandfather Francisco dies shortly thereafter, and the land itself appears desolate: "there was no telling of the sun, save for the one cold, dim, and even light that lay on every corner of the land and made no shadow, and the silence was close by and all around and the bell made no impression on it" (193).

The death of the ancestor and the decay of the land point to the profound implications of Abel's aphasia for the perpetuation of Native American culture and tradition. Momaday reduces the importance of particular cultural losses by insisting that loss is a part of an historical cycle in which each generation preserves and refigures its ethnic identity. This characterization, however, places a heavy responsibility on every generation to participate in this process. Otherwise, the cultural rift between generations could indeed become unbridgeable. Tosamah recognizes this threat when he asserts that the memories and stories of tribal life represent a tradition that is "always but one generation from extinction" (97). The absence of the generation between Francisco and Abel represented by the absent father already suggests a tenuous cultural linkage between them. To the extent that Abel is a figure for the experience of contemporary Native Americans, his enduring aphasia and displacement point to a bleak future.

The implication here that Abel has a basic moral responsibility to recall and retell the past despite his cultural estrangement resonates with Wyschogrod's assertion of the historian's moral responsibility. The responsibility to recall the dead in both Momaday and Wyschogrod applies not only to witnesses but also to the storyteller and historian. Wyschogrod, like Momaday, insists that this obligation remains even though the historian must recover the past through a process of constructing what she calls *ficciones*.[25] Wyschogrod argues that the construction of historical narratives is inevitably a process that involves a certain degree of fictionalization, particularly in the process of recovering the "negated possibles" of history. This does not diminish the legitimacy of the historian's work, however; the "absolute truth" of history is not a product of "a purely transparent language that would render discursive rectitude possible" (168). Indeed, the nineteenth-century goal of composing objective historical records is not only impossible but also misses the primary moral responsibility to recall the experiences of those who would be (and were) silenced by such records. Precisely because these voices have been silenced, the historian's task involves a reconstruction of the past that cannot be fully verified in all its details; hence, the historian's task involves a degree of fictionalization. Likewise, storytellers in Momaday preserve Native American traditions and histories through a process that cannot guarantee historical verifiability. But Aho, in particular, fulfills her responsibility as a storyteller whether or not her stories of the Crow and the Black Hills satisfy this criterion. Her recovery of the past makes it possible for others, like Tosamah, to identify with events and places of which they have no personal experience. In this light, Abel's aphasia appears to be less a physical malady than an unwillingness to engage in a process of imaginative recollection on behalf of others.

This is not to suggest that either Momaday nor Wyschogrod subscribes to a notion that any fiction is legitimate history or that readers cannot judge between competing depictions of the past. Put another way, neither Momaday nor Wyschogrod is a relativist. Although Wyschogrod accepts the poststructuralist precept that absolute historical accuracy cannot be guaranteed, she insists that a degree of certainty can nonetheless be arrived at, grounded in what she calls "non-events" (168). The elimination of "non-events," events that can be demonstrated not to have occurred on the basis of material evidence, establishes a limited range of possible histories. In this way, Wyschogrod argues that the histories created by Holocaust revisionists, for example, can be refuted. Denials of the mass genocide engaged in by the Nazi regime represent inaccurate histories even if historians cannot describe in precise detail the lives or numbers of those murdered in the camps. Wyschogrod's characterization of history writing as *ficciones* recognizes the inescapable degree of uncertainty in historical narrative and foregrounds this fact. Indeed, *ficciones* are distinct from other kinds of historical narrative, according to Wyschogrod, in that they continually point to their own "ontological errancy" (32). In so doing, *ficciones* are capable of drawing attention to silences in existing historical records; the self-consciousness and metacommentary of *ficciones* compose an ethical history by "bringing forth the silences of the other rather than by forcing silence into speech" (32).

For Momaday, the question of legitimate and ethical narratives comes to the fore through the character of Angela Martin St. John. Angela is a

Caucasian who comes to visit the reservation's mineral baths, and during her stay she has a brief affair with Abel. When Abel is hospitalized after the police beating in Los Angeles, Angela visits him in the hospital and tells him a story she has made up of a young Indian brave born of a bear and a maiden. Although the novel does not render any explicit judgment on the legitimacy of her story, it provides several clues to suggest that it is an unethical appropriation of Native American stories.[26] Angela herself lacks familiarity with tribal customs and traditions; more importantly, unlike other stories that are transcribed fully in the text, Angela's is merely paraphrased. In a text so preoccupied with the fragility of the oral tradition and the necessity of preserving stories, the decision to paraphrase her story suggests a rejection of it.

Momaday differs from Wyschogrod in that he finds an optimistic potential even in such cultural appropriations. Wyschogrod would, no doubt, note Angela's lack of self-consciousness as well as the fact that her story silences Abel. "He didn't ever say anything about it afterward," Ben Benally notes (187). But Angela's story causes Ben to recall a bear story told to him by his grandfather – a story that is transcribed in the text (187–89). The implication appears to be that culturally inauthentic stories like Angela's can facilitate genuine recollection, even if such stories were told with potentially disingenuous intentions.

It is against this possibility that the grave consequences of Ben Benally's refusal to remember Native American traditions publicly on behalf of others like Abel must be read. His unwillingness to remember denies Abel the possibility of recovery. "You have to forget about the way it was, how you grew up and all," Ben asserts, if you want to live in the city (148). These assertions represent not only a denial of tribal culture but also a self-denial. Unwillingness to speak is a moral failure in this context, a willful forgetting. "Everything is here, everything you could ever want. You never have to be alone," Ben explains. Yet Ben is continually alone, inhabiting an apartment that he does not own. He is so alienated from his dwelling place that he cannot even open a window for fear of his landlord's wrath. Ben is almost literally suffocated by lack of place. He sacrifices his cultural heritage in the desperate attempt to belong to the cityscape, rationalizing the discrimination he faces and his continued willingness to tolerate it. His eagerness to assimilate destroys his ability to serve as a tribal priest. This becomes apparent when Abel approaches Ben for help. Ben takes Abel to a hill away from the city and attempts to heal him by singing a song from the Navajo Night Chant. Yet Ben becomes self-conscious and "ashamed" when he hears other Indians

carousing near by (146). As a result, the ceremony is only partially
successful: Abel's body is healed but he remains aphasic. Ben's physical
displacement means that he has no *place* for the sacred songs in his world.
Even if he remembers them, he cannot remember them on behalf of
others. This failure of memory is even more pronounced in the 1989
edition of *House Made of Dawn*, in which he forgets the final petition,
"Restore my voice for me."[27] The failure of memory denies Abel an
opportunity to be cured of his aphasia. While Abel manages to recall
the words to a song in the final scene, his continued aphasia – his lack of
voice – suggests an inability to preserve and pass on the oral tradition.

Ben's failure to recall the Night Chant prayer correctly suggests a more
nuanced reading of Abel's function in *House Made of Dawn*. Up to this
point in my analysis, Abel has figured largely as a negative exemplar
against which other characters are read. Such an interpretation, however,
overlooks the ways in which he conditions how readers experience the
more successful instances of reclaiming place. To read Tosamah's sermon
against the counterpointing scenes describing Abel's fragmented psyche
after the police beating creates a very different experience from reading
Momaday's account of his trip to the mountain in *The Way to Rainy
Mountain*. The latter work claims a cultural restoration that is heavily
qualified in *House Made of Dawn*. Abel's story draws attention to the fact
that nostalgic recoveries occur against a background of fragmentation,
displacement, and loss that is not erased. If Tosamah finds healing and a
sense of purpose, Abel and others like him do not – and Abel's enduring
alienation stands as an implicit indictment of Tosamah for dismissing
him as a "longhair" (148).[28]

Abel himself becomes a figure associated with memory in the sense that
his progression toward despair inspires other characters and the narrator
to recall the past. These stories and memories are retained on the textual
level and passed on to the reader. Abel's progressive decline into frustration, violence, alcoholism, and alienation testify to the value of these
memories and the possibility that they could sustain and preserve the
cultural integrity of Native American communities. The contrasting
scenes offer precisely what Abel himself never recalls. Through the figure
of Abel, the novel asserts the value of these stories and implies that readers
are charged with the responsibility of recalling them. Even in the final
scenes of the novel, the narrator provides access to memories that Abel
lacks. In his last days, Francisco desperately attempts to relate his most
treasured memories to Abel. However, Abel cannot make sense of them:
"but it had no meaning. The random words fell together and made no

sense" (195). In contrast, the narrator conveys them to readers with absolute clarity, insisting that "the voice of [Francisco's] memory was whole and clear and growing like the dawn" (197). By imagining the "voice of his memory," the narrator "restores" these otherwise lost memories much as Aho "recalled" memories of the Crow and the Black Hills possessed by her ancestors.

Perhaps the most significant instance in which Abel inspires the recollections of others occurs during the canyon scene mentioned earlier. His failure to form a creation song out of the "colored canyon" and thereby heal himself sparks the narrator to do what Abel does not: to "recall" the promise of a future return in the ruins of an ancient civilization that lived in the canyon:

[The remains appeared] as if the prehistoric civilization had gone out among the hills for a little while and would return; and then everything would be restored to an older age, and time would have returned upon itself and a bad dream of invasion and change would have been dissolved in an hour before the dawn. (57–58)

The nostalgia for the lost "older age" establishes a promise for the future: the hope for restoration becomes marked in the landscape itself. The remains of the "prehistoric civilization" not only stand as a reminder of the passing of a people but also insist upon their eventual return. The narrator's description thus challenges perceptions that the ruins fore-shadow the fate of contemporary Native Americans, thereby rejecting the sense of historical determinism projected by Euro-American histories. Recollection has this capacity to refigure the dominant metaphors of history, for Momaday, whether it is the product of personal memories, stories passed down generations, or even imagined reconstructions guided by nostalgia. The ruins need not signify inevitable and irretrievable loss but can be recast within narrative as the source of a conditional promise of restoration. This is not, however, a passive rationalization for inaction. For the "older age" to be restored, the present community must continue to preserve the remains of the past; otherwise, there is nothing to restore, and Abel functions in the text to accentuate this bleak possibility. Com-memoration becomes a basic moral responsibility, then, because the promise associated with the ruins continues to exist only as long as it is conveyed within stories.

This idea clarifies why the nostalgia for lost sacred places is so essential to Momaday's moral vision. The narrator's nostalgic fantasy of the lost community's restoration not only refigures perceptions associated with the ruins; it also provides the basis for establishing solidarity in the present among those living at Walatowa who may not share any common historical or tribal linkage. If the present community is composed of individuals who lack a common heritage, they could come to share an identification with the nostalgic past, "the older age." Indeed, the vagueness of Momaday's description and the absence of any specific tribal affiliation attributed to the "prehistoric civilization" invite identification even by Native Americans like Abel who lack strong cultural roots or ties. The civilization's "prehistoric" status implies that it predates and thereby encompasses all tribal identities. Were Abel to identify with it, then, he would share a sort of Pan-Indian identity with others at Walatowa despite knowing little about his own ancestry. In other words, the nostalgic connection to the past substitutes for a common cultural heritage as the basis for shared experience and community among the living.

MEMORY AND RESPONSIBILITY

While the physically wounded and culturally alienated male protagonist has been a recurring figure in Native American fiction since *House Made of Dawn*, this figure consistently finds healing and integration within tribal life that Abel never achieves. This is apparent, for example, in the next Native American novel to achieve significant critical acclaim, James Welch's *Winter in the Blood* (1974). The unnamed Blackfoot narrator of the novel is, like Abel, a mixedblood without a father or other strong tribal ties; he, too, loses a grandparent toward the end of the novel. Yet, if the death of his grandmother means that the narrator loses a familial connection to someone who has experienced precolonial tribal life, the narrator nonetheless learns to recast the event as part of a process whereby he identifies with Blackfoot culture in ways he was previously unable to do. The last line of the novel notes that the narrator throws his grandmother's tobacco pouch into the grave, marking an acceptance of his responsibility to commemorate her death and thereby to assume his own place within tribal life. The narrator's success on this account is emphasized by his discovery shortly before this event of the identity of his true grandfather, Yellow Calf the hunter. While the narrator has not been physically healed in the final scene, still suffering from a bad leg that feels like a "tree stump," the social network of relationships he establishes through Yellow Calf points toward the recovery of cultural continuity.[29]

A broader recovery of tribal cultural life is claimed in Welch's later novel, *Fools Crow* (1986), in which he portrays Blackfoot life during the period when the Euro-American presence first becomes disruptive. The novel refuses to indulge in tragic lamentation even after it becomes clear to the eponymous protagonist that his tribe cannot triumph over the military forces of the United States government. Indeed, the final image of the novel belies any sense of defeat as the narrator describes the return of the buffalo herds and concludes with a pronouncement that "all around, it was as it should be."[30]

The novel most clearly written as an extension of and response to *House Made of Dawn*, Leslie Marmon Silko's *Ceremony* (1977), makes even stronger claims for the possibility of literary fictions to revitalize or recover Native American traditions and culture. The novel's protagonist, Tayo, shares with Abel not only a sense of alienation born of his mixedblood heritage and uncertain parentage but also an ailment incurred while serving in World War II. Like Abel, Tayo returns to reservation life diseased and haunted. In stark contrast to Momaday's novel, however, *Ceremony* depicts its protagonist finding physical recovery, integrating himself within tribal culture, and reclaiming an identification with sacred spaces appropriated by the United States government. Indeed, Silko's novel makes much more radical claims about the possibility of nostalgia to "restore" the longed-for past than any of the other novels this study will consider. Even in the face of obvious signs of deteriorating artifacts, sacred spaces, and cultural practices, characters in the novel insist that memory itself preserves a kind of ontological essence. Observing a cliff painting whose outlines have been washed away almost completely, Tayo's lover/guide Ts'eh assures him that "as long as you remember what you have seen, then nothing is gone."[31]

Silko's claims are difficult to evaluate in terms of Western poststructuralist-influenced theories of historiography like Wyschogrod's. For Wyschogrod, the fallibility and fragility of memory limit the extent to which historians can claim a sense of certainty; the transparency of memory that Ts'eh takes for granted implies that a much higher degree of historical certainty is possible, and hence she can assert that through remembering "nothing is gone." Wyschogrod would be unlikely to accept such a claim because the theories of representation on which her work is based assume a basic inadequacy of language to reflect transparently the objects it depicts. The problem facing a historian is thus not solely one of ideology but of language itself. Even the most well-intentioned and self-conscious historian cannot claim, on Wyschogrod's understanding, to move beyond *ficciones* because he or she cannot guarantee the stability of the signifiers that would compose an historical document. Following the predominant Western theory of linguistics dating back to Saussure, Wyschogrod characterizes language as fundamentally unstable because no particular word has any inherent relation to the thing it describes. Rather, the significance of a word arises from its interrelations with the other words and signs that constitute a language.

The great difficulty of interpreting *Ceremony* in these terms becomes apparent from the novel's first sentences. Drawing on Pueblo creation stories, Silko asserts an inextricable and inherent link between word and thing:

> Thought-Woman, the spider,
>   named things and
>   as she named them
>   they appeared.

> She is sitting in her room
> thinking of the story now
> I'm telling you the story
>   she is thinking. (1)

According to this idea, Ts'eh's claims for memory are perfectly sensible. If the act of naming creates the object that the word describes, then the act of remembering offers the promise of re-creation.[32] And Silko's insistence that the creation of the cosmos, for the Pueblo, is an ongoing process implies that reclaiming a connection to lost sacred spaces is a feasible and, indeed, logical task for Native American literary texts to undertake. The radical conclusion of these claims is that Native American fiction offers even the most highly acculturated Native American the possibility of recreating a viable cultural connection to the tribal life of previous generations.

Silko resists the implications of her own claims, however, particularly with respect to the restorative capacities of language. The novel characterizes the precolonial past in quasi-prelapsarian terms. The first Native American healer to whom Tayo turns, old man Ku'oosh, laments his inability to heal diseases that were once curable. "There are some things we can't cure like we used to [. . .] not since the white people came," Ku'oosh states (38). This sensibility echoes throughout the text, and can be found in assertions made by the narrator that for thousands of years Native Americans shared a single clan name and even a single consciousness. The "simple certainty of [. . .] how everything should be" is only lost, on this account, after the first contact with European explorers (68). Yet no character in the text claims the possibility of restoring a precolonial cultural purity despite assertions that the material world is continually reproduced through stories, that Euro-Americans are nothing more than creations of Indian witchery, and that time itself is cyclical rather than linear. Indeed, the endorsement of cultural hybridity by the healer Betonie later in the novel at least implicitly acknowledges the impossibility of restoration and return. Instead, Betonie's model of hybridity suggests that the preservation of Native American cultural practices requires abandoning the very principle of restoration. "I have made changes in the rituals," Betonie asserts. "The people mistrust this greatly, but only this growth keeps the ceremonies strong" (126).

Silko's unwillingness to depict the kind of restoration that her own theories promise can be explained in part by arguing that the generative capacity of language limits its restorative potential. On this understanding, storytelling still creates the material world, but every act of storytelling adds new dimensions to the same universe. Or, more glibly put, nothing can be unsaid in Silko's world. This becomes most apparent during the scene describing the creation of Euro-Americans. Betonie tells Tayo of a contest among Indian witches to determine who has the most power. The contest culminates when a witch puts forward a story that proves more terrifying than all the other charms or powers demonstrated previously. The story brings into existence entities whose fear of the world leads them to find fulfillment only in destruction. Yet when the other witches plead for the winner to "[c]all that story back," and thereby to uncreate Euro-Americans, the witch replies that it is impossible (138). Betonie's story suggests an understanding of language that shares affinities with the Bakhtinian notion of heteroglossia. Every utterance reshapes and revises the significance of previous statements, causing them to take on multiple layers of meaning. Thus, the "original" statement or story, for Silko, no longer exists as such because it cannot be rearticulated without reference to subsequent utterances. Hence, the logic of cultural hybridity in *Ceremony* can be read as a response to the recognition that Native American identity and practices have become inextricably tied to the identities and practices of other Americans.

This explanation does not fully resolve the question why Silko repeatedly depicts the past in prelapsarian terms. Even Betonie seems to cast the precolonial past in such a manner, noting that "[a]t one time, the ceremonies as they had been performed were enough for the way the world was then" (126). Wyschogrod's theory of alternative history is of some use here. Wyschogrod can be read to argue that challenging historically deterministic accounts of American "manifest destiny" and other myths of the "vanishing Native American" demands the creation of alternative historical narratives that have sufficient plausibility that they cannot be falsified by available material evidence. As described earlier, Wyschogrod achieves this end through a self-conscious reconstruction of voices silenced by existing historical narratives. But more obviously mythical narratives like Silko's stories of a prelapsarian Pueblo past can also meet Wyschogrod's criterion for alternative history. Precisely because she accepts a radical discontinuity between the past Betonie describes and the late imperial present, Silko gains greater freedom to describe the past according to a very different set of philosophical and cultural biases from those currently in circulation. Mythical narratives describe realms of possibility that are sufficiently removed from present reality that they can be neither verified nor falsified on the basis of material evidence. Thus, even if many readers are unlikely to read the story of the witches conference as an historical event, it represents a form of historical knowledge in that readers are afforded the opportunity to understand the social relationships between ethnic American groups in ways that differ from the predominant model of white majority-Native American minority. Native Americans are not cast as incidental aspects of lands that Europe discovered; rather, they are depicted as the center of an historical narrative in which the Europeans are peripheral characters.

Thus, Tayo's quest for physical healing and a sense of connection to Native American sacred spaces provides Silko with the opportunity not only to rethink Native American identity but also to redefine the basic terms of discourse about American identity more broadly. *Ceremony* does not deny the universalism characteristic of Western histories, but recasts the normative subject within history as Native American rather than Euro-American. As Tayo prepares for a final confrontation with "the destroyers" outside the mine shaft where uranium for the first atomic bombs was extracted, Tayo experiences a fantasy of being reunited with his relatives, both living and dead. This fantasy of restoring kinship ties also claims much broader, metaphorical connections across space and time to include a family of all humankind. And this broader identification enables the narrator to make a rather provocative assertion: "From that time on, human beings were one clan again, united by the fate the destroyers planned for all of them, for all living things" (246). The language of restoration implied here, "one clan again," is crucial to addressing anxieties about endorsing cultural hybridity, that it might lead to assimilation or what has popularly been called the "melting pot" model of multiculturalism. *Ceremony* allays these concerns by redefining the basic terminology of American identity according to Pueblo conceptions, referring to a united clan rather than country. Indeed, the implication here is that Silko's model of hybridity will paradoxically lead to the restoration rather than loss of tribal cultures. Multiple identifications – as Pueblo, Native American, and American – do not necessarily come at the expense of one another, for Silko. The Pueblo participation within contemporary American society is cast as part of a broader, ongoing narrative of Native American history rather than the final chapter in a tragic narrative of cultural annihilation.

The vision of alternative history proposed here, like that proposed by both the Native American novelists and the academic theorists explored earlier, requires a reevaluation of the dominant Western model of memory and the values it implies. As Edward S. Casey notes in *Remembering: A Phenomenological Study*, memory is increasingly understood in terms of a computer metaphor. On this understanding, memory represents discrete bits of data to be deposited and stored. To remember something involves a passive process of registering and storing incoming sensory impressions as they occur. Thus, the person remembering is significant to this process only in so far as he or she is capable of accurately representing the event or image to be remembered. This idea of what Casey calls passivism has philosophical roots tracing back to Aristotle, and extends into the twentieth century in the works of Bertrand Russell. According to this model, the basic criterion for useful memory is its accurate representation of what happened, and the act of remembering should be one in which the subjectivity of the rememberer is bracketed off as much as possible. Factors related to the rememberer's desires, beliefs, or other memories never contribute to remembering, but threaten to reduce the mimetic accuracy of memory. Wyschogrod's *ficciones*, Betonie's story of creation, and Tayo's discovery of a universal human clan identity are all flawed forms of recollection, on this account, because they privilege creative and highly subjective engagements with the past.

Recognizing that every model of memory implies a set of value judgments about what acts of remembering are culturally useful or acceptable, Casey defends a model that places the activities of the rememberer at the center of concern. In particular, Casey focuses on the kinds of knowledge and experience that can be gained by a more activist model. He asserts, "Rather than a mere repository *of* experience, remembering becomes thereby a continually growing fund *for* experience: a source itself, indeed a resource, on which not only future acts of remembering but many other experiential modes can draw as well."[33] Casey's argument suggests that memory provides a crucial contribution in many circumstances in which accurate replication of an event or image is not of primary concern. Mourning represents only one significant instance in which memories are used to redefine a person's experience of the world and the ways in which he or she can interact with others. Mourning, as an act of remembering, involves not only the effort to preserve accurate images of the lost loved one; it also involves a process through which the mourner redefines his or her relationship to the dead by deliberating over which memories are foregrounded in the act of commemoration and how they are presented. As demonstrated by the narrator of *Winter in the Blood*, mourners often reassess their values in the process of remembering. This sense that remembering involves introspection, self-analysis, claims of affiliation, and other features not necessarily tied to retrieving exact sensory impressions invites a more open attitude toward purportedly inaccurate or "inauthentic" memories like those associated with nostalgia. Nostalgia, on this understanding, can be viewed as a form of remembering that provides crucial experience without necessarily preserving an accurate replica of the lost homeland.

As was the case with Wyschogrod's theory of history discussed in the last section, Casey's rejection of the computer model of memory implies neither that all acts of remembering are equally valuable nor that accuracy is unimportant. Casey rejects extreme theories of activism, which suggest that memory literally creates the past by bringing it into being. As Casey notes, memories often appear without deliberate effort, and what is recollected frequently does not correspond to what a person might desire. Rather, his thesis is more restricted to suggest that while memory should be true to the past in certain respects, remembering as mimicry or replication would not represent the only way for this to be possible. On this point, Casey's emphasis differs somewhat from Wyschogrod's. For Wyschogrod, as detailed earlier, depictions of the past are bound by a basic criterion of accuracy that denies "non-events" – occurrences that can be disproven on the basis of material evidence – the same status as those that cannot be refuted. For Casey, acts of remembering are differentiated on the basis of the extent to which they create useful sources of experience on which individuals can draw for guidance. This understanding would suggest, for example, that nostalgia could be useful in instances in which the idealized past does *not* represent a means of escapism or a refusal to confront present dilemmas. When it does, though, nostalgia is pernicious because the fantasy of the past prevents the nostalgic from using the resources of memory and imagination to discern the sources of present disappointment.

The moments of nostalgia in *Ceremony*, like those in *House Made of Dawn*, would be considered in Casey's terms to be useful acts of remembering because they enable characters and readers to experience the present in ways they might have been otherwise unable to do. After Tayo's final confrontation with the destroyers, for example, the novel indulges in one of its most nostalgic moments. Tayo is met by the spirits of his Uncle Josiah, Cousin Rocky, and grandmother – and this reunion occurs despite the fact that the first two died years earlier: "He dreamed with his eyes open that he was wrapped in a blanket in the back of Josiah's wagon. [. . .] Josiah was driving the wagon, old Grandma was holding him, and Rocky whispered 'my brother.' They were taking him home" (254).

The moment represents the "restoration" of a sense of place and community that Tayo never felt before. This is most evident in the image of Rocky referring to him as "my brother." In life, Rocky referred to his mixedblood cousin as brother only once. This restoration of a longed-for world is apparent in the physical landscape as well. In the sky, "clouds with round heavy bellies had gathered for the dawn," signifying the end of the seven-year drought linked to Tayo's illness. The land itself is reconsecrated, and Tayo's successful integration within tribal cultural life is marked by a counterpointing mythic narrative describing Hummingbird's and Fly's quest to undo a similar curse of drought in their world. Yet, the narrator immediately qualifies her previous claims of restoration, deemphasizing their importance and necessity. If Tayo is carried home in a spirit wagon accompanied by his relatives, the narrator notes that Tayo "had come a long way with them; but it was his own two feet that got him there" (254–55). Likewise, the narrator describes the return of the rain clouds poetically, only to dismiss their significance several sentences later: "It was not necessary, but it was right, and even if the sky had been cloudless the end was the same. The ear for the story and the eye for the pattern were theirs; the feeling was theirs: we came out of this land and we are hers" (255).

The fantasies of recovering an idealized home, then, prevent neither Tayo nor the narrator from recognizing the reality of loss. For the purposes of the novel, accuracy about the presence or nonpresence of the rain clouds is unimportant because the text is concerned more about rethinking identity than recovering some putative lost purity. The description of the lost world enables the articulation of solidarity across tribal and ethnic lines belied by obvious differences in the present. And this idea of solidarity retains its force as an ideal whether or not the nostalgic world with which it is initially associated can be realized. The shift in perception enabled by such fantasies is apparent in the narrator's pronoun shift: the move from third-person plural to first-person plural in the quotation above is possible because characters and readers now share, theoretically at least, a common fantasy of restoration. Henceforth, the novel suggests, the struggle Americans face is not one defined by ethnic conflict, Euro-Americans versus Native Americans, but by those committed to ecological awareness and preservation of the environment versus those committed to selfish gain.[34]

Whether or not *Ceremony*'s efforts to recharacterize identity debates in the United States seem overly optimistic, they point toward the increasing politicization of Native American literature since *House Made of Dawn*. Momaday's characterization of Native American identity eschews specific political ideologies, focusing instead on the ethical values implicit in identity claims. His assertion that an American Indian "is a moral idea" which a person has of himself or herself establishes a broadly inclusive identity category that avoids direct links to specific political claims to land and treaty rights.[35] Such a redefinition has political implications, of course, and serves to reposition Native Americans within American society. Momaday's characterization asserts that the long history of Native Americans inhabiting the Americas has cultivated in them an acute sense of the ecological needs of the country, thereby granting Native Americans a unique and vital voice within American discourses. But notably, Momaday's claim of Native American expertise is cast as a means not of excluding other populations' claims to land but of establishing a model for the United States as a whole to endorse what he calls "an American land ethic."[36]

Silko largely accepts this conception of Native American identity in her first novel, a conception that shuns any particular political affiliation, yet she demonstrates much greater eagerness to identify her work in terms of specific political ideologies in her second novel, *Almanac of the Dead* (1991). In this novel, Silko repeatedly asserts connections between Marxism and tribal philosophies about history. Marxian notions about the irreversible processes of history driving toward the realization of a socialist utopia provide a kind of materialist grounding for Native American prophecies predicting the recovery of tribal lands from European colonizers. Land reclamation thus becomes not merely an idyllic fantasy but an historic inevitability to which fictional texts have a responsibility to testify. And although Marxism as a political force on the world stage is fading even as Silko is completing her novel, she claims that Marx and Engels were not the originators of revolutionary history but interpreters who grasped incompletely how forces of nature act within the political realm.[37] The character Angelita La Escapía reflects late in the novel that "[Engels and Marx] had been close, but they hadn't quite got it. [. . .] They had not understood that the earth was mother to all beings, and they had not understood anything about the spirit beings."[38]

The image of the longed-for homeland becomes the basis for political activism in other more recent Native American novels, particularly Linda Hogan's *Solar Storms* (1995). Following the tradition established by Momaday, *Solar Storms* traces the returns by Native American characters to homelands from which they have been separated or of which they have no recollection. Yet the novel differs from *House Made of Dawn* and other previous Native American novels in that almost half of the plot is devoted to the political struggle against developers trying to exploit Native American lands. Hogan depicts a series of peaceful and violent protests engaged in by the protagonist, Angel, and her maternal ancestors. Such activities create political solidarity across generational and tribal lines by invoking an idea of a lost unity and wholeness. "To fight has meant that we can respect ourselves, we Beautiful People," Angel asserts toward the end of the novel. "Now we believed in ourselves once again."[39] As Momaday and Silko did before her, Hogan depicts solidarity not in terms of new affiliations but as the restoration of what should have been all along. Even here, however, the differences from Momaday are strikingly apparent. For the Pan-Indian solidarity envisioned by *Solar Storms* links literary characters to existing political organizations including the American Indian Movement, whose members take part in the protests described in the novel. Literary production and political activism are seen as mutually constitutive, and this connection is cast as crucial to the future of Native Americans.

The implied function of Native American fiction here begs comparison with Wyschogrod's understanding of history as a gift of hope. The second epigraph of this chapter identifies two interrelated questions that Wyschogrod poses: 1) what is the possibility of community in the wake of cataclysm; and 2) what is the role of the historian in this process? This chapter's analysis has demonstrated that the answer to the latter provides an answer to the former. The historian is uniquely capable of restoring a sense of possibility to the present by recovering the "negated possibles" of the past. This recovery depends on both rigorous research to uncover the contingency of historical events and a self-conscious writing style, *ficciones*, that draws attention to voices silenced by history. Wyschogrod is less optimistic than the literary authors in this chapter about the degree to which the silenced past can be made to speak. Even if Momaday, Welch, Silko, and Hogan repeatedly admit that the recollection of the past depends on the imagination, they nonetheless see these "memories" as providing a legitimate, perhaps privileged, access to the past. The gift of history, for Wyschogrod, is more modest. By recovering the "negated possibles" of history, the historian enables others to see the future as the realm of possibility, not determinism. The contingency that governs the past governs the future as well. And by casting the future in terms of a more just present, Wyschogrod argues that the historian provides a sense of hope that is a "spur to activity" (248).

This last assertion recalls this chapter's initial thesis, that ethics in much of contemporary Native American fiction and in Wyschogrod's work depends on the hypothetical reconstruction of pasts that have never occurred. The sense of hope that provides an ethical orientation or a "spur to activity," as Wyschogrod calls it, hinges on the recovery of "negated possibles" or the nostalgic past. A simple chronicle of the past would not provide hope, as understood either by literary authors including Momaday, Welch, Silko, and Hogan or by scholars including Wyschogrod, Bernstein, and Morson; such a chronicle would only record a history of unameliorated suffering that grants a sense of determinism and inevitability to the future as well as the past. Hope can exist only in a situation where individuals perceive the possibility that the future might be different from the present, and Wyschogrod's historian and the story-tellers in Native American fiction all turn to the past to assert that such a sense of possibility previously existed. By the same token, however, hope cannot exist without recalling loss. Loss profoundly shapes the possibilities that the future can be imagined to take. Wyschogrod's historian can envision a future of multiple possibilities only by recovering past possibilities that were annihilated by the passing of time. Tosamah's pilgrimage to Rainy Mountain and Tayo's confrontation at the uranium mine both suggest that the future is imagined in terms of a "restoration" of a nostalgic past. Hence, every effort in the novel to reclaim place depends on a prior act of recalling its loss.

Although Momaday, Silko, and Wyschogrod all assert that their work provides hope for reestablishing communities in the wake of displacement or cataclysm, their visions of community are ultimately irreconcilable. Following Levinas, Wyschogrod rejects what she calls "communities of immanence" (218). This refers to the Platonic and Aristotelian ideals of autochthony (common soil or place); it also refers to the capitalist and

Marxian ideals of production and exchange as the basis of community. Wyschogrod envisions a "community of hospitality" that is informed by poststructuralist notions of exteriority and deterritorialization. The literary authors in this chapter would all reject this latter notion; one of the most basic claims of contemporary Native American fiction has been that viable communities must be grounded in some common experience of place, even if the connection to place is retained only through nostalgia. As the Native American activist and thinker Vine Deloria, Jr., puts it, "Sacred places are the foundations of all other beliefs and practices because they represent the presence of the sacred in our lives."[40] Otherwise, individuals like Abel and Tayo feel no moral responsibility for their tribal community. The destruction Abel causes, as much as his own ailments, testifies to the importance of identifying with place. Momaday does not insist that tribal sites must be restored to an historical or mythical precolonial purity. Nostalgia opens up the possibility of refiguring the relationship to the past so that individuals might identify with places not historically associated with their tribal identities. The promise of Rainy Mountain in the late imperial context is that it functions as a Pan-Indian site. And authors like Momaday have used nostalgia to claim a broader Indian heritage for themselves: "I thought of myself as an Indian rather than Kiowa," he notes in a conversation with Charles Woodward.[41] But *House Made of Dawn*, *Winter in the Blood*, *Ceremony*, and *Solar Storms* all make it clear that some basic attachment to place is the precondition for community.

Momaday's and Wyschogrod's conflicting visions of community provide useful correctives for each other. Momaday identifies the limits of Wyschogrod's attempt to conceive of history "in the wake of the cataclysm" (218). If the term "cataclysm" helps her to link disparate experiences of suffering into a common history – much as I discussed Ricoeur doing in Chapter 2 – it effaces the various ways in which suffering was experienced historically. For Native Americans, "cataclysm" is associated with the loss of sacred places, and Wyschogrod's vision of a deterritorialized community fails to address this experience. On the other hand, Wyschogrod points to the dangers of Momaday's nostalgia. If nostalgia refigures the past so that individuals may claim memories of events and places not experienced personally, it diminishes the distinction between direct and vicarious experiences. The danger, for Wyschogrod, would be effacing the alterity of other individuals in the process of identifying with their experience and thereby perpetuating their historical silencing. Indeed, this corrective becomes all the more necessary later in Momaday's career as he increasingly endorses what has become his most controversial notion: blood or racial memory.[42]

Momaday's claim that certain stories are preserved and passed along genetic lines as if they were personal memories threatens to appropriate the voices and experiences of his ancestors. Blood memory also diminishes the moral claim that aphasia places on readers. Abel's malady asserts the enduring consequences of governmental policies against Native Americans – Abel provides a concrete image of the "silenced others" that Wyschogrod calls on the historian to depict. Indeed, Abel provides in *House Made of Dawn* precisely the corrective for Tosamah that Wyschogrod might offer for Momaday's later works. If Tosamah's nostalgic fantasies offer the hope of restoring a vital connection to the past despite cultural dislocation, Abel's presence attests to the fact that such "restorations" cannot erase loss but only transform how it is experienced. The idea of blood memory attenuates Abel's claim on readers by suggesting that he will retain the potential for his own recovery indefinitely. Wyschogrod's emphasis on "cataclysm" asserts the absolute alterity and uniqueness of each person's experience – experience that can never be fully recovered. In this sense, she restores readers' responsibilities to individuals like Abel, and thereby reaffirms the original moral power of the novel itself.

CHAPTER 4

Refiguring national character: the remains of the British estate novel

> The simultaneity of the Nation – its contemporaneity – can only be articulated in the language of archaism, as a ghostly repetition; a gothic production of past-presentness.
>
> – Homi Bhabha

> The lesson of the Falklands is that Britain has not changed and that this nation still has those sterling qualities which shine through our history.
>
> – Margaret Thatcher

The last two chapters focused on literary movements whose genesis was explicitly linked to broader efforts to confront the enduring legacies of imperialism and modernity. The novel form, crucial to the conceptualization of national identities in Europe and the United States in the nineteenth century, is appropriated by writers from marginalized groups in the second half of the twentieth century as a means of representing and recasting experiences largely effaced by endorsed histories and canonical literary texts of the First World. The self-conscious use of nostalgia to refigure experiences of the past is apparent not only in Caribbean and Native American novels discussed in the previous two chapters, however, but also in literary works composed throughout the contemporary Anglophone world. Indeed, the longing for lost or imagined homelands has been a central feature of novels written in England as much as it has been in its former colonies; as Great Britain has had to confront the decline of its Empire and the vast influx of refugees from the colonial peripheries, literature has provided a medium for exploring questions of Englishness and the future of the nation. By tracing developments in what might be called the "British estate novel" over the course of the twentieth century, it becomes apparent that liberals and conservatives alike identify the future of Great Britain in terms of reclaiming or redefining what constitutes the nation's "true" spirit or *ēthos*. The finest modern and postwar examples of this genre – Evelyn Waugh's *Brideshead Revisited* (1945) and Kazuo

Ishiguro's *The Remains of the Day* (1989) respectively – both employ nostalgia to reclaim the lost *ēthos* of England despite their conflicting views of what defines the nation. This chapter's analysis of the estate novel genre, then, can contribute to this study's understanding of nostalgia in contemporary Anglophone literature in two ways: 1) by focusing on authors who define themselves more explicitly in terms of the colonial centers rather than peripheries, as has been the case for the majority of authors explored so far; 2) by contrasting the uses of nostalgia in modernist and postwar novels.

THE STATE OF THE ESTATE

The decay of the English country estate in both *Brideshead Revisited* and *The Remains of the Day* evokes a powerful yearning for lost national glory. Brideshead, in Waugh's novel, has been requisitioned as a temporary military barracks in preparation for the war against Hitler, all but the first floor sealed off, the estate fountain fenced in and filled with the cigarette butts of soldiers. Shortly after the war, Darlington Hall, in Ishiguro's novel, has been purchased by an American, Mr. Farraday, its staff cut from eighteen to four; the house itself is empty and hardly used, no longer the gathering place of the wealthy and influential. Indeed, the diminished condition of the estate is taken to be emblematic of the nation as a whole. The casual disdain for Brideshead and the general sense of purposelessness among the soldiers under the command of Captain Charles Ryder are of a piece. Ryder finds himself lamenting: "it was not as it had been."[1] Ishiguro's Mr. Stevens, butler of Darlington Hall, finds a similarly faltering commitment on the part of his younger contemporaries, who lack the dignity appropriate to their station. The English character, like the estates that are the definitive places of England for Ryder and Stevens, has been neglected, uncultivated, and left to decay in the postwar period.

   The nostalgia in *Brideshead Revisited* and *The Remains of the Day* is so intriguing because both novels invoke a tradition within the British novel that had previously degenerated into satire: the "crisis of inheritance" narrative that reads the fate of the nation through the condition of the English country estate. Even by the 1920s, the linkage between nation and estate is ridiculed by novels such as Aldous Huxley's *Crome Yellow* (1921) and D. H. Lawrence's *Lady Chatterley's Lover* (1928). Waugh himself satirizes the tradition in his earlier novel, *Handful of Dust* (1934). Yet, by 1944 he would insist that the English ancestral seats were "our chief national achievement" and he mourned their decay.[2] Ishiguro, too, makes a notable though certainly less startling departure from his earlier work in *Remains of the Day*. His interest in Darlington Hall and its butler Mr. Stevens bears little topical similarity to his previous explorations of Japanese immigrants in postwar England in *A Pale View of Hills* (1982) and the guilt experienced by postwar Japanese in *An Artist of the Floating World* (1986).[3] *The Remains of the Day*, like *Brideshead Revisited*, appears to hearken back to the novels of Jane Austen, Henry James, and E. M. Forster with its interest in the grand country estate and questions of what constitutes English character.

The revival of the estate novel tradition in *Brideshead Revisited* and *The Remains of the Day* responds to an increasing nostalgia in British politics and culture. This nostalgia represents a reaction to the social, economic, and cultural tensions that have accompanied the loss of the Empire and international prestige culminating in the 1956 Suez Canal fiasco. Ryder himself anticipates this trend when he asserts that only "in the last decade of their grandeur" are the estates given their due; the English "salute their achievements at the moment of extinction" (226–27).[4] The country house becomes a prominent object of nostalgia in this context because of its longstanding associations with continuity, tradition, and Englishness.[5] Since the eighteenth century, Virginia C. Kenny argues, the country house has served as a metaphor for a good society.[6] It becomes a central icon of British heritage in the postwar era because its presence belies the cultural turbulence caused by increasing emigration from the colonies; chronic unemployment and economic depression; and the resurgence of regionalism within Scotland, Ireland, and Wales.[7] The restoration effort begun in the 1970s has seen large sums of public money devoted to reversing the decades-long decline of the estates; indeed, by the time *The Remains of the Day* is published in 1989, historian David Cannadine is lamenting the "cult of the country house" in Great Britain.[8] Precisely when the nation's international stature is declining, the estate is proclaimed to be "one of the greatest British contributions to European civilization."[9]

As Benedict Anderson, Eric Hobsbawm, and Homi Bhabha have demonstrated, assertions about national heritage are never ideologically neutral; nationalisms forge solidarity through "the invention of traditions" that depend on monuments like the English estates to function as sites for commemorating the putative national past.[10] Within this context, Waugh and Ishiguro can be read as participating in a national debate over the perceived legacy of Great Britain. Considerable attention has been devoted to the nostalgia employed by Conservative politicians like Margaret Thatcher, whose call for a return to "Victorian values" justified an array of political policies from tightening money supply to union busting to war over the Falkland Islands; numerous studies have demonstrated how her political ideology depended on the reformulation of history.[11] However, literary scholars of both Waugh and Ishiguro have been at pains to deny the nostalgia in their novels. Ian Littlewood, for example, insists that Waugh's "ultimate concern" in *Brideshead Revisited* is "not to indulge nostalgia but to transcend it."[12] Likewise, readers of Ishiguro emphasize the irony rather than nostalgia in *The Remains of the Day*.[13] This tendency to downplay nostalgia in literary texts carries over into more general studies of literature and nationalism;[14] even Homi Bhabha's work focuses on the ways in which literature challenges the nostalgia employed by nationalist narratives. For Bhabha, literature opens up a "sepulchral 'otherness' of national identity" that disrupts efforts to establish "a settled and continuous national tradition."[15]

This tendency in criticism, however, overlooks how nostalgia is used by both *Brideshead Revisited* and *The Remains of the Day* to reenvision what constitutes "genuine" Englishness. By contrasting memories of the estates in their glory with their present state of disrepair, Waugh and Ishiguro establish an "originary" set of national ideals whose betrayal is indicated by the condition of the estate. The betrayal of the nation, for both Waugh and Ishiguro, is specifically a moral failure because both authors cast national identity in ethical terms. The expression of disappointment thereby establishes an ethical critique that insists on a return to the "true" *ēthos* or spirit of nation. This *ēthos*, however, is constituted in the process of remembering it. Hence, the novels intriguingly suggest that only in the midst of decline can the purportedly true ideals of Britain be recognized. As was the case in novels looked at in earlier chapters, nostalgia in *Brideshead Revisited* and *The Remains of the Day* is crucial to their visions of how social relations could be organized differently. The contrasting visions these novels present, however, points to the potential for nostalgia to be used by conservative and progressive writers alike in ways not apparent so far in this study. Waugh's imagery and language foreshadows that used by postwar Conservative politicians, particularly Prime Minister Margaret Thatcher; both ultimately conceive of an essentialistic idea of national identity. In contrast, Ishiguro uses nostalgia to reject such essentialisms and to redefine key terms associated with national character: dignity and greatness. This refiguration of national character is mapped spatially as the novel ultimately associates the nation's *ēthos* with the pier at Weymouth rather than the estate.

FALL OF THE HOUSE OF ENGLAND

At least since Jane Austen's *Mansfield Park* (1814), the English estate has been positioned both as a defining aspect of the nation's *ēthos* and as a crucial site of cultural debates about national identity.[16] The physical structure of the estate suggests an inherited structure of society, morality, manners, and language, according to Alastair Duckworth.[17] The endurance of the estate creates the illusion of national continuity. And this illusion imagines that cultural changes modify the essential structure, not to challenge it. Duckworth's analysis suggests that the estate novel tradition explores such "improvements" in order to distinguish proper and improper attitudes toward social change. Proper social change, in this context, threatens neither to undo the status of the estate nor to change its essential character. The critique of the Crawfords in *Mansfield Park* comes from Austen's distrust of their attitude toward cultural heritage. The Crawfords represent improper agents of social change because of their wish to widen the gap between church and house, a connection that will also be essential to Waugh.

The estate appears to provide the ideal metaphor for the enduring nation whose individual members might change but whose essential structure remains relatively consistent. Precisely because the fate of the country house is so closely intertwined with the fortunes of the British Empire, however, the precarious situation of the former points to that of the latter.[18] The crisis in *Mansfield Park*, for example, is precipitated by the economic losses that Sir Thomas experiences in his West Indies estate – losses that demand his immediate departure from Mansfield to Antigua. The corrupting influence of the Crawfords on the inhabitants of Mansfield and the "improvements" they would bring to the estate become possible only because its lord is absent and preoccupied with colonial matters.[19] Sir Thomas' timely return and restoration of order to the house points to an important fact about the estate novel tradition: the promise of reconciling conflicting cultural attitudes into a unified national spirit depends on not only the economic stability of the estates themselves but also an unquestioned lord who exemplifies the ideals of Englishness.

Hence, the struggle over inheritance in later novels in this tradition, like E. M. Forster's *Howards End* (1910), is deeply rooted in cultural arguments about what embodies the national *ēthos* and what direction the nation will take. Determining the appropriate heir of Howards End is important to its dying owner, Mrs. Wilcox, because the estate embodies the *ēthos* of England: "to her it had been a spirit, for which she sought a spiritual heir," the narrator states.[20] The novel imagines the conflicts between the Schlegels and the Wilcoxes over Howards End as a mini-drama of the social and ideological tensions of a national collectivity.[21] If the novel leaves the question of the appropriate heir unsettled, it nonetheless concludes with an uneasy reconciliation between the two families. This reconciliation makes the restoration of the estate possible, a restoration marked by the renewed fertility of the fields surrounding Howards End. And this revival is imagined as promising a more general revival of *ēthos* against what Rae Harris Stoll refers to as "the dehumanizing social order" of mass culture and mass consumption.[22] The house itself is cast as the site of resistance against the "craze for motion" sweeping England, a site that promises to maintain "civilization" itself (268). In the final pages of the novel, Margaret Schlegel asserts that "our house is the future as well as the past" of the nation (268).[23]

Forster struggles to envision a cultural reconciliation simply not possible during either the wartime years that produced the sentiments of *Brideshead Revisited* or the Thatcherite years that led to *The Remains of the Day*. Such reconciliation is possible only under conditions in which social change does not threaten to eradicate the estate space as the privileged marker of nation. Yet even in Forster this is a fragile, fleeting promise.[24] The Wilcoxes' willingness to cede their claim to Howards End suggests that for them the estate no longer signifies the *ēthos* of the nation. This attitude shift foretells the decline of the estate. Helen Schlegel foresees this outcome and declares, "Life's going to be melted down, all over the world. [. . .] Howards End, Oniton, the Purbeck Downs, the Oderberge, were all survivals, and the melting-pot was being prepared for them" (268). Indeed, Forster's novel represents one of the final prewar examples of a novel committed to imagining the destiny of the nation through the metaphor of the country house. After World War I, the continuing economic difficulties Great Britain suffered, if nothing else, guaranteed that the rate of estate closures would increase for decades to come. And if Waugh and Ishiguro revive the estate novel tradition, Brideshead and Darlington Hall nonetheless experience the decline foretold by Helen Schlegel. As a result, the vision of the estate as a model of society that reconciles conflicting ideals of nation into a unified spirit is rendered inescapably nostalgic.

By the time Lawrence's *Lady Chatterley's Lover* is published, the cultural reconciliation imagined by earlier estate novels is neither possible nor even desirable. World War I, changing attitudes toward modernization, economic difficulties, and the inevitability of another worldwide conflict increasingly undermine the estate as a symbol of nation. The estate appears isolated, aloof, and unsustainable. Wragby Hall, in Lawrence's novel, is polluted by the fumes from nearby Tevershall pit; Wragby's lord, Clifford Chatterley, is crippled by a wound received during World War I. His injury is telling: rendered impotent, Clifford is prevented from establishing a legitimate heir. The promise of continuity sought by authors from Austen to Forster is gone. Lawrence does not perceive this occurrence as tragedy, however; if he condemns modernization and its pernicious consequences on people and the landscape, he refuses to endorse the ideals associated with the estate even nostalgically. Its helplessness to prevent the onslaught of modernization leads Lawrence to envision a restoration of the spirit associated with the uncorrupted forest away from Wragby Hall. Lady Chatterley must leave the estate and abandon its lord in order to find restoration for her body and soul. If Britain is to have a future, Lawrence suggests, it will not be determined from the estates.

BURNING ANEW AMONG THE "OLD STONES"

Waugh reverses Lawrence's formulation: if the estate is in decline, this is the fault of the nation for failing to preserve its greatest legacy. If Britain is to have a future worth having, for Waugh, it can only come from restoring the estates and the spirit of nation they signify. No less than Lawrence, Waugh rejects Forster's dream of reconciliation between conflicting ideals of nation. The forces of modernization have produced a generation that is morally and culturally bankrupt, according to Waugh. This "age of Hooper," as it is referred to in *Brideshead Revisited*, has allowed the national spirit to be extinguished through neglect. Thus, a sense of disappointment becomes the dominant tone in *Brideshead Revisited*: even at the close of the novel, the estate fountain – the symbol of baptism and renewal – remains shut off and filled with the cigarette butts of soldiers listlessly waiting for the endlessly deferred struggle against Hitler's armies to begin.[25] Witnessing this weariness and indolence among his men, Ryder laments his own lost commitment to the Army: "Here my last love died" (5). The image suggests the sloth that has come, for Waugh, to infect "our national virtues of magnanimity and good temper."[26]

The function of Catholicism in the novel needs to be read in the context of Waugh's search for a value system that could restore a declining nation. This reading moves away from the tradition of reading *Brideshead Revisited* as a Catholic novel; Catholicism in the novel is inseparable from Waugh's longing to restore a notion of Englishness. The inseparability of Englishness and Catholicism for Waugh becomes apparent in his assertions about England's past: "England was Catholic for nine hundred years, then Protestant for three hundred, then agnostic for a century. The Catholic structure still lies lightly buried beneath every phase of English life."[27] Catholicism is not opposed to Englishness here but central to it. Only the restoration of Catholicism can restore English heritage to the present, this passage suggests. The death of the English spirit that Waugh perceives in the Army is the inevitable result of a nation having "buried" the value system that sustained it for 900 years.[28]

It should come as little surprise, then, that the first scene of *Brideshead Revisited* that Waugh wrote was the description of Lord Marchmain's deathbed repentance.[29] If the estate itself is the physical marker of the national spirit or *ēthos*, then its lord has a responsibility to be both guardian and representative of Englishness. Lord Marchmain's casual indifference to his responsibilities, his loathing of the English countryside, and his unwillingness even to live in England demonstrate his failure to preserve the estate and national character (99). His ultimate return to England and penitence just before his death signify a longing to return to the religious tradition of his ancestors and a desire to repent from a life that neglected the spiritual and national ideals to which he was heir. In this way, Catholicism and Englishness become linked, and this redefines Lord Marchmain's life story so that prior events are retroactively understood to lead up to this "restored" connection to the estate and church.

The deathbed scene establishes a narrative paradigm whereby the estate *ēthos* is itself revised through a process of retrospection that casts change as "restoration." For the majority of the novel, Ryder's nostalgia takes the form of a longing to return to the Brideshead associated with the drawing-room: "But as the years passed I began to mourn the loss of something I had known in the drawing-room of Marchmain House and once or twice since," he recalls (227). Shortly after Ryder's recollection of Lord Marchmain's affirmation of faith, however, the estate becomes associated with the chapel rather than the drawing-room. Indeed, the reopening of the chapel at the end of the novel leads Ryder to revise his earlier conclusion that the estate space and its spirit have been lost: "the place was desolate and the work all brought to nothing," as he puts it (351). Rather, Ryder perceives that the true spirit of the place lives on in its chapel. For here he witnesses "the flame which the old knights saw from their tombs, which they saw put out [. . .] I found it this morning, burning anew among the old stones" (351). Ryder's discovery of the chapel as the true heart of the estate allows him to merge Catholicism and Englishness; this in turn makes it possible for Ryder to recommit himself to a floundering Army and to rejoin his compatriots and face the tasks at hand, even if this means working with men who share his commanding officer's contempt for Brideshead (345). Here, Ryder becomes the spiritual heir of the estate, the one man to retain memories of its past.[30]

Nostalgia is essential to *Brideshead Revisited* not only because it drives individuals like Ryder to recall the past. Indeed, in the novel, the full significance of events can be perceived only retrospectively. Ryder suggests as much when he describes his own path to maturity: "again and again a new truth is revealed to us in whose light all our previous knowledge must be rearranged" (79). In his own life, this becomes a gloss for understanding his changing associations with Brideshead and, by extension, England. This conception suggests that the Brideshead associated with the drawing-room and that associated with the chapel are not conflicting notions of the estate; the latter is truer, if less obvious. But this reality cannot be appreciated in the moment because only a maturity born of a sense of loss can establish the insight necessary. The failure of Hooper and the "Young England" that he symbolizes, then, is the result of their cultural amnesia and lack of respect for the past. And this failure guarantees that they never experience the nostalgia that is the precondition of perceiving the true English *ēthos*.

Intriguingly, Waugh does not conceive of a Britain that reverses the sense of decline that has defined its history, according to Andrew Gamble, for more than a century. Ryder's nostalgia engages him in a process of retrospection that depends on decline. He cannot witness the flame burning anew until he has already concluded that the estate is in disrepair. For this initial recognition leads him to question his own associations with the estate and the centrality of the drawing-room to his memories of it. His final recognition insists that the spirit of England is not limited to the physical structure of the estate; the image of the flame suggests an essential spirit that endures. Hence, Ryder can recognize the nation's true *ēthos* only after its apparent loss.

Nostalgia does not function here primarily to lament past grandeur; rather, it allows Waugh to transform what memories the estate evokes. Nostalgia, as demonstrated earlier, enables the novel to shift the primary associations of Brideshead from the drawing-room to the chapel. This shift can occur only retrospectively and in the face of loss; as long as the estate retains its status and prestige, it is inescapably associated with aristocracy, leisure, and high culture. Against a backdrop of wartime rationing and privation, these associations limit the ability of the estate to function as a representative *national* space. After its transformation into a military barracks, however, Brideshead becomes emblematic of a national commitment to the war effort and the sacrifice across all social classes that this commitment necessitates. Putting this in more theoretical terms, nostalgia in *Brideshead Revisited* resolves tensions between conflicting images of the estate (and the national traditions that they evoke) through an act of narrative synecdoche: one part is cast as the remnant of the estate in its totality. By marking the chapel as the final fragment untouched by the "age of Hooper," Waugh claims the heritage of the estate in its entirety and subordinates aspects that do not correspond to his vision of Catholic Englishness. In other words, Ryder mourns the loss of the drawing-room and its aristocratic cultural ideals *in order* to establish the primacy of the spirit associated with the chapel. His lament that "all is vanity" is immediately corrected, and Ryder quickly concludes that the flame that burns within the chapel "could not have been lit but for the builders" (351). Even if the estate as a physical structure lies in ruin, the novel implies, Ryder nonetheless "inherits" its spirit and retains it within his memory.

This analysis provides an interesting counterpoint to David Rothstein's argument that collective memory in *Brideshead Revisited* is maintained by individuals living in a society unsympathetic to and uninterested in the past.[31] The novel also assures this situation by reading the past of the nation with respect to the decayed estate. For, among the soldiers camped at Brideshead, only Ryder has memories of it. This makes him the sole and uncontestable spiritual heir not only to the estate but also to the past itself because, as noted earlier, Waugh casts the national past through the story of the estate. Hence, the estate provides a unified vision of nation in ways it did not for Forster; whereas the Schlegels and the Wilcoxes each represent a long tradition of how the nation might be defined, no tradition exists in *Brideshead Revisited* to stand as a legitimate contrast to the one embodied by Ryder. Retrospection in *Brideshead Revisited* allows Waugh to depict the crisis of the estate as the culmination of a struggle to preserve an essential national spirit precisely because he occludes questions of class, race, and the Protestant tradition. Rather than serving as the space for contesting visions of nation to be played out, the estate in *Brideshead Revisited* stands as the last bastion against "false" visions of England.

Waugh's efforts to "restore" the true spirit of England anticipate the nostalgic politics of postwar Britain. Repeatedly, British politicians have invoked a nostalgic vision of national unity in order to establish a moral ground for their policies. Anthony Eden justified his efforts to retain the Suez Canal by casting Nasser alternately as the reincarnation of Hitler and Mussolini. Enoch Powell allegedly sought to build a politics of racial hatred through claiming a putative unified national spirit that had become polluted. And, as noted earlier, Margaret Thatcher invoked a moral framework of "Victorian values" in order to justify a host of economic, social, and military policies. Indeed, in the aftermath of the Falkland Islands conflict, Thatcher's imagery hearkens back to Waugh's vision of the flame "burning anew among the old stones": "[Britain has] rekindled that spirit which has fired her for generations past and which today has begun to burn as brightly as before."[32]

Like Waugh, Thatcher invokes a national spirit that burns again in the face of adversity. Indeed, the restoration of *ēthos* becomes possible only through the very obvious and inescapable reality of the decay of the Empire. As Patrick Brantlinger suggests, the nostalgic politics of Thatcherism depended on a myth of national origins constituted in the purported struggle to "reclaim" Britishness.[33] The apparent failures of Britain and the British only clarify that the nation possesses an essential and unchanging character, which Thatcher claimed to have personally renewed.[34]

It would be a mistake, however, to cast Waugh simply as a "forerunner" to Thatcherism. The nostalgic essentialism of the latter represented a strategy designed to draw electoral support. In contrast, Waugh accepted and even embraced the inevitable unpopularity of his vision of Catholic Englishness. The irony is that *Brideshead Revisited* nonetheless gained immense international popularity because it answered a nostalgic longing among British and American audiences for a "simpler" time; Waugh's effort to articulate a viable and essentialistic national identity that established Englishness in moral terms went largely unnoticed. Nor has the tendency in criticism to read *Brideshead Revisited* as a Catholic novel drawn sufficient attention to his efforts to refigure national character. The image of the flame "burning anew" in the final pages of the novel is as much nationalist as religious. Indeed, the novel bends Catholicism to the needs of the nation. The flame, Ryder asserts, was first witnessed by the Crusaders and now it "burns again for other soldiers" (351). The choice of imagery here is telling – Christianity offers a host of images that could have justified Ryder's repudiation of the army. But he chooses to link the flame to a Christian image explicitly associated with political and military commitment – and by casting himself as a latter-day crusader, Ryder recommits himself to a nation at war.

THAT'S WHAT WE FOUGHT HITLER FOR

If Ishiguro also revives the estate novel tradition, he rejects the essentialism that for Waugh defines national identity. Like previous novels in this tradition, *The Remains of the Day* links the crises of estate and nation: the sale of Darlington Hall to an American comes at the moment of Great Britain's eclipse as a world power.[35] The decline of the estate in *The Remains of the Day* mirrors the decay of the British Empire – at a time when ever larger sections of Darlington Hall are being closed off and dust-sheeted, Great Britain finds itself shedding its colonies. Stevens undertakes an expedition to the West Country in the hope of enticing the former housekeeper, Miss Kenton, to return to Darlington Hall just months before Great Britain embarks on a disastrous military expedition to reclaim the Suez Canal. And like Ryder before him, Stevens experiences a profound disappointment with the condition of the estate and his countrymen, a disappointment that initiates a series of nostalgic reflections on individual ethics that ultimately revises national ideals. Ishiguro's novel differs from Waugh's, however, in a fundamental way: the restoration of the "original" promise of a national *ēthos* is not found in the return to the English estate. Whereas Ryder ultimately returns both physically and mentally to the estate, Stevens stands at the pier at Weymouth at the end of his narrative quest.

The shift in physical space from estate to the pier is motivated by Ishiguro's distrust of the nostalgia that Waugh endorses and which dominates the postwar political scene. In an interview with Allan Vorda and Kim Herzinger, Ishiguro notes that he writes against the "enormous nostalgia industry" going on in Britain.[36] While much of it is "harmless," nostalgia has also been used as a "political tool," according to Ishiguro. He notes:

This [nostalgia] can be brought out by the left or right, but usually it is the political right who say England was this beautiful place before the trade unions tried to make it more egalitarian or before the immigrants started to come or before the promiscuous age of the '60s came and ruined everything.

Implicit in his statement is a recognition that the myth of England was invoked to justify the Falkland Islands conflict, union busting, and immigration quotas during the years leading up to the publication of *The Remains of the Day*. Particularly during her 1979 campaign, Margaret Thatcher invoked imperialist nostalgia and the subliminal racism that it implies, Joel Krieger suggests.[37] Her evocations of national "greatness" – the very term that Ishiguro makes central to *The Remains of the Day* – represented a tacit but widely recognized code for white England.

Hence, the novel's formulation of national identity based on the category of "greatness" is both nostalgic and ironic. In a speech resonating with Thatcher's own rhetoric, Stevens links landscape to national character early on in the novel: "the English landscape at its finest," he declares, "possesses a quality that the landscapes of other nations, however more superficially dramatic, inevitably fail to possess. [. . .] T]his quality is probably best summed up by the term 'greatness.'"[38] The greatness of the land and its people are of one kind, even if such landscapes are becoming increasingly rare. Thus, Stevens declares his merit in speaking of "*Great* Britain" (28; italics in text). Greatness is revealed to be an empty term, however, when Stevens attempts to characterize it. He suggests that "it is the very *lack* of obvious drama or spectacle that sets the beauty of our land apart" (28; italics in text). In an unconsciously ironic deflation of Thatcherite rhetoric, Stevens defines greatness as a purely negative quality, a "lack."

This definition of greatness undermines a notion that national identity can be cast in essentialistic terms. By refusing to take for granted the basis of national identity, Ishiguro foregrounds the fact that the significance of greatness is constituted by those who employ the term; the national spirit or *ēthos* does not preexist the attempts to formulate or define it. Stevens's inability to formulate a positive definition of nation suggests that the essentialisms of Waugh and Thatcher depend on a tacit understanding that race, class, and religion define a set of unchanging characteristics. Much as Slavoj Žižek has suggested in his own analysis of Thatcherite Britain, *The Remains of the Day* suggests that "Englishness" is an empty signifier deployed to legitimate particular ideological positions.[39] Precisely because the term does not signify anything specific, it can be used to justify any number of unrelated goals, much as Thatcher used the term to defend her domestic and foreign policy.

In the context of the novel, greatness is understood to reproduce and enforce class hierarchies. The notion of greatness, of course, does not have consistent characteristics across social, sexual, and ethnic lines. Stevens's aspirations for greatness foreground the ways that national character is construed vis-à-vis class position, for he does not ask what constitutes a "great" Englishman but "what is a 'great' butler?" (29). Social position determines for Stevens the ways in which he can be "great." He takes for granted that the call to greatness makes very different demands on Lord Darlington and himself. Stevens' own definition of greatness endorses class stratification. From the outset, he defines moral virtue in terms of inhabiting one's social role successfully – the primary duty of the average citizen is to serve gentlemen who are "furthering the progress of humanity" (114). In other words, virtue comes from serving the virtuous. This vision, of course, depends on the ethical expertise of the "great gentlemen," creating a social hierarchy of experts and nonexperts, where the latter are understood to be dependent on the former for ethical insight. The failure of experts, then, necessarily leads to the failure of their servants, and the shame of Lord Darlington's activities on behalf of the Third Reich haunts Stevens years after his employer's death. But he insists on the ethical expertise of great men and the inadequacy of judgment on the part of "normal" citizens like himself and the implied reader:

One is simply accepting an inescapable truth: that the likes of you and I will never be in a position to comprehend the great affairs of today's world, and our best course will always be to put our trust in an employer we judge to be wise and honorable, and to devote our energies to the task of serving him to the best of our ability. (201)

The *ēthos* embodied by the estate presupposes a hierarchy in which only one individual, the lord or spiritual heir (in the case of Ryder), is capable of ethical judgment. The ethical failures of the experts, however, suggest that Stevens' plea of ignorance conceals a desire to exonerate himself retroactively of his own culpability. Hence, Stevens can carry out Lord Darlington's wish to fire his Jewish employees without perceiving himself to be performing a racist action: "There are many things you and I are simply not in a position to understand," Stevens rationalizes to Miss Kenton, "concerning, say, the nature of Jewry. Whereas his lordship, I might venture, is somewhat better placed to judge what is for the best"

(149). Linking expertise and ethics frees Stevens from having to assume responsibility for his own actions.

The sense that the legitimate representative of the estate possesses a special ethical expertise lies at the heart of the British estate novel. In *Brideshead Revisited*, for example, the burden to restore *ēthos* falls on Ryder's shoulders exclusively. Although the "flame" witnessed by Ryder in the chapel represents the spirit of the nation, his moral quest is independent of the soldiers under his command. He tells them nothing about the history of Brideshead and reveals to Corporal Hooper only that he had stayed there previously. To the extent that the novel envisions a community that takes Brideshead as the embodiment of national *ēthos*, it is defined exclusively by the unitary prophetic voice of Ryder. Difference or dissent from the representative figure results from a poverty of vision. Lord Darlington, in *The Remains of the Day*, echoes these same sentiments. He claims to speak on behalf of the nation, "We English" (87), and even claims to know (better than the other "We English") what is best for it: "Democracy is something for a bygone era. [. . .] The few people *qualified to know* what's what are talked to a standstill by ignorant people all around them" (198; italics mine). For Lord Darlington, those who lack expertise, those not "qualified to know," hinder ethics. Both Lord Darlington and Ryder endorse ethical positions that reinforce class hierarchies in an age when they are threatening to collapse. Both men claim to possess ethical expertise – an expertise that has no obvious mechanism for acquisition by the working class. Thus, ethics becomes the final ground from which the privileged lay claim to their "entitlement" and assert their right to govern the nation.

The Remains of the Day, however, challenges the viability of such claims to ethical expertise. Lord Darlington, for all his worldliness, remains blind to his promotion of the totalitarian regime in Nazi Germany. Mr. Lewis, the senator from Pennsylvania, fails to provide a viable alternative vision, though he has the courage to challenge Lord Darlington publicly. Lewis' own bungled and heavy-handed attempts to disrupt Lord Darlington's conference, however, undermine his own claims to expertise. Expertise proves disappointing on more mundane levels as well in the novel. Mr. Stevens' aging father, whom the son holds to be a paragon of a "great" butler, fails to perform his duties; the definition of a "great butler" put forward by the Hayes Society (a society that claims to admit butlers of "only the very first rank") does not establish clear criteria but only vague principles. Even the guidebook that Mr. Stevens intends to follow on his trip to visit Mrs. Benn (the former Miss Kenton) proves disappointing. The most beautiful and moving sites that Stevens comes across are those pointed out by locals, not by experts.

Stevens' deference to and ultimate disappointment with Lord Darlington reflects an attitude toward the English *ēthos* as embodied by the estate. The blind presumption of expertise by men like Lord Darlington led them to tolerate and even aid the Nazi regime in Germany. Stevens, like many of his countrymen, loyally served the "great gentlemen" of the nation, confident that their service and their trust were being put to good ends. The absolute disregard for the majority of the British population demonstrated by Lord Darlington and his peers, however, suggests that this trust was misplaced. Darlington remains from beginning to end aloof, isolated, and even parochial. He believes that occupying the representative space of *ēthos*, the estate, grants him not only the right to represent the entire nation but also an inherent knowledge about the concerns of its people. Such disregard is not exclusive to Lord Darlington but continues to be the predominant attitude of the postwar British government. While Stevens undertakes his journey to visit Mrs. Benn, the government under Prime Minister Eden is leading the nation toward a conflict over Suez without consulting the general population or even the majority of parliament. In the name of protecting a colonial empire, on which the estate depends for economic support, the government disregards the desires of its own populace.[40]

The movement away from the estate to the space of the pier in the novel, then, suggests an attempt on Ishiguro's part to relocate the *ēthos* of England and to challenge the primacy of the estate as its representation. As Stevens progresses toward the pier at Weymouth, he finds himself increasingly revising his vision of the past and particularly his blind faith in the moral authority of the "great gentleman." His physical movement away from the estate mirrors the novel's move away from an "ethics of expertise" exemplified by Lord Darlington.

The revision of *ēthos* depends on the narration of personal disappointment much as it does in earlier estate novels, for the betrayal of trust drives Stevens to question ethical identity and thereby national identity. Initially, these revisions concern his father as a role model. Stevens likes to repeat a story that his father, himself a lifelong butler, was also fond of repeating. The story concerns a butler who remained unperturbed in his role when a tiger entered the dining-room. It is important not for the truth of actions related but for its ethics, "what it reveals concerning my father's ideals" (37). In fact, the story concretely embodies virtues that

Stevens' father strives for but fails to attain, and he tells the story in order that others might recognize what he hopes to become.

The effort by Stevens' father to convey desired virtues in narrative points to the novel's shift away from ethical principles based on expertise to a notion that they are a product of conversation. The absence of an essentialized ethical foundation or national character denies the basis of expertise – principles, like national character, are *constituted* not given. Hence, a story like the one that Stevens' father tells acts as a proposition regarding the defining terms of moral and national character, a proposition that is subject to scrutiny, debate, and revision. In this sense, storytelling opens up the ethical conversation about Englishness, freeing it from the provenance of "experts." Without abandoning the terms "greatness" and "dignity," Ishiguro nonetheless shifts their significance: they become thick concepts (to recall Williams' term) whose employment in stories provides a common vocabulary for debating and envisioning ethical action. They remain crucial to a conception of *ēthos* because they provide the basic terminology through which conversations about ethics can be entered.

Thus, as Stevens revises his understanding of greatness and dignity, his vision of ethical duties changes. He gains ethical insight by retelling the story his father told him so many times because it forces him to cast his story with an audience in mind and to anticipate their questions. In fact, only after he retells the story does he recognize that his father tells it in order to represent the character he longs to possess. The nostalgia for ideal butlers felt by both Stevens and his father represents neither an unguarded praise of the past nor an unqualified sense of present decline; it seeks to project into the past particular characteristics that are longed for in the present. To say they existed once suggests that they could exist again, perhaps in an even better form. By retelling the story, Stevens learns to praise the qualities of his father and yet distinguish himself and the ideals of his generation from those of his father, something he could not do while he understood ethics in terms of expertise. Stevens' story opens a conversation in which he redefines the role inhabited by his father and himself.

By opening a conversation, however, Stevens unwittingly destabilizes his own claims to expertise. As his journey progresses, Stevens' narrative recalls not only his own vision but also that of the deceived working class. Running out of gas during his road trip, he is forced to spend the night in a small rural village where, though he is mistaken for a wealthy gentleman, his own definitions of *ēthos* are challenged by the local activist, Harry Smith, who believes that dignity is "something every man and woman in this country can strive for and get" (186). For Smith, dignity comes from service, and his village, he points out, gave more than their share to the war effort. By right of birth each English man and woman can claim dignity, for all alike fought for their country: "That's what we fought Hitler for," he says. In making this assertion, Smith argues for a different understanding of the nation itself, not only his own community. He lays claim to the legacy of *ēthos* on behalf of all the English, though his notion of freedom does not extend to those living in the colonies.[41]

The moral force of Harry Smith's claim for "universal" dignity is based on the sacrifices made by the working class in the name of defending the nation. Men and women who never experienced the privileges of the estate life were called on to defend England against Hitler's armies. To claim subsequently some share in the privilege enjoyed by men like Lord Darlington asserts that service represents the original spirit of *ēthos* more than the material trappings of its representative space, the estate. By accepting the call to fight against Hitler, Smith declares, the working class defends a dignity that they were never offered.

This challenge to the fundamental assumptions and claims of the estate can only come from *outside* of it. The social space of the estate itself does not permit such challenges to class hierarchy. Within Darlington Hall, all manners of requests, demands, and inquiries are made, but little conversation. The few genuine moments of conversation are quickly interrupted by the social pressures and expectations everyone feels within the house – pressures that even Lord Darlington's godson feels whenever he comes. And Miss Kenton's protests operate within the social hierarchy without ever threatening it. She questions the butler Stevens, never Lord Darlington. Hence, conversation itself is structured and delimited so that it challenges neither the authority of nor the terms associated with *ēthos*. It is only when Stevens steps outside of the estate space that his foundational premises are questioned and his own actions made to appear suspect.

Stevens does not return from his nostalgic quest as the spiritual heir of *ēthos*, as Ryder does. *The Remains of the Day* refuses to declare national character to be the special province of a prophetic figure or expert. Rather, it is the product of an ongoing conversation. And despite his unwillingness to heed the voices of working-class people, Stevens finds that his conversations with them alter his experience and understanding.[42] His recognition that he has ignored a "whole dimension to the question" of dignity represents only one moment of insight resulting from conversation with real and imagined others (116). These conversations lead Stevens to reinterpret the past, to recognize that Lord Darlington has no inherent claim to dignity or expertise, and to recognize the complicity in his lifelong silence concerning Darlington's progression toward Nazism. Stevens' nostalgia leads him to redefine his ethical concepts, for the act of concretely representing these concepts through stories begins a communicative circuit with an imagined audience that resists foreclosure by the teller. Stevens may begin a story in which his own dignity is implicitly guaranteed but nonetheless he must finally confront his own moral failure.[43] He fails to live up to his own ideal of dignity and greatness because he has chosen not to choose. He fails to defend *ēthos*, and if he continues to occupy the estate of England, it will be an empty and haunting place that has lost its definitive character: "what dignity is there in that?" he laments (243).

This is not to suggest that Ishiguro's work represents an unqualified endorsement of a national character produced by unending conversation. Ishiguro recognizes that conversations often reproduce hierarchies of power – the bantering that Stevens comes to admire in Mr. Farraday and the people at the pier at Weymouth is not a wholly innocent example of open interaction. As Susie O'Brien points out, bantering is subject to rules that frequently conceal particular relations of power.[44] And if the novel wrestles with conflicting notions of dignity, the centrality of the concept to a British *ēthos* is never disputed. Even Harry Smith does not offer a vision to replace the estate *ēthos*. For better or for worse, he is enamored of it himself. However, he does demand a notion of Englishness that accommodates a wider class spectrum: individuals outside of the estate have a legitimate, if not privileged, claim to national character because they have acted ethically. Implicitly, Smith's demand for a more inclusive *ēthos* envisions a future that would have a place for difference and marginality in ways excluded by earlier estate novels like *Brideshead Revisited* and by Smith himself, who remains blind to his own racism toward colonized subjects. Within the novel, such blindness is only ever revealed and challenged through conversation, and the pier becomes the space most associated with the open interactions necessary for genuine conversation. Ending the novel with Stevens at the pier recognizes the need for and inevitability of a shift in representative national spaces and welcomes it, even if Stevens himself will probably return to the emptiness of Darlington Hall.

If postwar British novelists like Ishiguro have been critical of the nationalism that culminated in the Thatcher years, many have been unwilling to abandon the concept of a British character altogether. It is certainly true that nostalgic appeals to a concept of nation have been met with suspicion after Nazism. Despite misgivings about many of its manifestations, however, the notion of a national character maintains a powerful appeal. Even in the work of an immigrant writer like Ishiguro, the examination of thick ethical concepts like "loyalty" and "dignity" is not independent of conceptions of a national character.[45] For authors like Ishiguro and Waugh, the wounds of national loss provide the means to imagine not the types of political agency sought by nationalism but an ethical character. These moral explorations are central to *Brideshead Revisited* and *The Remains of the Day*. The linking of ethical and national character stems from the fact that the nation has become one of the central grounds for envisioning moral duties. Nationalisms depend on merging nation and *ēthos* in the collective imaginations of their putative communities; thus, national character and ethics have become intimately linked in modernity. This remains true even if a postnational era has begun to emerge, a period defined by what Tom Nairn refers to as the "break-up of Britain."[46]

In terms of his ethical vision, Ishiguro appeals to a national character, though it is defined in opposition to the Englishness that embodied the Empire. The image of people gathered together on the pier waiting for the lights to come on represents an imagined national community that preserves the incompatibilities and conflicts that are often effaced or willfully forgotten in nationalistic narratives. Implicitly, Ishiguro suggests that if Britain is to have a future, it must embrace what it meets on the pier – the country houses and the ideals of Englishness associated with them are no longer sustainable in elitist isolation. The fact that such claims remain largely implicit in *The Remains of the Day* and in Ishiguro's two subsequent novels, *The Unconsoled* (1995) and *When We Were Orphans* (2000), however, points to the limitations of nostalgic narratives in providing useful social critique. This chapter has explored how nostalgia can encourage the exploration of unacknowledged disappointment and resentment, yet such explorations do not necessarily lead individuals to engage in a sustained effort to change the conditions that led them to pine for the past. The likelihood of Stevens' eventual return to Darlington Hall testifies to this point. Self-critique remains palatable when cast in the indirect and sentimentalized terms characteristic of nostalgia; hence, Stevens might return to his old life despite a new awareness of his ethical failings.

For the same reason, the critique of British society in *The Remains of the Day* may be sufficiently palatable for the novel to remain widely popular despite its unflattering observations. Indeed, it could suffer the same fate as *Brideshead Revisited*: to become a novel that is admired and loved, but whose ideas for redefining national identity are largely overlooked. More than any other author in this study, Ishiguro demonstrates how a pervasive and often escapist rhetoric of decline may be appropriated within literary narratives to provide a critical reflection on how social and economic conditions might be altered. But this achievement must be tempered by the recognition that the novel's prominence in no way commands a broader shift in national discourse.

CHAPTER 5

Appeasing an embittered history: trauma and nationhood in the writings of Achebe and Soyinka

The struggle to redefine a purportedly lost national *ēthos*, discussed in the previous chapter in relation to the British estate novel, is apparent in various forms throughout the contemporary Anglophone world. It is complicated in many postcolonial contexts, however, because national boundaries were typically imposed by colonial powers without any regard to traditional tribal, ethnic, or cultural affiliations. Particularly among African nations, the articulation of a precolonial solidarity cast in national and/or continental terms has been crucial to independence movements. At the same time, the nostalgia underlying many national-ist narratives has encouraged the idea that a national homeland is the special provenance of a particular people. The civil strife, war, and geno-cide that have characterized so much of postcolonial Africa testify to the dangers of such claims. The 1994 genocide of an estimated 800,000 Rwandan Tutsis and moderate Hutus provides only one graphic exam-ple of a connection between nostalgia and what Reed Way Dasenbrock calls "a politics of genocide."[1]

Dasenbrock's assertion points to a nagging possibility that has haunted African political theorists, activists, and artists alike since the 1960s: namely, that the past provides a source not of inspiration and guidance but of trauma. The idea that the colonial encounter inculcates a kind of collective trauma subsequently replayed in the postcolonial context was articulated as early as the 1950s by the Martinique-born psychiatrist Frantz Fanon, whose work during the French-Algerian war led him to diagnose a variety of psychic disorders resulting from colonial policies. Explicit references to psychological disorders induced by colonialism appear subsequently in the works of literary authors across the contin-ent, including the South African Bessie Head and the Zimbabwean Tsitsi Dangarembga, whose novel *Nervous Conditions* (1988) takes its title from a passage in Fanon's *The Wretched of the Earth*. Literary explor-ations of the consequences of colonialism for individual and collective psyches have employed the language and metaphors of not only Western psychoanalytic discourses but also traditional African beliefs. In particular, the idea of what is called *ogbanje* in Igbo and *abiku* in Yoruba has figured in the writings of Nigerian novelists, perhaps most famously in Ben Okri's Booker Prize-winning novel, *The Famished Road* (1991). The terms refer to a child who dies shortly after birth and whose spirit returns repeatedly to its mother's womb, only to suffer an early death after each successive birth. In Okri's novel, the *abiku* becomes a metaphor for Nigeria itself, whose birth as a democratic nation seems repeatedly thwarted. "Our country is an abiku country," the narrator is told near the end of the novel. "Like the spirit-child, it keeps coming and going. One day it will decide to remain. It will become strong."[2]

Not surprisingly, debates about the role the past should play in the imagination of the postcolonial nation figure prominently in the works of the two towering figures of Anglophone African letters in the twentieth century, Okri's fellow Nigerians Chinua Achebe and Wole Soyinka. Despite the fact that Achebe and Soyinka have come to embody opposing tendencies in postcolonial African literature, what Biodun Jeyifo terms "simplicity" and "complexity" respectively, both authors have increasingly confronted the idea of collective trauma in their writings.[3] As the optimism they felt in the 1960s about the future of Nigeria as "the Great Exemplar" of Africa waned, both have struggled with the reality that the consequences of colonialism continue to be felt long after independence. Indeed, in subsequent decades, trauma has become the prevailing metaphor in their descriptions of Nigerian history. Achebe asserts that the nation is still confronting "the traumatic effects of our first confrontation with Europe";[4] Soyinka likewise identifies the inhuman conduct of postcolonial regimes as part of a pattern caused by the "collective racial trauma" of the slave trade.[5] Perhaps the most sustained engagement with the idea of collective trauma occurs in Achebe's fifth and possibly final novel, *Anthills of the Savannah* (1987). Here, Achebe explores the struggle facing the citizens of the mythical state of Kangan as they attempt to comprehend the failure of their nation to flourish after gaining independence. The violence and chaos into which the nation descends lead to a profound sense of despair among the characters, a sense of despair that is formulated into a single question late in the novel by the female protagonist, Beatrice. Mourning the violent deaths of both her friend Ikem, editor of *The National Gazette*, and her lover

Chris, Minister of Information, she asks, "What must a people do to appease an embittered history?"[6]

Exploring this question with respect to Achebe and Soyinka has implications that extend beyond the study of Nigerian and even African literature more broadly. The kind of embittered or traumatic history that Achebe describes has become a central preoccupation for literary, historical, and psychological research. Trauma is one of the central terms of discourse within Holocaust studies; it has also been used to describe a wide variety of historical incidents in Germany, Chile, Japan, Spain, and elsewhere.[7] Shoshana Felman even characterizes the twentieth century as a whole in terms of trauma, labeling it a "post-traumatic century."[8] Beatrice's question is relevant to these discourses because it reopens debates over the role that narrative can play in the healing process. For the pathology of trauma, Cathy Caruth argues, lies not in the event itself but in how it is subsequently experienced: "The pathology consists [. . .] solely in the *structure of its experience* or reception: the event is not assimilated or experienced fully at the time, but only belatedly, in its repeated possession of the one who experiences it."[9] Narrative, according to a long line of clinicians from Pierre Janet and Sigmund Freud to Judith Herman more recently, has a unique capacity to restructure experience in ways that contain trauma within a larger life story and thereby limit its pernicious effects.[10]

Yet, the very fact that *Anthills of the Savannah* comes two decades after his previous novel, *A Man of the People* (1966), suggests a crisis of confidence on Achebe's part about the efficacy of literary narratives. These two decades witnessed several military coups, the secession of the Biafran region and subsequent civil war, and the squandering of Nigeria's oil wealth. In many respects, the publication of *Anthills of the Savannah* is surprising, for Achebe asserted after the publication of *A Man of the People* that the nation's violence left him unable and unwilling to write novels.[11] Despite building a career that established the legitimacy of African literature and his own international stature – despite decades of claiming that the novelist has a unique pedagogical responsibility on behalf of his or her people – the "inventor of the African novel" had apparently ended his career as a novelist.[12] Beatrice's question, then, goes to the heart of Achebe's own hopes and anxieties about the novel's ability to intervene in the nation's crises. Hence, the question of how a people appeases an embittered history might be read to imply a more specific question: how can *literature* appease an embittered history?

Literary representations of trauma are particularly relevant to this study because of the suggestion made by Julia Hell and others that trauma induces nostalgia.[13] Hell's exploration of German culture after the dismantling of the Berlin Wall in 1989 concludes that a rather unsettling longing for the German Democratic Republic has arisen among many former East Germans. In the face of radical cultural change and the need to construct a new national identity, traces of the Communist past have gained a new cultural cachet and the GDR's "legitimatory discourse of antifascism" has found new credibility.[14] Hell's analysis points to nostalgia in its most dangerous form: the longing to reconstruct a simplified and unproblematic past as a means of avoiding confrontation with unpleasant realities in the present. Such sentimentality legitimized Nazism in Germany and ethnic cleansing in the former Yugoslavia; on a much less dangerous scale, it legitimized British foreign policy from Eden to Thatcher and Reaganism in the United States.

Answering Beatrice's question, then, requires analyzing the extent to which nostalgia in contemporary Anglophone literature ameliorates or unwittingly exacerbates trauma. For both Achebe and Soyinka, nostalgia represents a necessary and often productive response to trauma that enables the restoration or creation of solidarity by restructuring how individuals experience the past. Both authors recognize the risks associated with nostalgia and even critique its usage by nationalist politicians to conceal social tensions and to construct falsely idealized pasts; both nonetheless remain attracted to its potential to refigure the past in ways that establish shared ethical ideals while still preserving cultural and religious differences. Indeed, the amorphous quality of nostalgia is precisely what attracts Achebe and Soyinka; more than any of the other authors explored in this study, Achebe and Soyinka utilize nostalgia's capacity to evoke concrete images that are nonetheless vague enough to have multiple and conflicting fassociations.

RECLAIMING THE PAST

Fanon highlights the complexities facing African artists, intellectuals, and politicians who wish to reclaim and rehabilitate precolonial cultural traditions. Recognizing the importance of reestablishing vital links to traditional African cultures as a means of counteracting the pernicious effects of colonialism, he nonetheless cautions against the obvious response to colonial indoctrination. Unqualified affirmations of precolonial

African culture and essence, according to Fanon, are ultimately counter-productive to liberation movements because they do not address the Manichean logic underlying colonial narratives that classify the world into hierarchical binaries of black/white, savage/civilized, child/parent, and so forth. Such binaries are hierarchical in the sense that one of the two terms is defined either as the negation of the other or as its rudimentary or immature form. "Black," in other words, does not embody a set of virtues that are a legitimate alternative to "white"; rather, "black" simply signifies "not white." A "child" is a person who has not yet matured into adulthood, and is unable to handle the responsibility of being a "parent."[15] Thus, efforts to rehabilitate the denigrated terms may grant to them a certain positive valence but not independence from the terms against which they are opposed. The result is that movements such as *négritude* ultimately reaffirm European culture and its dominance over Africa. This recognition was bitterly confirmed for Fanon by the repeated failures of those associated with *négritude* to support independence movements in Algeria, Martinique, and elsewhere; his stinging critique of *négritude* in *The Wretched of the Earth* comes in response to the realization that assertions of African essence do not imply continental political solidarity.[16]

Fanon's more positive attitude toward *négritude* in earlier works such as *Black Skin, White Masks*, however, indicates the complexity of the problem facing postcolonial African nation states. Taking his works together, it becomes apparent that the central challenge is to reconceive Africa as a positive identification that can be shared by groups across the continent while still recognizing that the concept of Africa has historically served the interests of European colonizers. Fanon asserts that "Colonialism did not dream of wasting its time in denying the existence of one national culture after another. Therefore the reply of the colonized peoples will be straight away continental in its breadth."[17] The denigration of African cultures by the colonial powers succeeded in altering the dynamics of social relations among African communities to the degree that it limited the range of psychological identifications these communities could subsequently take. A continental identification henceforth became inevitable to some degree because the disparagement of various African cultures was achieved by means of a consolidation of difference into a single black essence. Cultural variations between the Yoruba and Igbo, for example, were considered by the colonial powers irrelevant for the determination of colonial boundaries and racial characteristics. As such, local or tribal identities could not provide a satisfying basis for national identity because they did not directly address the racial denigration apparent in colonial discourses. Hence, the paradox facing African intellectuals, artists, and political activists has been the need to rehabilitate the idea of continental identity in the process of achieving national liberation.

Fanon himself wavers on the extent to which the reconstruction of African identity should be accomplished through the restoration of precolonial societies or the creation of entirely new solidarities through revolution.[18] A similar ambivalence has characterized the works of African artists and politicians he has influenced, from the Guinean Amilcar Cabral to the Kenyan Ngugi wa Thiong'o, the Ghanaian Ayi Kwei Armah, and both Soyinka and Achebe in Nigeria. The fact that they have all flirted with essentialistic conceptions of identity at some stage in their careers points to the allure of a connection to a precolonial past uncontaminated by the colonial era. Even Soyinka, who gained notoriety early in his career for his vociferous assault on *négritude*, found himself endorsing a kind of essentialist thinking later. Nonetheless, the tradition of the African novel since Achebe has demonstrated a nuanced sensitivity to the risks as well as the promise of envisioning the nation state as the restoration of previous systems of social relations. In one of his most famous pronouncements on the challenge facing the postcolonial artist, Achebe cautions against the longing to cast the past in idyllic terms:

> The question is how does a writer re-create the past? Quite clearly there is a strong temptation to idealize it – to extoll its good points and pretend that the bad never existed [. . . But the] credibility of the world [the writer] is attempting to re-create will be called into question and he will defeat his own purpose if he is suspected of glossing over inconvenient facts. We cannot pretend that our past was one long technicolor idyll. We have to admit that like other people's pasts ours had its good as well as its bad sides.[19]

Similarly to Fanon, Achebe insists that a "return to sources" fails to challenge European portrayals of Africa and Africans unless it depicts both the vitality of and the social tensions within precolonial cultures. Europeans established normative ideas of Africans that could not simply be dismissed after independence, and Achebe's concern about "credibility" points to the extent to which European norms have been internalized. An idealized version of precolonial life would either lack any credibility in the light of the undeniable existence of social tensions and ethnic and tribal rivalries, or describe a world so far removed from present circumstances as to be useless as a resource for building nations in the aftermath of colonialism.

Achebe's self-consciousness about the dangers of idealizing the past, however, does not eliminate a longing for lost worlds in his own writings. Even his first novel, *Things Fall Apart* (1958), depicts characters who express a longing for a more glorious past in pointed contrast to a disappointing present. The novel's protagonist, Okonkwo, mourns for his clan, "which he saw breaking up and falling apart" after its initial encounters with British missionaries and colonists.[20] This sentiment is echoed by Ezeulu in Achebe's third novel, *Arrow of God* (1964), "True medicine [. . .] had died with his father's generation. Practitioners of today were mere dwarfs."[21] Nor is nostalgia confined to Achebe's fictional characters; a nostalgic tone has increasingly permeated his nonfiction writings and interviews as his disappointment and frustration with Nigeria's rulers have grown in the decades since independence. In *The Trouble with Nigeria* (1984), Achebe laments the series of governments in postcolonial Nigeria, whose leaders "may already have betrayed irretrievably Nigeria's high destiny" with their corruption and disregard for democracy.[22] By the late 1980s, he confessed in an interview with Bill Moyers that he wished he could start the "whole story" of his country over again.[23]

The Biafran War (1967–70), more than any other event, confirmed a sense that the "story" of postcolonial Nigeria only replays the history of colonial violence and exploitation. This struggle, which claimed an estimated two million lives, demonstrated the consequences of the ethnic and tribal tensions that the British encouraged during the colonial era as a means of forestalling any united opposition front. The secession of the eastern, Igbo-dominated provinces was a direct result of targeted ethnic violence in the northern region by the Hausa-Fulani and the 1966 coup overthrowing the military government of Major-General Ironsi, which was dominated by Igbo officers. The brutal campaign to crush Biafra over the next three years, Achebe notes, "was such a cataclysmic experience that for me it virtually changed the history of Africa and the history of Nigeria. Everything I had known before, all the optimism, had to be re-thought."[24]

If nostalgic language or rhetoric is to provide a useful response to the trauma of embittered history, it needs to provide authors with the means to address the failure of optimistic narratives of liberation that had guided independence movements throughout the colonial world. These movements, Simon Gikandi argues, envisioned the nation as the basis for the fulfillment of human freedom.[25] The continued corruption and violence in postcolonial nation states cast doubts on this promise and even on the basic legitimacy of these narratives. Events such as the Biafran War defied the vision of history proposed by narratives of liberation and shattered the vision of national solidarity on which they were based. Nor have subsequent reconciliation efforts managed to revitalize a genuinely national narrative, in large part because postwar policy discouraged public discussions of the conditions that gave rise to the war and any official commemoration of Biafra. This policy was already outlined in General Yakubu Gowon's victory speech in January 1970, and quickly implemented thereafter.[26] Indeed, it is striking that Biafra continues to be considered "a wound that has not healed, an issue of conscience in our collective memory" not only by those who supported the secession, including Achebe, but also by those who opposed it, such as Soyinka.[27] Although the physical conflict itself ended in 1970, Soyinka has insisted as recently as 1998 that the Biafran War has still not ended.[28] The trauma that he and other writers and scholars describe results less from specific experiences of the conflict itself than from its transformation of how history more generally can be perceived. Achebe's statement earlier underlines this fact – the war is "a cataclysmic experience" not simply because of the lives it claimed but because "it virtually changed the history of Africa and the history of Nigeria."

In the absence of a compelling narrative for the postcolonial nation, Achebe and Soyinka find Nigeria doomed to traumatic repetition. Nigeria's politicians are consumed with a "strange forgetfulness" that leads them to repeat the same tragic mistakes and to return to corrupt leaders of earlier republics.[29] "The politics of the Second Republic," Achebe laments, "have demonstrated the Shavian conceit that the only thing we learn from experience is that we learn nothing from experience" (54). Like the patient suffering from trauma, Nigeria seems compelled to reenact in detail the event of betrayal without recognizing its repetition. Soyinka similarly describes a "recurrent cycle of human stupidity" that belies hope for national growth and progress.[30]

Achebe's and Soyinka's characterizations of trauma resonate with psychoanalysis in suggesting that "rehabilitation" requires the refiguration of past experiences. Trauma, as understood by psychoanalytic theory and both Achebe and Soyinka, inhibits an individual's or community's ability to access knowledge and process experiences in ways that enable change or growth. This failure to process the knowledge of an overwhelming occurrence constitutes what Cathy Caruth calls the "enigmatic core" of trauma, and it is this failure that leads to the characteristic and insistent return of the traumatic event.[31] As long as the knowledge of this event remains incompletely assimilated within narrative or symbolic systems, the traumatized individual or community is doomed, in Achebe's words, to "learn nothing from experience." The challenge facing the writer, then, is to locate and recover experiences that a community has failed to understand and assimilate. Writing provides a useful intervention to the extent that it can represent seemingly incomprehensible events and provide some sense of their meaning.

This is not to say that any explanation of events is productive. Through the character of Ikem in *Anthills of the Savannah*, for example, Achebe rejects efforts to replace older nationalist narratives of liberation with newer neocolonial narratives of economic exploitation because the latter do nothing to change the perception of Nigeria's continued victimization and helplessness. "To blame all these things on imperialism and international capitalism as our modish radicals want us to do is, in my view, sheer cant and humbug," Ikem asserts (147). As was the case with Momaday and Silko in Chapter 3, only narrative refigurations of experience that use the past to envision some degree of agency rather than victimization can enable a community to move beyond its traumatic history and to imagine a more satisfying future.

Achebe's longstanding claims for the pedagogical value of literature can be read in this light. While Achebe has made somewhat varying statements over the years regarding the precise pedagogical value of literature, one of the most provocative comes in a conversation with Charles H. Rowell. Achebe states that "This is what literature, what art, is supposed to do: to give us a second handle on reality so that when it becomes necessary to do so, we can turn to art and find a way out."[32] The value of literature identified here does not result primarily from its testimonial function, though this is certainly important to Achebe. As the metaphor of the anthills of the savannah in the eponymous novel indicates, literature can and must record events that colonial and even postcolonial histories suppress. The anthills survive, Achebe claims, "so that the new grass will have memory of the fire that devastated the savannah in the previous dry season."[33] By extension, the novel as a metaphorical anthill provides a similar function for the Nigerian people, providing memories of prior catastrophes. Achebe, however, attributes more importance to literature's ability to redescribe already known events, "to give us a second handle on reality." On this understanding, literature can modify the significance of a given event in the minds of readers by redescribing it imaginatively. And it is this ability to modify how events are perceived that allows literature to reformulate past experience and to counter, theoretically at least, the effects of traumatic history.

The reformulation or redescription of experience is a recurring motif in *Anthills of the Savannah*. In a central scene of the novel, for example, Ikem in his capacity as the editor of *The National Gazette* visits a group of protesters from his native province of Abazon who have come to the capital in order to petition for drought relief. During this visit, Ikem is told a story of a leopard and tortoise as an allegory to describe the protesters' own struggle against the authority of the capital and Kangan's dictator, Sam. The story describes a tortoise's last wish to a leopard before the latter eats him. Granted his wish for a few moments' respite, the tortoise furiously scratches the ground; the act, he explains, serves to mark the ground for future passers-by: "Because even after I am dead I would want anyone passing by this spot to say, yes, a fellow and his match struggled here" (117). The story asserts the importance of establishing an historical record of the struggle against power; however, the story also asserts the need to redescribe how the struggle was fought. It calls for a reformulation of the initial experience in order to find in it retroactively a potential that may not have initially existed. The protesters from Abazon recognize that they have no more ability to overcome the military government than the tortoise has to overcome the leopard. The hope is that subsequent generations will remember their defiance and read in it the possibility of more successful resistance at some later date.

If literary narratives can undo traumatic history to some degree by redescribing the past in ways that enable individuals to learn from it and not repeat past mistakes, nostalgia may contribute to this process. Indeed, nostalgia has been crucial to the efforts by all the literary authors in this study to experience the past in new ways. Their visions of longed-for communities, previous chapters have shown, do not always come at the expense of "what really happened" but instead provide a richer and more complex picture of the past by drawing attention to moments of lost possibility and communities that were never fully realized. The longing for a lost or imagined homeland certainly *can* reinforce trauma, as Hell suggests, by oversimplifying the past and repressing uncomfortable events, but it *need* not do so. As the previous chapter's analysis demonstrated, such longings frequently inspire a process of imagination whose end cannot be anticipated or fully controlled. Hence, even disingenuous uses of nostalgia might facilitate an individual's or community's efforts to move beyond trauma. The real question, then, is the extent to which the nostalgia employed by specific authors such as Achebe and Soyinka enables the refiguration of the past in ways that might not otherwise be possible.

Simon Gikandi's seminal book on Achebe, *Reading Chinua Achebe: Language & Ideology in Fiction*, provides an important lead in this direction. Gikandi's reading of *Anthills of the Savannah* draws out the deeply retrospective character of the novel. Retrospection is first established as the predominant tone by the narratorial perspectives of Chris, Ikem, and Beatrice, all of whom are concerned with the past far more than with the present or future. Beatrice is most explicit in this regard, describing herself as engaged in a process of "bringing together as many broken pieces of this tragic history as I could lay my hands on" (75). The novel's retrospective character is heightened by the hindsight that readers are granted about the fate of the various narrators. Chris and Ikem are dead by the time their narratives are read; Beatrice is the subject of a political smear campaign depicting her as a modern-day Madame Pompadour. Retrospection is not limited to the novel's tone, moreover, but is essential to Achebe's ideological concerns. The novel, on Gikandi's reading, is committed to the task of reclaiming "an original moral sense" that has been eroded beyond recognition by postcolonial politics.[34] This task requires a series of contrasts between the past and present to highlight the betrayal of the nation by its leaders. Gikandi writes, "Writing is hence a retrospective moment which seeks to recapture a past of promise and to contrast it with a present of failure; at the postcolonial moment of narration, the narrators must contrast the nationalist longing for a homogenized form and culture with the fragmentation engendered by the politics of power and betrayal."[35]

Nostalgia becomes a crucial feature of Achebe's novel in that the "past of promise" that retrospection identifies is a reconstruction of the past in terms of present longings. Within the context of the novel, there is no prelapsarian moment before the promise of national solidarity, democracy, and prosperity was inflected by self-interest, the desire for power, and what Achebe calls "tribal politics."[36] Even the picture of youthful idealism that Chris paints of Sam (the current dictator of Kangan), Ikem, and himself as students at Lord Lugard College training themselves to lead an independent postcolonial Kangan is tempered by Beatrice's recognition of their egotism: "Well, you fellows, all three of you, are incredibly conceited. The story of this country, as far as you are concerned, is the story of the three of you" (60).

Beatrice herself engages in a nostalgic reconstruction of the past. Her claim to be collecting the "broken pieces of this tragic history" implies that there was once an unbroken wholeness or totality subsequently shattered. But the novel gives no indication of this world. At no point does Beatrice or any other character ever identify this unbroken world or the supposedly broken promise of democracy in the present tense. The promise itself, like Beatrice's unbroken world, comes into being in clear and articulate terms only after it has purportedly been betrayed or broken. In other words, the "past of promise" exists only as an inaccessible moment that has never been present, and it only becomes accessible only through the fantasy of returning to a world that never was.

Nostalgia is similarly crucial to the articulation of Achebe's political vision in *The Trouble with Nigeria*. Early on in this work, Achebe identifies the crisis facing the nation to be the result of the "death of a dream-Nigeria" in which all citizens could live and work in equality.[37] What is striking about Achebe's statement is the date he attributes to this "death": 1951. The ideal of Nigeria thus does not survive even to the moment of the nation's birth some nine years later. And, interestingly, Achebe does not suggest that the passing of his "dream-Nigeria" or the ideal itself could have been recognized in the moment; he recognizes them only "in retrospect." Like *Anthills of the Savannah*, *The Trouble with Nigeria* suggests that such ideals come into existence retroactively through the nostalgic refiguration of past experience.

To begin to understand Achebe's motivations here, the nostalgia in his writings should be read with respect to his long-term ideological commitment to iconoclasm. Repeatedly, Achebe has insisted that the "storyteller has a different agenda from the emperor," and this agenda is guided by a moral responsibility to challenge those in power.[38] The artist serves his or her country by pointing to the excesses of power and criticizing ideals that threaten to become rigid orthodoxies. It is this guiding "critical intelligence" that makes the artist a true patriot, and anyone who fails in this task betrays his or her country.[39] Nostalgia sharpens the critique of existing political regimes by enabling Achebe to cast present disappointments in concrete and widely recognizable terms. Achebe's "dream-Nigeria" provides an image of what is missing in the current state – an environment in which a person could "pursue any legitimate goal open to his fellows" – even if Achebe himself cannot articulate what precise policies might be necessary to achieve this ideal.[40] He is thereby able to locate in moments of the past heretofore unrecognized potential in the light of present desires.

When Chief Obafemi Awolowo "stole" the leadership of Western Nigeria from Dr. Nnamdi Azikiwe in 1951, few parties could have perceived in the moment the "death" of a national ideal that Achebe can identify thirty years later. Retrospectively, however, Achebe can find in that moment the potential for what could have been and recast it as a sort of utopian image that is persuasive precisely because it is cast within the past, and is hence theoretically recoverable.

Achebe's commitment to critique applies even to the nostalgic images on which his critique draws. He notes, for example, that his "dream-Nigeria" was perhaps "an unrealistic dream at the best of times."[41] He directs a similar critique at the literary characters that evoke the most nostalgia in his own work: Okonkwo and Ezeulu. These characters have often been cast in elegiac terms by Achebe. In his preface to the second edition of *Arrow of God*, for example, Achebe asserts that Ezeulu is a role model for the Nigerian people, "a magnificent man." Similarly, he insists that when men like Okonkwo fall, their entire society is shaken: "When a man like Okonkwo crashes, there are echoes left by his death and these echoes continue to resound in the community."[42] Yet if Okonkwo and Ezeulu represent powerful figures of Igbo tradition – paragons of strength, determination, and willpower – Achebe insists that they fail their people in the moment of greatest need. When his village refuses to support military action against British colonizers and missionaries, Okonkwo commits suicide; facing a threat to his own role as priest, Ezeulu refuses to perform the ceremony that would allow his people to harvest their crops. Indeed, Achebe's depictions of his protagonists suggest that the colonial encounter only makes manifest problems that already existed within Igbo culture, and the conflict with the British simply foregrounds the moral failure of a particular kind of Igbo role model – one who is unwilling to sacrifice his pride in the name of the community's need.[43]

This reading of Achebe develops my earlier characterization of his nostalgia. The depictions of characters like Okonkwo and Ezeulu suggest that Achebe not only locates moments of lost potential in the past but also highlights particular moments of failure in the light of present political and cultural issues. In other words, nostalgia provides Achebe with a rhetorical mode of critiquing present social and political visions by recasting them within the realm of the past; this helps to explain why in the midst of efforts by his countrymen to construct a postcolonial Nigerian state, Achebe writes stories of the failure of precolonial and colonial heroes and the ways in which such figures betray the communities they represent. In a 1963 conversation with Lewis Nkosi and Wole Soyinka, Achebe links Okonkwo and nationalism, and the failure of the former points to that of the latter. When Achebe is asked about the fall of Okonkwo, he links it to the weakness of the society as a whole. "The weakness of this particular society, I think, is a lack of adaptation, not being able to bend. [. . .] I think in his time the strong men were those who did not bend, and I think this was a fault in the culture itself."[44] Okonkwo and Ezeulu presage a postcolonial Nigerian government that would valorize authoritarian practices and denigrate dissent.

Achebe's concern with Okonkwo and Ezeulu as leaders points to his more basic rejection of political, cultural, and ethical absolutism. The rejection of absolutism, for Achebe, draws its basis from traditional Igbo culture, and he invokes proverbs such as "wherever something stands, something else will stand beside it" to insist that absolutism represents not a legitimate moral position but ideological blindness.[45] The most obvious target of this critique would be Christianity, which Achebe faults for its insistence on the idea of "one way, one truth, one life." However, this critique is also directed toward Igbo culture and Nigeria more generally. On this understanding, single-mindedness, stubborn traditionalism, and fanaticism of all kinds represent attitudes that inevitably produce disastrous results for the individual and his or her community – and it is when Okonkwo and Ezeulu fail to remember this that tragedy occurs. Likewise, the civil war that engulfs the mythical state of Kangan at the end of *Anthills of the Savannah* is precipitated in large part by the unwillingness of the nation's leaders to converse with representatives from the province of Abazon and listen to their needs. As a result, the military government that came into power promising stability ends as one more instance in an embittered history of violence.

The rejection of absolutism in Achebe's thought, however, does not imply a complete rejection of moral foundationalism. Over the course of his career, Achebe has inconsistently though repeatedly insisted on the existence of basic and universal moral distinctions. "[T]he frontier between good and evil must not be blurred [. . .] no matter how fuzzy it may be to us, there is still a distinction between what is permissible and what is not permissible," Achebe asserts.[46] Most obviously, such claims provide Achebe with some nonculturally specific grounds on which to critique colonialism. As Michael Valdez Moses suggests, Achebe cannot endorse antifoundationalism without reducing the social collapse experienced by the Igbo during the colonial period into merely an instance of social and ideological "change." Antifoundationalism, Moses argues, would negate the possibility of making strong moral claims through literature, for "antifoundationalism implies a theoretical neutrality toward the kind of ethical and political conflict that Achebe dramatizes. [. . .] Achebe's novel suggests something quite different, namely that the very existence of certain societies depends upon their adherence to certain foundational premises."[47]

Thus, even though Achebe asserts that contingency and convention define the codes of behavior by which a community operates, he insists on the need for certain nonrelativistic standards. The proverb "wherever something stands, something else will stand beside it," for example, does not imply moral relativism, for it enables Achebe to clarify his critique of Christianity. A strong relativism would assert that Achebe cannot use the terms of one culture – here, the Igbo – to critique another, British missionary culture. Instead, the proverb endorses the idea of accommodation as a foundational moral principle. This principle acknowledges a high degree of variation and contingency among different cultures, but it does not imply that all evaluation is purely culturally bound. Rather, it assumes the need to account for difference and to accept the legitimate existence of contrasting beliefs within any community. The principle of accommodation insists on the legitimacy of Christian perceptions, then, but faults Christianity for not extending the same regard to Igbo beliefs.

The ideal of accommodation implies that political formations like the nation state need to tolerate and even embrace diversity as long as cultural differences do not challenge the basic source of unity – the nation itself. At the same time, the ideal insists that various ethnic and religious groups have a responsibility to offer the same regard to others that they would wish themselves to be accorded, and to work out disputes within the framework of the nation. The political application of the principle of accommodation is clearly evident in *Anthills of the Savannah*: the novel refuses to endorse the idea of secession for the province of Abazon, despite legitimate grievances with the capital. The preservation of Kangan remains an indisputable and unifying principle.

Achebe's claims regarding moral universalism, then, serve not only to critique agents of colonialism but also to guide efforts to imagine what form the postcolonial African nation might take. Given that nations like Nigeria will inevitably possess a diversity of ethnic, cultural, and religious traditions, a stable and sustainable national identity requires some minimal sense of shared beliefs. "For a society to function smoothly and effectively its members must share certain basic tenets of belief and norms of behavior," Achebe writes. "There must be a reasonable degree of consensus on what is meant by virtue and vice; there must be some agreement on the attributes of a hero, on what constitutes the heroic act."[48]

The naming ceremony at the end of *Anthills of the Savannah* represents an attempt to balance concerns about both absolutism and relativism as guiding principles for nation and ethics. In the final scene of the novel, the community that forms around Beatrice in the aftermath of the civil violence and coup that claim the lives of Chris, Ikem, and Sam takes upon itself the task of performing the naming ceremony for Ikem's child. Beatrice names the child Amaechina, "may-the-path-never-close," noting that this is their version of the name the biblical prophet Isaiah gave to one of his children, Shear-jashub, "the-remnant-shall-return" (206). After the child's grandmother and great-uncle arrive, the group collectively pledge to be parents to the child under the watchful auspices of the ghosts of Ikem and Chris. The ceremony seeks to balance the necessity to commemorate the past and the need to create a place for the future by selectively drawing upon a variety of cultural and religious traditions.[49] Indeed, Achebe emphasizes the diversity of the people present at the naming ceremony and their ability to overcome their differences. Despite disagreements about religion, and despite the fact that the participants do not even share a common language, those assembled at the naming ceremony are united by a desire to see Amaechina grow up in a world different from their own.[50]

The balance between cultural diversity and unity established during the naming ceremony is possible only because Amaechina becomes the focus of the participants' nostalgia, a figure for the lost promise of a postcolonial nation. The characters variously lament the loss of their loved ones and the tragic fate of Kangan since independence. Although the particular losses they feel are unique, they share a sense that these losses all reflect a broader national crisis. The characters perceive this all the more acutely as they look upon Amaechina, a child who will grow up without a father because her country could not live up to its promise. Hence, even though the characters have somewhat different grievances and different explanations for the failure of the nation, they do not perceive these differences to represent a source of conflict because they share a more basic foundational principle of caring for the child and providing for her future. This becomes apparent in the series of pledges and petitions the characters all affirm, culminating with a petition on behalf of the nation: "The life of Kangan" (212). The naming ceremony enables the translation of individual regret into communal solidarity, and the commitment to an individual person's wellbeing thereby comes to imply a more general commitment to the nation's. Indeed, what is particularly striking about this scene is that the characters feel more able to express their diverse modes of belief after agreeing that they share a common ethical charge.

Perhaps the most notable moment in this regard occurs when Beatrice's housekeeper, Agatha, bursts into an evangelical Christian song at the ceremony, something she had never previously done in front of her employer. After observing a Muslim participant in the naming ceremony, Aina, beginning to dance to Agatha's song, Beatrice revises her earlier contempt for Agatha's religious beliefs and joins in what rapidly becomes a communal dance (208). Nor does Agatha express resentment when another member of the group joins in the song with a nonreligious refrain.

In this ceremony of mixed traditions and innovation, nostalgia provides the basis for the formation of ethical solidarity. Although it is often associated with fear, anxiety, and xenophobia, the longing for what has been lost provides a common ground that had been prohibited previously by religious, cultural, and linguistic difference. Precisely because nostalgia tends to be characterized by ambiguous, incoherent, and unformed longings, a single object can be the source of nostalgia for a wide range of people. If a society needs to have its members "share basic tenets of belief and norms of behavior" – as Achebe claimed earlier – then the creation of a nostalgic image of what the country could have been accomplishes this by establishing a nexus for a collection of diverse beliefs. That is, Beatrice and Agatha need not share the same God if they both consider Elewa's child to be the enduring trace of a lost world of promise – a once and future world whose possibility requires labor in the present. Far from leading to disengagement, nostalgia provides the conditions to establish the hybrid identities that Edward Said and other postcolonial thinkers consider to be necessary to confront existing political conditions.[51]

The ideal of accommodation modeled by the naming ceremony, however, envisions a somewhat unfamiliar form of hybridity. Typically, the metaphor of hybridity refers to an identity that blends several different cultural traditions together in a way that does not prioritize certain cultures over others. This kind of blending is not present in *Anthills of the Savannah*. If the Muslim Aina chooses to dance to a Christian tune, this does not imply any endorsement or internalization of Christianity on her part. She may be joining Agatha in celebrating the naming ceremony and praying for a brighter future for Kangan, but the fact that the celebration utilizes Christian song is purely incidental to her. Nor is there any evidence that Agatha, on seeing others joining in her song, has any greater respect for other religions or any desire to incorporate aspects of them in her own daily life. Thus, the novel does not envision a sort of common hybrid identity taken up by all the characters. Rather, the characters are hybridized by the naming ceremony to the extent that they learn to accommodate the different beliefs of others who have similarly taken the pledge to care for Amaechina.

Achebe's vision of accommodation, then, does not preclude contest-ation between members of the community. On the contrary, it seems to guarantee conflict. Although the novel ends with the naming ceremony, it would not be difficult to foresee a great deal of disagreement shortly thereafter over how best to raise Amaechina. The community members do not yet have to decide the difficult questions of what religion(s) Amaechina will follow, where she will live, who will support her, and so forth. Indeed, hints of disagreement arise even during the ceremony. Amaechina's grandmother is angered by the nontraditional form the ceremony takes, though she is mollified eventually. Perhaps more sig-nificantly, Emmanuel, President of the Students Union, disputes one of the early toasts during the ceremony. Contradicting Beatrice, Emmanuel insists that the group should toast not only people but also what he calls "living ideas" – a point to which Beatrice ultimately concedes (207).

The foregrounding of disagreement in *Anthills of the Savannah* refines Achebe's earlier political critique in *The Trouble with Nigeria*. In Achebe's novel, disagreement between members of the community who share some basic tenets or principles is neither negative nor divisive. Instead, it appears to be the basis of growth. Because Beatrice and Emmanuel both share the basic principle that they must accommodate each other's beliefs, they do not perceive their different values to be necessarily incompatible. Hence, after Beatrice's concession, everyone can joyfully toast "People and Ideas" (207). Communal solidarity is achieved not by silencing or repressing dissent but by encouraging it.

This stands in stark contrast to what Achebe perceives as the prevalent interpretation of the Nigerian coat-of-arms. The coat-of-arms identifies two virtues – unity and faith – that are taken to be the foundational ideals of the nation state. For Achebe, the problem is that such ideals have been cast as absolute and unquestionable. Achebe quotes Ukapabi Asika as saying that Nigerian unity is "the absolute good."⁵² Achebe insists, however, that such interpretations encourage unquestioned loyalty and cast political dissent as inherently negative. "Unity can only be as good as the purpose for which it is desired. [. . . The] social validity [of unity and faith] depends on the willingness or ability of citizens to ask the searching questions," he writes.⁵³ *Anthills of the Savannah* models precisely this process of asking the "searching questions." Emmanuel's question, for example, does not seek to undermine Beatrice's authority or her right to lead the naming ceremony; he seeks to diminish neither her ideas nor the basic commitment to unity that brings the participants together. Achebe envisions here a mode of questioning that leads to ethical growth by demanding careful scrutiny of the assumptions underlying the ideals endorsed by a community.

TRANSFORMING PRESENT REALITY

The failure of Nigeria to implement such a vision of community, however, suggests that the novel form provides the space to describe a ceremony that would have little chance of occurring outside of the realm of fiction. *Anthills of the Savannah* presents a felicitous collision of cultural forces without the tension that has historically been prevalent. Even the military coup that occurs at the climax of the novel is quick and relatively bloodless in comparison to the Biafran War. From the perspective of trauma theory, Achebe's focus on an idealized resolution to the social tensions that led up to civil war seems misguided, if not escapist. Nor does he apparently believe that the representation of the traumatic past requires the use of a distinctly modernist literary language, as Hayden White and others have argued.⁵⁴ While Achebe's novel is certainly less in the realist mode than his previous works, it still bears few of the experimental formal features and metafictional characteristics of other contemporary Anglophone novels preoccupied with trauma, including Raymond Federman's *Double or Nothing* (1971), Toni Morrison's *Beloved* (1987), Ben Okri's *The Famished Road* (1991), and D. M. Thomas's *The White Hotel* (1981). Such differences might be attributed to different aesthetic sensibilities among various literary traditions; however, Achebe's use of the terminology and metaphors of trauma to describe the political crisis of postcolonial Nigeria demands at least some thought about why he departs so dramatically from other writers in his response. If he presents simplified and idealized resolutions to difficult political realities, does this not undercut the pedagogical value he claims for literature? More specifically, if the naming ceremony in *Anthills of the Savannah* imagines a solidarity that cannot be reproduced in Nigeria or anywhere else, can it genuinely provide a useful ethical guide or will it lead only to frustration?[55]

Over the course of his career, Wole Soyinka has actively refused to present such an idealized community in his work. The difference from Achebe is perhaps nowhere more evident than in his 1965 novel, *The Interpreters*. Like *Anthills of the Savannah*, *The Interpreters* depicts the crises facing the first generation after independence; Soyinka's novel also depicts a heterogeneous group of the new nation's best and brightest: a journalist, engineer, lawyer, aristocrat, academic, and artist. Yet Soyinka's "interpreters" fail to find a basis of solidarity comparable to that found by Achebe's characters. The character who is briefly identified as a potential "link" between them, the young thief Noah, is subsequently dismissed by the artist Kola as "simply negative [. . . an] unrelieved vacuity."[56] Even before this point, Noah becomes a source of dissension rather than solidarity as the various "interpreters" offer conflicting explanations for his descent into petty crime. Nor do the tensions between them lessen after Noah is apparently rehabilitated by the preacher Lazarus. In stark contrast to *Anthills of the Savannah*, the conclusion of Soyinka's novel depicts not a ritual affirmation of shared values and commitments but "a night of severance" in which "every man is going his way" (245).

Soyinka's refusal to present a community similar to that found in *Anthills of the Savannah* points to a fundamental difference in attitude toward the historical knowledge provided by recollection. While Soyinka agrees with Achebe that a "return to sources" is crucial to the conceptualization of the postcolonial nation state, he asserts that recollection often perpetuates a nation's embittered history by limiting the possibility for various cultural and ethnic groups to imagine themselves in terms of a broadly inclusive national identity. As early as 1960, Soyinka cast himself in opposition to writers such as Achebe who, he believed, focused their attention on the past to the exclusion of the present. In one of his most famous essays, "The Writer in a Modern African State," Soyinka blasts the author who is "content to turn his eye backwards in time and prospect in archaic fields for forgotten gems which would dazzle and distract the present."[57]

Even in his later, more modulated writing, Soyinka underscores the dangers of recollection as much as he praises its progressive potential. In

The Open Sore of a Continent (1996), he notes that "cultural memory" is the only weapon of resistance available to the citizens of a nation ruled by a dictatorship.[58] This is not because recollection leads citizens to conceive of a nation in more egalitarian terms, however; rather, it encourages people to revitalize older tribal or ethnic identifications. Thus, instead of providing the basis for broad solidarity and a progressive future, the preoccupation with cultural memory leads to "a period of internal retreat" in which the populace "withdraw[s] into the cultural sheath."[59] Whereas *Anthills of the Savannah* depicts recollection as ultimately leading to the articulation of shared national ideals, Soyinka insists that it leads to a retreat from a genuinely national discourse.

The risks of drawing upon cultural memory for models of social relations and systems of governance are apparent in Soyinka's earliest works. In his play *A Dance of the Forests* (1960), for example, Soyinka creates an allegory of the Nigerian independence celebrations, for which it was written and first performed. The ritual "Gathering of the Tribes" that precipitates the action of the play is an event that occurs only once in an historical epoch, and the host community calls upon its scattered ancestors to return for it.[60] The idealized vision of the past that the community has created for itself, however, leads it to misunderstand whom it is calling. The town elders assume they are summoning a stream of "Warriors. Sages. Conquerors. Builders. Philosophers. Mystics"; consequently, they are unable to recognize the Dead Man and Dead Woman who do return (31). Nor are the town dwellers ready to confront what the dead have to say. When the Dead Man pleads in the first lines of Part One, "Will you take my case?", he is repeatedly rebuffed (7). For the Dead Man does not appear as a majestic ancestral spirit but as a disheveled and terrifying presence wearing moldy armor over a bloated body; he does not speak words of congratulation but issues a moral claim for the redress of social injustices that preexist the colonial encounter. In his lifetime he was a captain in the army of Mata Kharibu, and he was sold into slavery for refusing his ruler's command to fight an unjust war.

The unwillingness of the town dwellers to recognize that his victimization occurs at the hands of Africans rather than Europeans points to the genuine dangers of their idyllic depictions of precolonial life. In the midst of celebrations for the newly independent postcolonial state of Nigeria, Soyinka provides a cautionary tale suggesting that appeasing an embittered history involves more than rejecting colonial rule. Indeed, the embodiment of collective trauma in Soyinka's play is the Dead Man, who lived hundreds of years before the British ruled Nigeria. The failure of the town dwellers to recognize who this character is and why his claim remains unsettled condemns them to replay the past, a point emphasized by Soyinka making the same actors who compose the court of Mata Kharibu play the roles of the town dwellers. Thus, they are very literally the same people who sold the Dead Man into slavery, and he returns like a traumatic memory to haunt them for their unexpiated crime.

While this critique of conservative idealizations of the past is consistent with his characterization of Nigerian history as a "recurrent cycle of human stupidity," Soyinka is equally critical of an "extreme ultra-leftism" that would deny any "progressive potential" to the past.[61] The weakness of the latter position, for Soyinka, is demonstrated through the character Egbo in *The Interpreters*. Egbo experiences the first memory described in the novel, recalling the creek in which his parents drowned. Yet his initial reaction is to deny the validity of the memory, noting that since the water in the creek continually moves on, the spot where his parents drowned no longer exists. Over the course of the novel, his reluctance to remember takes on increasingly bitter overtones. He rages against the ghosts of the dead for remaining among the living; when his friend and fellow "interpreter" Bandele challenges his attitude, Egbo insists that the dead have a single duty to the living: to be forgotten as quickly as possible. He extends this attitude to African politics, echoing Fanon's insistence on shedding emotional attachments to the past. "Can't you get it into your head that your global or national politics don't really count for much unless you become ruthless with the fabric of the past?" he insists (120).

Egbo is forced to reassess his position later in the novel when he runs into Noah again after the latter has fled Lazarus' church. Egbo is startled by Noah's transformation, uncertain if it is indeed him. The figure standing beneath a mango tree has been "cleansed of every moment of his past" (231). Failing to perform the ritual initiation ceremony into Lazarus' church, Noah flees all attachments. Detached from his past, he does not embody the New African envisioned by Egbo, capable of forging a new national and continental destiny. Rather, he lacks dynamism entirely; he is utterly passive, "a blank white sheet for accidental scribbles" (231).

The anxiety Soyinka demonstrates in *The Interpreters* about the tendency by the Left to dismiss the past as a useful source of knowledge is more explicitly stated in his nonfiction writings on what he terms the "newly surfacing mood of negation" among younger African writers and thinkers.[62] Soyinka identifies this attitude in Yambo Ouologuem's 1968

Bound to Violence (*Le Devoir de violence*), which represents for him the first fully realized African literary work to demonstrate an uncompromising iconoclasm toward all cultures, histories, and civilizations. The ideas presented here and in later works including Ayi Kwei Armah's *Two Thousand Seasons* (1973) suggest that the evolution of postcolonial African nations demands the rejection of all cultural sources – Western, Islamic, and precolonial African.[63] Efforts to reclaim precolonial African traditions are misguided, according to this view, because they have become inseparably linked to Western ideas of class, race, and imperialism.

While Soyinka grants that this attitude represents a logical and even inevitable response to *négritude* and other aesthetic and political movements that have exploited racial identity, he resists the conclusion that the solution to the "recurrent cycle of human stupidity" requires the wholesale repudiation of the past. Hence, despite his own affinities with the political Left, Soyinka characterizes such writings as presenting as much danger as the more politically conservative work of the *négritude* movement. He writes that "Icons can be positive or negative; a blanket iconoclasm is an undialectical proceeding on a par with blanket fetishization of myth and history."[64] A "blanket iconoclasm" is no more dialectical than *négritude* because it assumes that the critique of existing cultural, social, and political institutions is the sole imperative for the writer. Put another way, iconoclastic writers still essentialize Africa, only in negative terms. Instead of critically engaging with the past, they simply repudiate it.

While Soyinka is very explicit in his critiques of both the Right and Left in politics and *négritude* and iconoclasm in art, he is less specific in his explanation of how to utilize the "progressive potential" of the past, or even what constitutes this potential. One thing that does become apparent in his more mature writings is that his critiques are motivated by a concern that a younger generation of politicians and artists has lost touch with the vision of Pan-African identity that motivated members of his own generation during the 1960s. This concern becomes particularly apparent in *The Open Sore of a Continent*, in which Soyinka laments the loss of a sense that the nation state was only part of a broader continental idea. In a strikingly sentimental passage for an author who has repeatedly criticized sentimentality, Soyinka writes:

So how did it all go so badly wrong? [. . .] I know that as [my generation] came into self-awareness as productive beings, we brought our immediate national space into perspective, not narrowly as an idea from which we took a sociopolitical definition of ourselves but as a branch of an even larger idea, the idea of continental identity in formation. [. . .] Many students of my generation surely set their political sights on variants of continental oneness [. . .] We saw the continent, at least from the south of the Sahara to the southern tip of the continent, not as a conglomeration of nations but as one nation, one people. [. . . T]he boundaries of a communal identity are today set much more narrowly. The sights of the average nationalist are sadly contracted.[65]

The rise of national identity is inseparably linked here to the consciousness of transnational solidarity. Africa itself is cast as a nation, perhaps the only true nation on the continent. The shift away from Pan-African identity is troubling to Soyinka because he perceives no other viable basis for a heterogeneous nation state. Ethnicity and tribe are such unpalatable alternatives that Soyinka endorses a continental basis for solidarity despite the obvious similarity between his position and that taken by the *négritude* movement. The idea of continental unity is so compelling to Soyinka because it ironically promotes greater diversity within national boundaries. To see the nation as a local expression of a broader continental idea means that the existence of cultural differences is not an impediment to but a hallmark of a healthy state.

Indeed, on this point Soyinka emphasizes a contrast with *négritude*, characterizing the African continent and the states that compose it as ethnically and culturally heterogeneous, and continually evolving. In his essay "New Frontiers for Old" (1990), cultural diversity is the defining characteristic of the continental body: "Yes indeed, there is an entity called Africa," he writes, "but the creative entities within its dark humus – fecund, restive and protean – burst through the surface of a presumed monolithic reality, and invade the stratosphere with unsuspected shapes and tints of the individual vision!"[66] At the same time, Soyinka demonstrates affinities with *négritude* in identifying a sense of continental unity as the nonnegotiable basis for political thinking and artistic creation.[67] Liberation movements, in other words, do not arise from groups unifying out of a set of common interests; rather, they are the reflection of an *a priori* unity whose political reality had been denied initially by colonialism and subsequently by sectarian violence among Africans who have lost sight of their Pan-African identity.

This reading of Soyinka insists that the increasingly nostalgic character of his writings since the 1980s does not represent a failure of imagination or withdrawal from current debates over the future of Nigeria. On the contrary, Soyinka's lament for the disappearance of Pan-African thinking represents a response to the failures of more narrowly defined nationalisms that have flourished throughout Africa in the postcolonial era, and his self-conscious use of nostalgia enables him to reconfigure the ideal of continental unity as a political and ethical ideal that has continuing relevance. After witnessing three decades of postcolonial regimes failing to live up to promises of promoting democracy, prosperity, and solidarity, Soyinka's youthful vision of African unity could no longer be credibly portrayed as an imminent future waiting to be realized through revolutionary action. Rather than rejecting the ideal itself, however, Soyinka recasts it as a promise betrayed by greed and sectarian thinking. As a betrayed ideal, the vision of Pan-African unity establishes a definition of the nation state that has been repeatedly neglected by African nationalists but continues to endure. This sense of an enduring ideal clarifies Soyinka's notion of the "progressive potential" of the past, distinguishing it from the idea that the past might provide an explicit model for the present to emulate. "Potential" implies a possibility that has been neither realized nor extinguished. Nostalgic reflections on "How did it all go so badly wrong?" can access this potential because they are guided by specific experiences of how current political systems have failed to meet the hopes and needs of citizens.

Although Soyinka's more retrospective writings promote the continuing importance of the nation's existence in the face of seemingly intractable political and ethnic tensions, he is careful to avoid any implication that the form the nation will take is known in advance. Soyinka has been very critical of readings by Gerald Moore and others suggesting that he envisions traditional Yoruba society as the blueprint for Nigeria as a whole.[68] Indeed, what is striking about Soyinka in comparison with Achebe and other African writers of their generation is that despite his assertions about the importance of a continental if not explicitly essentialist identification, he rejects the idea that the past provides the basis for how the nation should be organized. This is apparent in his characterization of the role the past plays in the construction of Africa. Extending his discussion of what constitutes Africa in "New Frontiers for Old," Soyinka asserts that "the ancestors join in the festive dance to rhythms that have always lain latent in their veins, awaiting the solar eruption of new harmonics from their uninhibited, space-tuned off-springs."[69] The postcolonial nation state that Soyinka sees arising out of this "dance" does not represent the actualization of historical or even idealized African societies. The organization of social relations or "rhythms" are newly created, refiguring past cultural traditions to fit current circumstances.

The image of ancestral figures retroactively discovering within themselves the rhythms of a postcolonial nation recalls the broader claims of this study as a whole: the existence of a significant strand of contemporary Anglophone literature that eschews the idea of recovering some putative cultural memory or past totality in favor of recasting the present in the light of fantasies of social arrangements as they could have been. Soyinka's sense that literature has the capacity to discover a progressive potential to the past that was never fully realized is crucial to the preservation of a kind of idealism that Biodun Jefiyo finds Soyinka able to retain in his mature writings, despite the political failures of Nigeria and the imprisonment and exile he has had to endure.[70] On this point, Soyinka shares more with Achebe than with more "postmodern" writers including Samuel Beckett, J. M. Coetzee, and Salman Rushdie, who demonstrate similar commitments to critiquing the post-Enlightenment metanarratives but remain reluctant to articulate what more ethical communities might look like.

This persistent determination to move beyond critique is apparent even in Soyinka's recent collection of essays, *The Burden of Memory, The Muse of Forgiveness* (1999). In this collection, Soyinka links two concerns that have preoccupied him from his earliest days: *négritude* and the crises facing South Africa. Writing in the post-apartheid era, Soyinka considers the prospects for genuine reconciliation in Africa and the extent to which the kind of essentialist thinking motivating Léopold Senghor and other proponents of *négritude* might be useful to this process. Despite his pessimism about the capacity of the Truth and Reconciliation Commission or *négritude* to address the enduring consequences of colonial violence that prompted them, Soyinka senses in them laudable efforts to confront the ambivalence of recollection. Indeed, this ambivalence is foregrounded in the final image of his collection, a musical instrument called the sosso-bala. The instrument, which dates back to the twelfth century and was taken outside the Republic of Guinea for the first time in honor of the celebrations for Senghor's ninetieth birthday, symbolizes for Soyinka both "the near intolerable burden of memory" and "a recovery of lost innocence."[71]

The ambivalent associations that the sosso-bala evokes for Soyinka are consistent with the complex and often highly qualified positions he has taken toward recollection in all his writings – an ambivalence that has been a source of frustration for many younger Nigerian writers and critics, perhaps most notably the playwright Femi Osofisan.[72] Soyinka's ambivalence is not the result of an unwillingness to take a political stand, however, but a recognition of the genuine and inescapable complexity of efforts to make use of the past for the imagination of a viable postcolonial nation state. From the beginning of his career, Soyinka has claimed that artistic representations of the past are crucial to the transformation of how colonized peoples perceive themselves and their ability to govern their destinies.[73] Yet the transformative potential he ascribes to literature has nothing to do with its capacity to chronicle historical events or even to encourage readers to identify with heroic figures. This becomes apparent in a 1990 lecture at Cambridge University in which Soyinka attempts to distinguish his goals from those of *négritude* and nationalist movements presenting simplified idealizations of the past. Invoking the Edenic language and metaphor he will later use in his description of the sosso-bala, he argues:

The loss of paradise is a recurrent fable, the morality tale of the colonized world, of the very experience of colonization, not simply of expulsion and exile. For colonization is indeed a state of internal exile at its most spiritually debilitating. [. . .] Indeed, paradise can be regained; again and again, the artist does regain paradise, but only as a magical act of transformation of present reality, not through the pasting of a coy, anachronistic fig-leaf over the pudenda of the past in the present.[74]

Soyinka's ambivalence is again noteworthy. In the very passage claiming that the artist has the capacity to recreate the past and transform the present, he cautions against misguided idealizations. The tendency to idealize the past is not entirely negative, however; for Soyinka, the longing for a "prelapsarian" state has a kind of progressive potential if it is used to guide the imagination in exploring alternatives to present social circumstances. The failures of *négritude* and African nationalisms arise from their tendency to identify in the past an actual model for the postcolonial nation state.[75] Like Christian revisionists who painted over church frescoes depicting Adam and Eve's nudity, African nationalist movements ironically impose "postlapsarian" values on an image meant to depict the superiority of "prelapsarian" life. According to the Eden story, Adam and Eve are entirely comfortable with their naked bodies until they are convinced by the serpent to eat from the tree of knowledge of good and evil; viewers who are uncomfortable with the images of nudity demonstrate their own inability to perceive "paradise" as it actually was.

The postcolonial allegory that Soyinka reads into this scene establishes a critique of African politicians and artists who would conceal ethnic and intertribal tensions preceding the colonial encounter. Such efforts, for

Soyinka, are guided by a sense of shame that arises from the internal-ization of Western critiques of precolonial societies. The tree of know-ledge of good and evil thus becomes in Soyinka's allegory the Western epistemologies disseminated during colonial occupation, and Africans who would idealize the precolonial past unwittingly promote such theor-ies of knowledge and the notions of historical development they imply. Thus, the challenge Soyinka identifies is not to regain "paradise" or precolonial purity by attempting to recreate models of social relations apparently utilized by precolonial societies, but instead to use images of the past to revise present attitudes toward Africa and the West.

Soyinka's idea of a "transformation of present reality" provides a way of understanding his shifting attitudes toward the notion of a Nigerian nation. Early in his career, Soyinka rejected the idea that African nations should be organized according to colonial boundaries, and he blasted the Organization of African Unity for its endorsement of the so-called "in-violability principle" that such boundaries should determine the sovereign territories of postcolonial nations. Yet Soyinka opposed the secession effort by the Igbos in the Biafran region. In his later writings, he laments the fragmentation he observes throughout his native Nigeria, culminating with the annulment of the June 12, 1993 presidential elections by General Ibrahim Badamosi Babangida. When, in his most sustained response to the annulment, Soyinka asserts that Nigeria has never been a nation, his assertion provides the grounds not for disengagement but for renewed engagement in the political life of his country. While Nigeria is not a nation, it is an "unfulfilled promise" and a "duty."[76]

According to the argument of this chapter, such a characterization is not incompatible with his previous assertions that Nigeria as a concept signifies a holdover of colonial ways of organizing and thinking about the world; rather, Soyinka's characterization of Nigeria as an unfulfilled promise represents a reinterpretation of Nigeria as a concept in the light of a more acute awareness of what the past could have been. Thus, Nigeria as the "paradise" described above comes into being as artists, activists, and politicians work to transform the organization of society associated with that term and imposed by the British Empire. That is, the nation of Nigeria is an idea that has never existed as such but nonetheless can direct the ways liberation movements envision the future.

Soyinka's nostalgia here and in his description of the sosso-bala, then, is crucial to his concern with envisioning a stable basis of solidarity among African populations. Indeed, the importance of nostalgia becomes greater in the light of the fact that the ideal of harmonization associated with the sosso-bala is cast as his foundational principle of ethics. As outlined in one of his most famous essays, "The Fourth Stage: Through the Mysteries of Ogun to the Origin of Yoruba Tragedy" (1973), Soyinka argues that ethical determinations for the Yoruba are made on the basis of whether or not an action "creates harmony in the cosmos."[77] Yet, as Soyinka makes clear throughout his writings, the history of the Yoruba since the colonial encounter through to the present day is marked by violence and dissension. Soyinka likewise makes no effort in *The Burden of Memory, The Muse of Forgiveness* to deny that the ideal of harmonization associated with the sosso-bala represents the exception, not the rule. The "glimpses and echoes" the instrument provides cannot reverse the history of colonial violence nor guarantee any promise of a more utopian future in Guinea or Africa more generally; Soyinka admits that the instrument provides little more than consolation.[78]

His unwillingness to dismiss the instrument and the consolation it promises, however, suggests that its capacity to evoke the idea of a longed-for homeland has an importance that transcends any obvious political value the instrument might have as an icon of national heritage. The instrument neither stands as a fragmentary remnant of the glorious past nor represents a material marker of racial essence. Rather, like the child Amaechina in *Anthills of the Savannah*, the sosso-bala functions as a concrete sign with multiple and overlapping associations. Precisely because so many people can identify with this sign, if not the ideals others associate with it, it provides a marker of solidarity. The solidarity it signifies is fragile and tenuous in comparison with that witnessed in Achebe's novel, but it nonetheless provides an image of hope for Soyinka, that Africans will work through the crises dividing them.

The idea that the writer can create out of traces of a violent history an image of solidarity is most fully articulated by Soyinka in *Season of Anomy*. The village of Aiyéró as depicted in the novel represents perhaps the most utopian community in all Soyinka's writings. It was founded by a group who rejected the flourishing Christian religion and its apparent justification of the slave trade; the new community sought instead to return to traditional African religions. Such a return is not cast as a regression or effort at isolationism, however, for all Aiyéró's young men travel across the world to learn about the mores and values of other societies. The cultural conversations produced by such travel actually promote the cultural integrity of the community because the young men always return from their travels to take up their lives again within the Aiyéró community, and during their travels they all send back a portion of their earnings to the village's communal fund. As Dasenbrock argues, the idea of Aiyéró suggests a kind of biculturalism distinct from consumerist pluralism or what he terms "ambiculturalism."[79] The novel does not endorse the idea that traditions should be arbitrarily mixed and matched, but insists that communities need to remain rooted within a cultural tradition even as they selectively appropriate the practices and ideas of other cultures. In this way, the cultural conversations the community members engage in do not threaten the foundational ethics of the society but rather enable them to refine their values.

Aiyéró thus represents one of a series of images, including the sosso-bala and Africa itself, in Soyinka's writings whose nostalgic character has been crucial to establishing his claims of an enduring possibility of solidarity despite a history of a precolonial, colonial, and postcolonial violence. Even in *Season of Anomy*, however, Soyinka continues to emphasize that his fictional communities cannot and should not be directly imitated by postcolonial Nigeria. The village is described in the opening paragraph as a "quaint anomaly [. . .] primitive and embarrassingly sentimental."[80] Only a few pages later, the community marks the funeral of its leader, and the novel rarely depicts the community members interacting with each other. Thus, readers have fairly little concrete information on how the ethical values associated with the village shape its social organization. Even after Ofeyi, the novel's protagonist, attempts to import the ideals of Aiyéró society to the nation as a whole, readers are given access to such efforts only after they have been crushed by the cocoa cartel that rules the country. Ofeyi proudly asserts how projects like the Shage Dam initiated by the community transform the very principles guiding social relations. "New projects like the Shage Dam meant that we could start with newly created working communities," Ofeyi states. "New affinities, working-class kinship as opposed to the tribal" (170).

Yet, the image of the dam presented to readers a few pages later is one of horror, a literary evocation of the violence directed against the Igbo in the months leading up to the Biafran War and a terrifying picture of the failure to create harmony across ethnic and tribal lines. Ofeyi is stunned to witness hundreds of bodies floating in the waters around the dam, victims of ethnic rivalry encouraged by the cocoa cartel as a means of crushing the industry and social reforms that the Aiyéró community sought to enact. Indeed, the final third of the novel depicts the systematic destruction of the "Aiyéró idea" by the cartel (218), and the community members themselves are forced to flee. Although the most revolutionary member of the community, a man called the Dentist, insists that their retreat marks the route for their return, it is a promise that remains unfulfilled in the novel.

While the desire to preserve some indication of the traumatic violence leading up to the Biafran War precludes Soyinka from portraying his fictional community in the present tense, this does not altogether deny a sense of hope apparent in *Season of Anomy*. The end of the novel depicts the retreat of the Aiyéró community, but they are joined by a new convert, Suberu, a former guard at the Temoko prison where Ofeyi was held. Certainly, this is a rather muted presentation of hope, one further belied by the fact that Soyinka has not (at the time of writing) produced another novel and has expressed notable discomfort with *Season of Anomy* in subsequent interviews – indications that the sense of hope provided by the novel may have outlived that felt by its author.[81] But the final sentence of the novel, "In the forests, life began to stir," suggests a kind of enduring promise encoded within metaphorical language (320).

That this hope can be expressed only indirectly through the metaphor of seasonal rebirth recalls the initial question of this section, which asked if the ideas of community presented by Achebe might be counterproductive precisely because they can never be enacted in the lived world. While the absence of a more direct portrayal of successful revolutionary action in *Season of Anomy* might imply that Soyinka should be exempted from similar concerns, the implicit idealism of his final image suggests that he shares with Achebe a sense that literary narratives have the capacity to convey hope despite recognition of the nation's embittered history. Tobin Siebers' reading of *Anthills of the Savannah* provides a way of understanding this hope as a form of knowledge rather than an effort to conceal or deny brutal historical realities. Siebers argues that proverbs in Achebe's writings "align what the people knows of itself with what it hopes to know of itself, knowing that hope is also part of what a people hopes to know."[82] I take this suggestion to mean not only that literature assists ethics by providing a sense of hope but also that the hope produced by literature results from an acute awareness of the disjunction between what *is* and what *could have been*. This is precisely what the naming ceremony in *Anthills of the Savannah* and Aiyéró in *Season of Anomy* both offer – a vision of communal solidarity that preserves cultural difference in a way that is both desirable and scarcely feasible. Hope, on this understanding, does not result from a sense that these fantasies of community can be reproduced in daily life; rather, it results from a sense that the present can be imagined in terms different from what a traumatic history would seem to dictate.

This reading follows Ato Quayson in urging a multitiered approach to African literature rather than an exclusive focus on its realistic or mimetic qualities. The tendency to read African and other postcolonial literatures as realistically reflecting traditional beliefs and practices has, of course, made a crucial contribution to the critique of Western depictions of colonized cultures. The fact that novels such as *Things Fall Apart* are now on the reading lists of schools across the world testifies to the power such works have to invite readers who may never have seen Africa to appreciate the richness and diversity of African cultures. Representationalist readings, however, risk occluding other significant features of literary texts, and Quayson makes a compelling case for reading African novels as "*restructurations* of various cultural subtexts."[83] The historical knowledge provided by the works of Achebe and Soyinka, like that provided by the other texts in this study, is not limited to empirically verifiable data or accurate portrayals of past events. Such a narrow or even impoverished notion of literature reduces it to a weak form of sociology. Literature certainly makes sociological claims, but not in an unmediated way. Quayson's own reading of *Things Fall Apart* highlights how previous realist readings of the novel often overlook the ambivalent attitude toward the Igbo society evinced by the novel; the depiction of precolonial Umuofia, according to Quayson, is inseparable from a subtle critique of that society for its male-dominated hierarchy of power.

This study's focus on the nostalgic images in the literary works of Achebe and Soyinka similarly suggests that these texts represent real historical conditions, but not necessarily in a manner designed to reflect their subject matter with the greatest mimetic accuracy. Neither Achebe nor Soyinka claims that the naming ceremony or Aiyéró represent explicit models for Nigerian social reform. The communities they portray nonetheless represent significant forms of historical knowledge in that they clarify more precisely how Nigerian society has failed to meet the needs of all its citizens. Put another way, the ethics posited by the writers' fictional communities have relevance to nonliterary discourses and politics because they result from an imaginative exploration of crucial moments in the nation's history with the benefit of hindsight and a keen sense of the disappointment many Nigerians have felt.

To appease an embittered history, then, does not demand a restoration of things lost. Rather, it demands a sensitivity to the memories of loss that remain. Appeasing an embittered history requires an act of imagination that is also and always an act of commitment: to imagine the world in terms that recognize its inevitable traumas without conceding that history itself is traumatic and to recollect past suffering as a guide for imagining future promise. Yet, if nostalgia is crucial to efforts by Achebe and Soyinka to appease Nigeria's embittered history in that it provides them with a mode for reenvisioning a shared basis for postcolonial communities, it cannot guarantee any long-term stability. The communities at the end of both *Anthills of the Savannah* and *Season of Anomy* are held together by a shared sense of responsibility and a shared longing to build a nation that could live up to the potential that characters can identify but may not themselves achieve. Such communities, like the nations they resemble, remain vulnerable to future dissension along tribal, regional, and religious lines; an embittered history thus remains a possibility that can always return.

Conclusion: nostalgia and its futures

In her impressive study, *The Future of Nostalgia*, Svetlana Boym argues that the rise of nostalgia in politics and culture since the 1960s is not without a certain utopian quality. "The twentieth century began with a futuristic utopia and ended with nostalgia," she writes. "Nostalgia itself has a utopian dimension, only it is no longer directed toward the future."[1] Even as the predominant *Zeitgeist* of the century shifts from optimism to nostalgia, however, a utopian impulse identified with modernity remains. This continuity endures despite the fact that nostalgia in the latter half of the twentieth century so often rose out of dissatisfaction with modernity and its vision of linear, progressive time. Nor is Boym alone in attributing a utopian quality to nostalgia; even thinkers who label nostalgia as a "social disease" share this perception. Susan Stewart, for example, writes that "Hostile to history and its invisible origins, and yet longing for an impossibly pure context of lived experience at a place of origin, nostalgia wears a distinctly utopian face, a face that turns toward a future-past, a past which has only ideological reality."[2] Boym and Stewart share a sense that nostalgics cling to an idealized world even as they retreat from the future. And given that this perception is so widely shared, the question of utopianism will almost inevitably arise with respect to this study, even though utopia has not figured as a central term in my analysis.

My study has explored a prominent "strand" within contemporary Anglophone literature that rethinks current social conditions and relationships by creating lost or imagined places of origin. The fantasy of return that drives these literary narratives enables the articulation of disappointment with present social conditions; to this extent, "homeplaces" like Rainy Mountain, Darlington Hall, or the Kangan-that-never-was resemble utopias. These places mark a social network or community that has no equivalent in the lived worlds of the characters – such places are in the very literal sense of the word utopias, "no places." Beyond this etymological connection, the nostalgic places envisioned by contemporary Anglophone literature bear deeper semantic affinities with at least one common notion of utopianism. Often when the word "utopia" is invoked, it is meant to signify a place better than the location currently inhabited. This "better place" may or may not correspond to any existing alternative political system or arrangement – it may or may not even be attainable – but it is seen to provide an ideal toward which to labor. Such an understanding of utopia resonates with the longed-for places described in this study, with one important caveat: none of these literary places is cast as a *future* ideal but always as one that has already been lost or was never available.

This caveat is crucial because it helps to establish one of the defining features of nostalgia in contemporary Anglophone novels and the vision of ethics they endorse. Works such as *Anthills of the Savannah* and *Season of Anomy* assert that the particular historical, economic, and cultural conditions brought about by modernity render questionable the progressive, futuristic idea of utopia envisioned by nineteenth- and early twentieth-century philosophies. Indeed, as became apparent in the previous chapter, Achebe and Soyinka reject the most powerful utopian political philosophy of the past two hundred years: Marxism. No amount of imagination or political activism, the literary texts in this study suggest, can effect a radical transformation of current conditions toward a utopian future without first rethinking and redefining how the past is experienced. The "embittered history" that haunts so many communities in the literary texts within this study drastically limits opportunities for positive social change. Thus, the future appears to be a realm not of possibility but of constraint and predetermination, as Beatrice's fears relate: "Were [Chris and Ikem] not in fact trailed travelers whose journeys from start to finish had been carefully programmed in advance by an alienated history? If so, how many more doomed voyagers were already in transit or just setting out, fresh faces with illusions of duty-free travel and happy landings ahead of them?"[3] None of the other characters can respond to Beatrice's fears, for all alike have internalized the basic nationalist narrative of liberation as the guiding story for them and their nation. Hence, the future appears so radically limited after the characters discover that this narrative appears to be unable either to explain the existence of the string of dictators that follow independence or to provide effective solutions for overcoming cultural differences within a postcolonial nation. Only by turning to the past and expressing their individual disappointments can characters begin to articulate an alternative narrative that calls for the participants in the naming ceremony to accommodate differing beliefs among themselves in the name of protecting Amaechina.

Beatrice's fear that the embittered history of Kangan has "programmed" the future in advance recalls what has been an insistent question throughout this study, linking authors who otherwise have very different beliefs: how does nostalgia's orientation toward the past help to direct action in the present and future? As I have understood these texts, this question is fundamentally one of ethics – not in the sense of abstract normative principles but rather in the sense of interactive and ongoing debates over how to negotiate between various and often conflicting responsibilities. Nostalgic narratives can contribute to this process by offering palpable images of human needs that are not being met. If nostalgia does not necessarily assist individuals in articulating solutions to these needs, it at least enables them to register the needs themselves. The image of the convent school in *Wide Sargasso Sea*, for example, does not provide a model of a better world to be emulated. Rhys makes it clear that Antoinette was not particularly happy there. However, her effort to recollect childhood experiences in the convent enables her to clarify both for herself and others the disappointment she feels after being imprisoned in the attic of Thornfield Hall and denied the ability to write by her husband. And once these images of disappointment are narrated, they can be further revised or redefined by others who share similar experiences. As Chapter 4 suggested, places like the English country house can function as sites over which communal values can be articulated and debated. Thus, if nostalgia does not assist directly in imagining a better future, it enables a more precise sense of how previous systems of social relations failed to address genuine human needs; and, at least in the case of Antoinette, this is the necessary precondition for discerning what her future actions should be.

The shift in contemporary Anglophone literature away from the idea of ethics as providing normative codes of behavior toward an almost Levinasean attentiveness to the particular needs of others suggests why the literary texts in this study appear reluctant to depict utopian worlds in more familiar ways. The idea of utopia typically assumes that a single system will provide satisfaction and benefit for all individuals in a given community. The fact that Antoinette's needs, hopes, and aspirations differ radically from Jane's, however, makes it difficult to imagine a system in which they could both be satisfied. Not even the idea of a feminist, egalitarian society could provide such an ideal, for Jane's feminism does not prevent her from denying Bertha Mason's unique identity.

In contrast, the vague, ambiguous, and shifting characteristics of nostalgic worlds enable individuals with diverse and often conflicting beliefs to identify with a common image. This was most apparent in Chapter 5, where nostalgia was essential to envisioning an idealized nation-state in which a child like Amaechina could have grown up in safety.

Throughout this study, the gap between the world as it is and the world as it could have been provided the basis for establishing shared ethical ideals. At the same time, *Anthills of the Savannah* and many of the other novels discussed here do not see the pursuit of a common basis of community to be incompatible with the existence of conflicting and often irreconcilable differences among its members about how to achieve these ideals. More simply put, the idealized Kangan differs considerably for Beatrice and Agatha, yet both remain committed to acting on this ideal in order to make a better Kangan for Amaechina. The irony here is that the very qualities of ambiguity, partiality, and open-endedness for which nostalgia is often faulted are seen by literary authors to be crucial to imagining more egalitarian communities.[4]

The futures portrayed by nostalgic narratives, however, seem scarcely feasible outside of the textual realm. Where Achebe sees the possibility of ethnic and religious differences leading to ethical solidarity, the historical record of Nigeria and so many other postcolonial nations indicates otherwise. The Biafran War provides only one salient example of how the promise of an egalitarian nation state collapsed into violence. If critics of nostalgia often fault it for escapism and simplification, there are ample reasons for their critique. Even if readers ignore the instances in which nostalgia has been cynically exploited by political groups, nostalgia appears to have a fairly bad record in facilitating social progress, protecting human rights, and promoting the value of diversity.

But the nostalgic narratives in contemporary Anglophone literature do not conceal events like the Biafran War; as demonstrated in Chapter 5, Achebe and Soyinka are highly conscious of how such events challenge the possibility of producing literary texts. The conclusions drawn by the authors in this study indicate that the futures produced by nostalgic fantasies are not invalidated by political violence; indeed, the perception of "an embittered history" appears to call out for the imagination of alternatives. The alternatives provided by nostalgic narratives are valuable less for their potential to provide a blueprint for a better or more utopian world than for their potential to offer hope that alternatives continue to exist. The idea of an embittered history is itself a narrative construction of experience, and nostalgia's refigurative capacity suggests that it is not the only or even necessarily the best way of understanding historical events.

Nostalgia has been rejected as a legitimate response to political and cultural crises by other strands of contemporary Anglophone literature, particularly "postmodern" strands characterized by avant-garde aesthetics, metafictional prose, and experimental formal features. The work of Salman Rushdie is exemplary in this regard. From his Booker Prize-winning *Midnight's Children* (1980) to his more recent *The Ground Beneath Her Feet* (1999), Rushdie's works have linked nostalgia to political sectarianism, religious intolerance, and cultural stagnation. Almost without exception, the protagonists Rushdie creates are characterized as international migrants, traversing the boundaries of nations and religions. The journeys that Saleem Sinai, Saladin Chamcha, Vina Apsara, and others undertake may or may not enable them to articulate a coherent alternative to nostalgic narratives of nationalism, but they do reveal such narratives to be "a conservative myth, designed to keep us in our places."[5] Particularly within Rushdie's later works, the longing for moral and epistemological foundationalism – the longing to find a "ground beneath your feet" – proves self-destructive.[6] In one of Rushdie's most vivid images, the international rock star Vina Apsara is literally destroyed by the ground beneath her feet, swallowed by an earthquake.

Rushdie's wide-ranging critique of, among other things, nostalgia, sectarianism, fundamentalism, and nationalism does not imply a withdrawal from political and ethical questions, as many of his critics have suggested. Indeed, such suggestions lead to artificially rigid distinctions among strands of contemporary Anglophone literature. The so-called "postmodern" formal features of his writing in no way prevent very explicit meditations on the ethical implications of writing, as revealed in his novel devoted to the history of postcolonial Pakistan, *Shame* (1983). In the midst of one of his trademark passages blending historical events and fantasy, the narrator turns to the question of why he, who emigrated to England, should take up the story of the country he has left behind. He freely confesses that others would be better suited to the task, such as an unnamed poet friend who had been recently jailed and tortured. Yet, the narrator recognizes that his friend's story may never be told: "Maybe my friend should be telling the story, or another one, his own; but he doesn't write poetry anymore. So here I am instead, inventing what never happened to me [. . .] Is history to be considered the property of participants solely?" (23).

Thus, if the method of retelling is frustrating to many of Rushdie's readers, the motive behind his retelling does not differ significantly from that stated by many authors in this study and other canonical postcolonial authors from Ngugi to Assia Djebar. Rushdie insists here on the necessity of speaking truth to power, though the form his writing takes differs from both the kind of literary realism characteristic of many postcolonial and testimonial literatures and the nostalgia of the texts discussed in this study. Although *Shame* is admittedly somewhat unique among Rushdie's writings in this regard, it does articulate an alternative set of myths to the Islamic fundamentalism used by Pakistan's dictators to consolidate their hold on power. The narrator writes, "The third option [for challenging Pakistan's leaders] is the substitution of a new myth for the old one. Here are three such myths, all available from stock at short notice: liberty; equality; fraternity" (278).

The articulation of alternative myths of nation in Rushdie's work points to a central difference between him and the authors in this study. Rushdie calls for a set of universal ethical norms that have specific historical contexts out of which they arise, yet which can be divorced from such contexts. Rushdie is not calling for an assimilation of Western values per se; rather, he is calling on Pakistan to realize a set of values that have never fully been carried out in the West or anywhere else. Liberty, equality, and fraternity function as utopian ideals because they have never been fully actualized. And, though he never formally articulates this point, Rushdie appears to sense that such ideals have never been fully actualized in part because they have been linked to specific histories. Whereas the authors in this study use nostalgia to ground particular ideals with respect to lost or imagined homelands, Rushdie suggests that such fantasies would limit the capacity for Pakistanis to imagine how their ideals might be lived out.

Rushdie's nonfictional writings since September 11, 2001, suggest more significant convergences between his work and the literary texts explored in this study. The connection between place and ethics that has figured so centrally among the authors discussed here become strikingly apparent in Rushdie's piece "October 2001: The Attacks on America." In contrast to the self-identification as a citizen of the world and international migrant apparent in his earlier writing, Rushdie explicitly identifies himself here in terms of place: "They broke our city. I'm among the newest of New Yorkers."[7] And, as has been the case throughout this study, the identification with place implies a set of ethical and moral commitments, which Rushdie articulates only a few paragraphs later. In a passage that would startle readers familiar with Rushdie's reluctance to move beyond critique toward a specific articulation of values, he rejects the assertion by the United Nations Secretary-General Kofi Annan that the citizens of the world must now define themselves by what they are against. Rushdie counters, "But what are we for? What will we risk our lives to defend?"[8]

The problems with Rushdie's new or at least newly clarified position recall similar concerns raised throughout this study with the uses of nostalgia in contemporary Anglophone literature. Efforts to situate abstract values in terms of specific conceptions of place inevitably risk endorsing unethical actions or attitudes. Rushdie's recent critiques of Islam raise the question whether his new identification as a post-September 11 New Yorker has led to a more honest recognition of Islam and its own crises or to a kind of xenophobic distrust. And his call for the defense of, among other things, homosexuals, evolution theory, and a more equitable distribution of the world's resources assumes a set of ethical commitments that are not shared by many who claim to identify with the same city and nation. Similarly, the worlds that Antoinette, Abel, Mr. Stevens, Beatrice, and others glimpse at the end of their narratives stand in stark contrast to the disappointing realities that led the characters to nostalgia. Yet, the cautious idealism apparent in the novels explored in this study asks readers not to dismiss the importance of nostalgic worlds, nor even perhaps the America of which Rushdie fantasizes. These literary texts suggest that the near impossibility of enacting nostalgic fantasies is not only a sign of the failure of language but also a sign of its possibility. For novels *can* promise what they cannot enact. Nostalgic longings enable characters to articulate in clear and powerful terms the disappointment that the narratives containing them cannot resolve. Indeed, literature haunts readers with precisely those promises that it cannot itself keep.

Notes

INTRODUCTION: NOSTALGIA, ETHICS, AND CONTEMPORARY ANGLOPHONE LITERATURE

1 Swiss physician Johannes Hofer coined the term "nostalgia" in his 1688 thesis *Dissertatio medica de nostalgia*. The term combines two Greek roots: *nostos*, "return to one's native land," and *algos*, "pain." For a history of nostalgia and its mutations since the seventeenth century, see Edward S. Casey, "The World of Nostalgia," *Man and World* 20 (1987), 361–84; George Rosen, "Nostalgia: A 'Forgotten' Psychological Disorder," *Clio Medica* 10.1 (1975), 28–51; Jean Starobinski, "The Idea of Nostalgia," *Diogenes* 54 (1966), 81–103; and David S. Werman, "Normal and Pathological Nostalgia," *Journal of the American Psychoanalytic Association* 25.2 (1977), 387–98.

2 Susan Stewart, *On Longing: Narratives of the Miniature, the Gigantic, the Souvenir, the Collection* (Durham: Duke University Press, 1993), ix.

3 Jackson Lears, "Looking Backward: in Defense of Nostalgia," *Lingua Franca* 7.10 (1998), 59.

4 bell hooks, *Yearning: Race, Gender, and Cultural Politics* (Boston: South End Press, 1990), 147.

5 Toni Morrison, *Beloved* (New York: Plume, 1987), 6.

6 Stuart Hall, "Cultural Identity and Diaspora," in Patrick Williams and Laura Chrisman, eds., *Colonial Discourse and Post-Colonial Theory: A Reader* (New York: Columbia University Press, 1994), 402.

7 See Starobinski, "The Idea of Nostalgia," 95–96.

8 Svetlana Boym, *The Future of Nostalgia* (New York: Basic Books, 2001), xv.

9 Stewart, *On Longing*, 23.

10 Satya P. Mohanty, "Can Our Values be Objective? On Ethics, Aesthetics, and Progressive Politics," *New Literary History* 32 (2001), 829.

11 Renato Rosaldo, *Culture & Truth: The Remaking of Social Analysis* (Boston: Beacon Press, 1993), 70.

12 Rey Chow suggests that similar struggles with traumatic historical events are apparent in many contemporary ethnic communities. As the example of *Beloved* indicates, such communities struggle with the reality that there are often no living witnesses to many of the experiences that define them as a community. Chow writes, "The native's victimization consists in the fact that the actual evidence – the

original witness – of her victimization may no longer exist in any intelligible, coherent shape." See Chow, *Writing Diaspora: Tactics of Intervention in Contemporary Cultural Studies* (Bloomington: Indiana University Press, 1993), 38.

13 Kathleen Brogan, *Cultural Haunting: Ghosts and Ethnicity in Recent American Literature* (Charlottesville: University Press of Virginia, 1998), 4.

14 Ibid., 62.

15 Roberta Rubenstein, *Home Matters: Longing and Belonging, Nostalgia and Mourning in Women's Fiction* (New York: Palgrave, 2001), 6.

16 Janice Doane and Devon Hodges, *Nostalgia and Sexual Difference: The Resistance to Contemporary Feminism* (New York: Methuen, 1987), xiii.

17 Lynne Huffer, *Maternal Pasts, Feminist Futures: Nostalgia, Ethics, and the Question of Difference* (Stanford: Stanford University Press, 1998), 19.

18 Nicolas Dames, *Amnesiac Selves: Nostalgia, Forgetting, and British Fiction, 1810–1870* (Oxford: Oxford University Press, 2001), 6. Intriguingly, studies devoted to earlier literary periods are often more willing to recognize nostalgia as a central cultural force in the late twentieth century than studies devoted to contemporary literature. Ann C. Colley, for example, opens her study of nostalgia and recollection in Victorian culture by declaring "the role of nostalgia as an organizing force in the imagination and memory" at the end of the twentieth century. See Colley, *Nostalgia and Recollection in Victorian Culture* (New York: St. Martin's Press, 1998), 1. Her logic implies that the legitimacy of her own study comes in part from the fact that the present reflects cultural phenomena of a hundred years ago. Astradur Eysteinsson likewise declares nostalgia to be one of the chief features of contemporary Western culture in his study of literary modernism; however, for Eysteinsson, the modernist past stands in stark and heroic contrast to the postmodern present. See Eysteinsson, *The Concept of Modernism* (Ithaca: Cornell University Press, 1990), 122.

19 Dames, *Amnesiac Selves*, 7.

20 Quoted in Brian Shaffer, "An Interview with Kazuo Ishiguro," *Contemporary Literature* 42.1 (2001), 7–8.

21 T. S. Eliot, "Tradition and the Individual Talent," in *The Sacred Wood: Essays on Poetry and Criticism* (London: Methuen, 1960), 7.

22 Ibid., 4, 6.

23 Quoted in Michael H. Levenson, *A Genealogy of Modernism: A Study of English Literary Doctrine 1908–1922* (Cambridge: Cambridge University Press, 1984), 217.

24 Virginia Woolf, "Mr. Bennett and Mrs. Brown," in *Collected Essays* (New York: Harcourt, Brace and World, 1953), 320–21.

25 Adam Zachary Newton, *Narrative Ethics* (Cambridge, MA: Harvard University Press, 1995), 12.

26 Chinua Achebe, *Hopes and Impediments: Selected Essays 1965 – 1987* (London: Heinemann, 1988), 37.

27 David Palumbo-Liu, "The Politics of Memory: Remembering History in Alice Walker and Joy Kogawa," in Amritjit Singh, Jr., Joseph T. Skenett and

Robert E. Hogan eds., *Memory and Cultural Politics: New Approaches to American Ethnic Literatures* (Boston: Northeastern University Press, 1996), 212.

28 Michael Valdez Moses, *The Novel and the Globalization of Culture* (Oxford: Oxford University Press, 1995), xii–xiii.

29 The relationship and distinctions between postmodernism and postcolonialism have been taken up in Chapter 7 of Anthony Appiah's *In My Father's House*, entitled "Postcolonial and The Postmodern" (Oxford: Oxford University Press, 1992); Chapter 9 of Homi Bhabha's *The Location of Culture*, entitled "The Postcolonial, and the Postmodern: The Question of Agency" (London: Routledge, 1994); Linda Hutcheon's "'Circling the Downspout of Empire': Postcolonialism and Postmodernism," *Ariel* 20 (1989), 149–75; and Helen Tiffin's article, "Post-Colonialism, Post-Modernism and the Rehabilitation of Post-Colonial History," *Journal of Commonwealth Literature* 23.1 (1988), 169–81.

30 Ursula K. Heise identifies two primary strands of postmodern fiction. The first, to which her study *Chronoschisms: Time, Narrative, and Postmodernism* is devoted, achieves prominence in the 1960s and 1970s. Such fiction is defined by narrative experimentation and innovative forms of metafiction. The second strand, which corresponds to some of the texts explored here, gains prominence in the 1980s. These novels are not defined by their formal innovation so much as by "the publicization of those alternative histories of women, cultures colonized by Western powers, or racial and ethnic minorities that had been ignored or repressed by mainstream historiography." See Heise, *Chronoschisms: Time, Narrative, and Postmodernism* (Cambridge: Cambridge University Press, 1997), 3.

31 Doreen Massey, *Space, Place and Gender* (Cambridge: Polity Press, 1994). I shall discuss Massey's ideas in greater depth in Chapter 1.

32 Paul Ricoeur, "Memory and Forgetting," in Richard Kearney and Mark Dooley, eds., *Questioning Ethics: Contemporary Debates in Philosophy* (London: Routledge, 1999), 9.

33 For a discussion of thick ethical concepts, see Bernard Williams, *Ethics and the Limits of Philosophy* (Cambridge, MA: Harvard University Press, 1985), p. 129.

1   NARRATIVES OF RETURN: LOCATING ETHICS IN THE AGE
OF GLOBALIZATION

1 For Giddens, modernity effects a radical transformation in how space is perceived. In premodern societies, social life is dominated by what he calls "presence" or localized activity; modernity, in contrast, fosters relationships between individuals who are separated locationally. And this shift in social relationships leads to the separation of space and place. Fredric Jameson's account of modernity considers it to be focused more on temporality than space or place, and postmodernism becomes a distinctive phenomenon in large part because of its preoccupation with the latter. "A certain spatial turn has often

seemed to offer one of the most productive ways of distinguishing postmodernism from modernism proper," Jameson argues, "whose experience of temporality – existential time, along with deep memory – it is henceforth conventional to see as a dominant of the high modern." Massey's rejection of postmodernism as a period label to describe the increasing interest in space comes from a sense that the term itself describes a rather narrow academic philosophy rather than a broad set of cultural practices. In her own work, she differentiates between what she calls "locality studies" and postmodernism, arguing that similarities between the two are no more than "accidents of language." See Anthony Giddens, *The Consequences of Modernity* (Cambridge: Polity Press, 1990), 18; Fredric Jameson, *Postmodernism, or, The Cultural Logic of Late Capitalism* (Durham: Duke University Press, 1991), 154; and Massey, *Space, Place and Gender* (Cambridge: Polity Press, 1994), 132. Subsequent references are given in the text.

2 hooks, *Yearning*, 148.

3 Charles Chamberlain, "From 'Haunts' to 'Character': The Meaning of *Ethos* and Its Relation to Ethics," *Helios* 11.2 (1984) 97.

4 Ibid., 100

5 Eugene Victor Walter, *Placeways: A Theory of the Human Environment* (Chapel Hill: University of North Carolina Press, 1988), 15.

6 There are certainly numerous exceptions to my claim that the ideals of modernity are incompatible with a positive connection between place and ethics. Various regionalist, ethnic, and environmentalist movements call for the restoration of more intimate connections to place. Many of these movements, however, consciously define themselves as antimodern, and hence make no claim to embody the ideals of modernity. Nor, I would argue, should nationalism more generally be perceived as an exception to my claim. As Benedict Anderson suggests, nationalism depends on attenuating connections to local places in favor of a much more abstract national identity. See Anderson, *Imagined Communities: Reflections on the Origin and Spread of Nationalism* (London: Verso, 1983).

7 Immanuel Kant, *Groundwork of the Metaphysic of Morals*, translated by H. J. Paton (New York: Harper & Row, 1964), 105.

8 Kant asserts that both the mechanism of reasoning and the basic ideals of human nature are common to all rational people. "There is no one," he argues in *Groundwork of the Metaphysic of Morals*, "not even the most hardened scoundrel – provided only he is accustomed to use reason in other ways – who, when presented with examples of honesty in purpose, of faithfulness to good maxims, of sympathy, and of kindness towards all (even when these are bound up with great sacrifices of advantage and comfort), does not wish that he too might be a man of like spirit" (122).

9 Zygmunt Bauman, *Life in Fragments: Essays in Postmodern Morality* (Oxford: Blackwell, 1995), 275.

10 E. M. Forster, *A Passage to India* (San Diego: Harcourt Brace Jovanovich, 1984), 131.

11 James Joyce, *A Portrait of the Artist As a Young Man*, edited by R. B. Kershner (Boston: Bedford, 1993), 213.

12 David Morley and Kevin Robins, *Spaces of Identity: Global Media, Electronic Landscapes and Cultural Boundaries* (London: Routledge, 1995), 7, 26.

13 Michel de Certeau, *Heterologies: Discourse on the Other*, translated by Brian Massumi (Minneapolis: University of Minnesota Press, 1986), 221.

14 Ernesto Laclau, *New Reflections on the Revolution of Our Time* (London: Verso, 1990), 42–43.

15 Edward Soja, *Postmodern Geographies: The Reassertion of Space in Critical Social Theory* (London: Verso, 1989), 11. The rhetoric of Massey's *Space, Place and Gender*, a text which has since become a touchstone for studies of place, reveals that even as late as 1994 place is still widely regarded in terms of essentialism and reactionary politics. Throughout her study, Massey characterizes her work as challenging the dominant position within the academy. She writes, "Within the academic literature as well as more widely there has been a continuation of the tendency to identify places as necessarily sites of nostalgia, of the opting-out from Progress and History" (4–5).

16 Laclau, *New Reflections*, 68.

17 Jameson, *Postmodernism*, xvi.

18 David Harvey, "From Space to Place and Back Again: Reflections on the Condition of Postmodernity," in Jon Bird et al., eds., *Mapping the Futures: Local Cultures, Global Change* (London: Routledge, 1993), 24.

19 Ibid., 24.

20 In *The Condition of Postmodernity*, Harvey argues that place-bound politics may in many cases support capitalism by fragmenting the national political scene and increasing a sense of regional differences between groups: "such oppositional movements become a part of the very fragmentation which a mobile capitalism and flexible accumulation can feed upon." See Harvey, *The Condition of Postmodernity: An Enquiry into the Origins of Cultural Change* (Cambridge: Blackwell, 1990), 303.

21 Maggie Sale, "Call and Response As Critical Method: African-American Oral Traditions and *Beloved*," in Barbara H. Solomon, ed., *Critical Essays on Toni Morrison's* Beloved (New York: G. K. Hall, 1998), 178.

22 Here, I am seeking to qualify Sale's assessment of "call-and-response patterns" in *Beloved*. According to Sale, such patterns draw on African-American oral traditions and produce a version of history that challenges "master versions" by emphasizing performativity and multiple perspectives. But the absence of similar patterns in the conclusion of the novel suggests that it is not necessarily the basis for communal narratives endorsed by the text. Indeed, the subsequent version of this pattern presented by the text – the "threnody" of Sethe, Denver, and Beloved – presents not only the instability of this model but its potentially tragic consequences. See Sale, "Call and Response," 179.

23 Toni Morrison, *Beloved* (New York: Plume, 1987), 89. Subsequent references are given in the text.

24 hooks, *Yearning*, 47.
25 Edward S. Casey, *Getting Back into Place: Toward a Renewed Understanding of the Place-World* (Bloomington: Indiana University Press, 1993), xv
26 Ibid., 265.
27 Arthur Redding connects the trees that constitute the "forest" that springs up between Paul D and Sethe with the trees that surround the Clearing. On Redding's reading, trees in *Beloved* represent "barriers to understanding" that are products of the slave past. See Redding, "'Haints': American Ghosts, Ethnic Memory, and Contemporary Fiction," *Mosaic* 36.4 (2001), 169.
28 Satya Mohanty suggests that Paul D's moral growth depends on learning to identify with the experiences of Sethe. "This transformation from law to human understanding," Mohanty writes, "from abstract humanity to real feeling, is predicated on the enlargement of Paul's personal capacity to experience." As with my own analysis, Mohanty suggests that Paul D's basic problem is that his moral judgments are based on abstract ethical ideas, and it is only his subsequent process of gaining knowledge about Sethe's experience of slavery that enables him to translate these abstractions into more concrete beliefs that are attuned to the histories that have shaped both Sethe's and Paul D's identities. See Mohanty, *Literary Theory and the Claims of History: Postmodernism, Objectivity, Multicultural Politics* (Ithaca: Cornell University Press, 1997), 227.
29 My analysis here challenges a common idea within Morrison criticism that the community formed by Sethe, Denver, and Beloved represents what Carolyn Rody calls "a momentarily utopian resolution." See Rody, "Toni Morrison's *Beloved*: History, 'Rememory,' and a 'Clamor for a Kiss'," *American Literary History* 7 (1995), 111. My argument suggests that this community does not represent a utopian moment that fails because of economic constraints and outside pressures; rather, it is a flawed model of community that appears utopian only insofar as it subordinates Denver's needs.
30 Toni Morrison, *Song of Solomon* (New York: Plume, 1987), 235.
31 Ibid., 236.
32 Toni Morrison, *Paradise* (New York: Alfred A. Knopf, 1998), 6.
33 Ibid., 5.
34 Ian McEwan, *Black Dogs* (New York: Bantam, 1992), xvi, xxi, xxv. Subsequent references are given in the text.
35 Toni Morrison, "Rootedness: The Ancestor as Foundation," in Mari Evans, ed., *Black Women Writers (1950–1980), A Critical Evaluation* (Garden City: Anchor, 1984), 340.
36 Toni Morrison, "Home," *The House That Race Built: Black Americans, U.S. Terrain*, edited by Wahneema Lubiano (New York: Pantheon Books, 1997), 10.
37 Morrison similarly describes how Enlightenment notions of rationality have been used to rationalize inhuman behavior. The character of school-teacher is most obviously identified with Enlightenment rationality in

Beloved, using pseudo-scientific methods to maximize production regardless of the human cost. Indeed, it becomes quickly apparent that his preoccupation with organizing the world into taxonomic structures enables him to deny any ethical responsibility for his slaves. By classifying them as animals, schoolteacher denies them any right to question his judgment or to earn freedom.

38 While distinctions between morality and ethics are inevitably fuzzy, this does not necessarily invalidate them, but suggests the fluidity of the concepts. In the case of both Bernard Williams and Zygmunt Bauman, the distinction serves the practical function of distinguishing between what they consider to be better and worse forms of deliberation. Both are suspicious of efforts to define narrowly or to codify what constitutes a legitimate way of decision-making, and ironically Williams faults morality and Bauman faults ethics for this tendency. Beyond distinguishing between modes of deliberation, distinctions between morality and ethics can be useful to emphasize the inevitable tensions that individuals and communities face when struggling with a dilemma. As Williams notes, there are always a range of ways of considering how to arrive at a resolution to a particular dilemma, and it is important to recognize that disagreements are inevitable and not inherently an indication of a failure. "Disagreement does not necessarily have to be overcome," Williams argues. "It may remain an important and constitutive feature of our relations to others, and also be seen as something that is merely to be expected in the light of the best explanations we have of how such disagreement arises." See Williams, *Ethics and the Limits of Philosophy*, 133.

39 Bauman, *Life in Fragments*, 43.

40 Alasdair MacIntyre, *After Virtue: A Study in Moral Theory* (Notre Dame: University of Notre Dame Press, 1984), 3.

41 Ibid., 8.

42 Emmanuel Levinas, *Totality and Infinity: An Essay on Exteriority*, translated by Alfonso Lingis (Pittsburgh: Duquesne University Press, 1969), 43.

43 See Zygmunt Bauman, *Postmodern Ethics* (Oxford: Blackwell, 1993), 69–77.

44 Bauman, *Life in Fragments*, 1–2.

45 Bauman, *Postmodern Ethics*, 80.

46 Ibid., 67.

47 Ibid., 60.

48 Animosity toward Sethe arises the day after Baby Suggs holds a celebration in honor of Sethe's escape from slavery. The "reckless generosity" of the party is perceived by members of the African-American community to be a demonstration of inappropriate pride (137).

49 Sethe is restrained by the women because she mistakes the visit of abolitionist Mr. Bodwin for the return of her former owner, schoolteacher.

50 My argument for the interdependence of ethics and morals implies substantial agreement with Geoffrey Galt Harpham's *Shadows of Ethics: Criticism and the Just Society*. Harpham argues that "It is morality that realizes ethics, making it ethical. [. . .H]owever, morality negates ethics, and needs

ethics in order to be moral." This understanding recognizes the legitimacy of the nonrational demands to which characters like Sethe feel themselves subject without dismissing or overlooking the fact that these demands are not cast in ethical terms. "Morality" provides a term to describe these feelings. At the same time, the relationship between ethics and morality proposed by Harpham, *Beloved*, and *Black Dogs* recognizes the importance of negotiating and even mitigating such demands, and Harpham uses the term "ethics" to refer to this process. See Harpham, *Shadows of Ethics: Criticism and the Just Society* (Durham: Duke University Press: 1999), 33.

Although Terry Otten uses somewhat different terminology to describe the threat that an unrestrained morality represents, his argument expresses a similar concern with unrestrained impulses. Otten writes that, for Morrison, "even the most noble and innocent assertion of will can generate the most heinous criminality." See Otten, "Horrific Love in Toni Morrison's Fiction," *Modern Fiction Studies* 39 (1993), 652.

51 Joan Riley, *The Unbelonging* (London: The Women's Press, 1985), 28. Subsequent references are given in the text.

52 Quoted in Donna Perry, *Backtalk: Women Writers Speak Out* (New Brunswick: Rutgers University Press, 1993), 269.

2 NOSTALGIA AND NARRATIVE ETHICS IN CARIBBEAN LITERATURE

1 Patrick Taylor, *The Narrative of Liberation: Perspectives on Afro-Caribbean Literature, Popular Culture, and Politics* (Ithaca: Cornell University Press, 1989), 4.

2 George Lamming, *The Pleasures of Exile* (London: Allison & Busby, 1984), 214.

3 Derek Walcott, *Omeros* (New York: Farrar Straus Giroux, 1993), 133.

4 Lamming, *The Pleasures of Exile*, 35, 36.

5 V. S. Naipaul, *Finding the Center: Two Narratives* (New York: Alfred A. Knopf, 1984), 34.

6 Naipaul himself has resisted the term West Indian or Caribbean to describe his writing. "One doesn't have to be a West Indian or Indian or English writer," he insists, "just a writer." See Evelyn O'Callaghan, "The 'Pleasures' of Exile in Selected West Indian Writing since 1987," in Glyne Griffith, ed., *Caribbean Cultural Identities* (Lewisburg: Bucknell University Press, 2001), 82. Reportedly, Naipaul even dropped a publisher for describing him as a West Indian writer. Despite such efforts to divorce his writings from specific geographical localities, however, Naipaul is considered within the literary tradition of Caribbean writing for my purposes because he demonstrates significant continuities with more canonical Caribbean writers in terms of subject matter and background.

7 Of the three main views on how narrative assists ethics, Martha Nussbaum and Frank Palmer represent eloquent spokespeople for the

first. Nussbaum argues that literature aids ethics by virtue of its ability to provide a compelling interpretive description of life: "The point is that in the activity of literary imagining we are led to imagine and describe with greater precision, focusing our attention on each word, feeling each event more keenly – whereas much of actual life goes by without that heightened awareness, and is thus, in a certain sense, not fully or thoroughly lived." See Nussbaum, *Love's Knowledge: Essays on Philosophy and Literature* (Oxford: Oxford University Press, 1990), 47. Palmer likewise argues that literature contributes to moral understanding by acquainting us with unfamiliar worlds; however, Palmer also claims that literature can acquaint us with the world in ways that direct, personal experience cannot because literature both draws readers' attention and distances them from the object it describes: "[fiction] conveys both the involvement and the detachment of our response to imagined situations. [. . .] We therefore experience a kind of intellectual activity that may not be present in cases of actual acquaintance with, say, anxiety, war, boredom, earthquakes, or bereavement." See Palmer, *Literature and Moral Understanding: A Philosophical Essay on Ethics, Aesthetics, Education, and Culture* (Oxford: Clarendon Press, 1992), 203. Paul Ricoeur represents an advocate for the second view of how narrative assists ethics. From Ricoeur's perspective, the ethical value of narrative comes from its ability to provide multiple descriptions of an event. This descriptive power destabilizes the authority of institutionally sanctioned histories: "Why are narratives helpful in this ethical respect?" Ricoeur asks. "Because it is always possible to tell another way. This exercise of memory is here an exercise in *telling otherwise*, and also in letting others tell their own history, especially the founding events which are the ground of a collective memory." See Ricoeur, "Memory and Forgetting," 9. This claim is particularly relevant to postcolonial literatures, whose authors have self-consciously worked to retell the past in terms other than those endorsed by colonial histories. Representing the third view, Geoffrey Galt Harpham's recent book *Shadows of Ethics: Criticism and the Just Society* proposes a somewhat different contribution of literature to ethics. For Harpham, the descriptive power of literature "actually exposes the shadowed, chiaroscuro character of ethics itself, which achieves a purified view of the ideal through methods that are themselves ethically dubious." See Harpham, *Shadows of Ethics*, ix–x. According to this view, literature cultivates respect for life in all its imperfections, rejecting "the strict respect for the ethical law that some philosophers would urge."

8 Ricoeur, "Memory and Forgetting," 9.

9 Rhys, in particular, felt deeply uncertain that readers would share her concern for Bertha Mason. This uncertainty is apparent even in letters to her most fervent supporters. In a 1958 letter to Selma Vas Diaz, for example, she writes, "The Creole in Charlotte Brontë's novel is a lay figure – repulsive which does not matter, and not once alive which does. She's necessary to the plot, but

always she shrieks, howls, laughs horribly, attacks all and sundry – *offstage.* For me (and for you I hope) she must be right *on stage.*" See Rhys, *The Letters of Jean Rhys*, ed. Francis Wyndham and Diana Melly (New York: Viking Penguin Books, 1984), 156.

10 Ellen G. Friedman, "Breaking the Master Narrative: Jean Rhys's *Wide Sargasso Sea*," in Ellen G. Friedman and Miriam Fuchs, eds., *Breaking the Sequence: Women's Experimental Fiction* (Princeton: Princeton University Press, 1989), 117.

11 As part of her attempt to rewrite *Jane Eyre*, Rhys "reveals" that Bertha is not the real name of Rochester's first wife; according to Rhys, Rochester renames Antoinette in an effort to erase all vestiges of her past.

12 Veronica Marie Gregg, *Jean Rhys's Historical Imagination: Reading and Writing the Creole* (Chapel Hill: University of North Carolina Press, 1995), 114.

13 Carine Melkom Mardorossian provides a useful survey of the history of Rhys criticism. Mardorossian argues that the study of Rhys' work has been characterized by "a succession of polarizations" between autobiographical versus fictional sources for her novels, Caribbean versus feminist influences, and the extent to which her work represents a critique versus a reproduction of colonial and patriarchal values. See Mardorossian, "Double (De)coloniza-tion and the Feminist Criticism of *Wide Sargasso Sea*," *College Literature* 26.2 (1999), 80.

14 Jean Rhys, *Wide Sargasso Sea* (New York: W. W. Norton & Company, 1966), 190. Subsequent references are given in the text.

15 Andrew Gibson, "Sensibility and Suffering in Rhys and Nin," in Andrew Hadfield et al., eds., *The Ethics in Literature* (New York: St. Martin's Press, 1999), 191.

16 In arguing that Antoinette's dreams depict her internalization of colonial narratives, I seek to qualify Mary Lou Emery's assessment that they give her the chance to "rewrite her own myth." See Emery, *Jean Rhys at "World's End": Novels of Colonial and Sexual Exile* (Austin: University of Texas Press, 1990), 36. With the exception of her final dream, I would argue, they are characterized by a sense of helplessness and self-destructiveness.

17 Jane's narrative evokes images of slavery even in its first chapter, where Jane refers to Master John as a "slave-driver" and "tyrant." See Charlotte Brontë, *Jane Eyre* (London: Penguin Books, 1985), 43.

18 By accepting Rochester's diagnosis of Bertha's madness, Jane is able to rationalize his cruelty to his first wife: "you are inexorable for that unfortunate lady," Jane declares, "you speak of her with hate – with indicative antipathy. It is cruel – she cannot help being mad." See Brontë, *Jane Eyre*, 328. This rationalization forestalls any consideration of whether Bertha's fate is in anyway the result of Rochester's cruelty.

19 Gayatri Chakravorty Spivak, "Three Women's Texts and a Critique of Imperialism," *Critical Inquiry* 12 (1985), 253.

20 The Enlightenment war on suffering never sought to eliminate all suffering, according to Zygmunt Bauman. See Bauman, *Postmodern Ethics*, 225. The

philosophical and political practices of the Enlightenment rationalized or concealed the sacrifices of minorities on behalf of the "greater good." Wai Chee Dimock makes a stronger claim in this regard, arguing that the Western idea of justice cannot ensure the redress of effaced suffering because the concept assumes "ethical primacy and descriptive adequacy." No exercise of justice can ever establish these goals, for Dimock, because individuals have different conceptions of good and evil. Following Isaiah Berlin and Bernard Williams, Dimock asserts that there "is no translation without loss [. . .] nor conflict-resolution without residue." See Dimock, *Residues of Justice: Literature, Law, Philosophy* (Berkeley: University of California Press, 1996), 7. Because of the inevitability of different conceptions, colonial missionaries or novelists including Brontë can do violence to figures such as Bertha Mason without perceiving themselves to be unjust.

21 Brontë, *Jane Eyre*, 477.
22 Rhys, *Letters*, 24.
23 Paul Ricoeur, *Time and Narrative*, translated by Kathleen McLaughlin and David Pellauer, 3 vols. (Chicago: University of Chicago Press, 1984–88), I, 81.
24 Laura E. Ciolkowski, "Navigating the *Wide Sargasso Sea*: Colonial History, English Fiction, and British Empire," *Twentieth Century Literature* 43 (1997), 340.
25 The function of narrative repetition in *Wide Sargasso Sea* has been treated by several critics. See Gregg, *Jean Rhys's Historical Imagination*, 96–100; Kenneth Ramchand, *An Introduction to the Study of West Indian Literature* (Middlesex: Thomas Nelson, 1976), 96; and Margaret Paul Joseph, *Caliban in Exile: The Outsider in Caribbean Fiction* (New York: Greenwood Press, 1992), 34. These analyses focus primarily on how Antoinette's story is prefigured by her mother's. David Cowart reads repetition in Lacanian terms, arguing that it serves to depict Antoinette's "lifelong frustrated desire to restore the illusion of identity between self and other." See Cowart, *Literary Symbiosis: The Reconfigured Text in Twentieth-Century Writing* (Athens: University of Georgia Press, 1993), 62.
26 Bhabha, *The Location of Culture* 253; Edward W. Said, *Culture and Imperialism* (New York: Alfred A. Knopf, 1993), 214.
27 Readers of Ricoeur such as Richard Kearney would find Rhys' use of nostalgia particularly troubling. Kearney reads Ricoeur to argue that narrative becomes ethical only if it "acknowledges its origin and end in the world of action." See Kearney, *Politics of Modernity: Toward a Hermeneutic Imagination* (New Jersey: Humanities Press, 1995), xv. On one level at least, Rhys betrays this ideal. Antoinette's preoccupation with regret and loss does not acknowledge an end in the world of action; her fantasy of an impossible reunion with Tia – a reunion that leads to suicide – implies that she does not believe that she can create a better world for herself. However, Antoinette's suicide leap occurs within a dream, and her retelling of it leads to a recognition of purpose that does indeed

appear to lead Antoinette toward action at the conclusion, though the text gives no definite indication of what she will do.

28 Stewart, *On Longing*, ix, 135.
29 V. S. Naipaul, *A House for Mr. Biswas* (New York: Penguin Books, 1992), 15.
30 V. S. Naipaul, *A Bend in the River* (New York: Vintage International, 1989), 3.
31 See Fawzia Mustafa, *V. S. Naipaul* (Cambridge: Cambridge University Press, 1995), 22–23.
32 Ibid., 25.
33 V. S. Naipaul, *The Return of Eva Perón with the Killings in Trinidad* (New York: Alfred A. Knopf, 1980), 216; Sara Suleri, "Naipaul's Arrival," *Yale Journal of Criticism* 2.1 (1988), 27.
34 Edward Said, "The Intellectual in the Post-Colonial World," *Salmagundi* 70–71 (1986), 53.
35 Conor Cruise O'Brien, Edward Said, and John Lukacs, "The Intellectual in the Post-Colonial World: Response and Discussion" *Salmagundi* 70–71 (1986), 68.
36 In a 1981 interview with Charles Michener, Naipaul makes one of his most explicit assertions about the moral sensibility at the heart of literary narrative. Countering Michener's claim that "great art can have so little moral sense," Naipaul asserts, "Ah, but not literary art, which *must* have that sense." While Naipaul does not further specify what kind of moral sense literary art has, his statement implies that a preoccupation with formalist concerns does not preclude an engagement with ethical questions, as Suleri's critique suggests. If literary art differs from other kinds in necessarily having a moral sense, and a distinctive feature of literary art is the presence of "words and people," then the implication is that language itself is intimately related to Naipaul's idea of moral sensibility. See Feroza Jussawalla, ed., *Conversations with V. S. Naipaul,* (Jackson: University Press of Mississippi, 1997), 69.
37 V. S. Naipaul, *The Enigma of Arrival: A Novel* (New York: Vintage Books, 1988), 130. Subsequent references are given in the text.
38 *Conversations with V. S. Naipaul,* 29, 46.
39 V. S. Naipaul, *The Mimic Men* (New York: Vintage International, 2001), 10. Subsequent references are given in the text.
40 Nana Wilson-Tagoe, *Historical and Literary Representation in West Indian Literature* (Gainesville: University Press of Florida, 1998), 65.
41 Ian Baucom, *Out of Place: Englishness, Empire, and the Locations of Identity* (Princeton: Princeton University Press, 1999), 178.
42 *Conversations with V. S. Naipaul,* 29.
43 Slavoj Žižek, *The Sublime Object of Ideology* (London: Verso, 1989), 59.
44 O'Callaghan, "The 'Pleasures' of Exile," 81, 84.
45 Satya P. Mohanty, "Can Our Values Be Objective? 804.
46 Bhabha, *The Location of Culture*, 86.
47 Graham Huggan, "A Tale of Two Parrots: Walcott, Rhys, and the Uses of Colonial Mimicry," *Contemporary Literature* 35 (1994), 655.

48 Mary Condé, Introduction to Mary Condé and Thorunn Lonsdale, eds., *Caribbean Women Writers: Fiction in English* (New York: St. Martin's Press, 1999), 2.
49 Jamaica Kincaid, "I Use a Cut and Slash Policy of Writing: Jamaica Kincaid Talks to Gerhard Dilger," *Wasafiri* 16 (1992), 21.
50 Paule Marshall, *Brown Girl, Brownstones* (New York: The Feminist Press, 1981), 310.
51 Paule Marshall, *The Chosen Place, The Timeless People* (New York: Vintage, 1992), 21. Subsequent references are given in the text.
52 Drawing on the work of Dean MacCannell, Kaplan writes, "A distinctive aspect of this form of modernity lies in a complicated tension between space and time. When the past is displaced, often to another location, the modern subject must travel to it, as it were. History becomes something to be established and managed through tours, exhibitions, and representational practices in cinema, literature, and other forms of cultural production." See Kaplan, *Questions of Travel: Postmodern Discourses of Displacement* (Durham: Duke University Press, 1996), 35.
53 Katherine Sugg, "'I Would Rather Be Dead': Nostalgia and Narrative in Jamaica Kincaid's *Lucy*," *Narrative* 10.2 (2002), 157.
54 Quoted in Angelita Reyes, "Reading Carnival as an Archaeological Site for Memory in Paule Marshall's *The Chosen Place, The Timeless People* and *Praisesong for the Widow*," in Amritjit Singh, Jr., Joseph T. Skerrett, and Robert E. Hogan, eds., *Memory, Narrative, and Identity: New Essays on Ethnic American Literatures* (Boston: Northeastern University Press, 1994), 185.
55 Hortense J. Spillers, "Chosen Place, Timeless People: Some Figurations on the New World," in Marjorie Pryse and Hortense J. Spillers, eds., *Conjuring: Black Women, Fiction, and Literary Tradition* (Bloomington: Indiana University Press, 1985), 166.
56 Paule Marshall, "Shaping the World of My Art," *New Letters* 40 (1973), 111.
57 My argument is informed by Simon Gikandi's claim that Marshall's reluctance to depict a more sustained sense of solidarity or recovery of cultural traditions comes from the sense that it would be futile for Afro-Caribbeans to seek to recover "African objects of knowledge in a continuous and holistic way." See Gikandi, *Writing in Limbo: Modernism and Caribbean Literature* (Ithaca: Cornell University Press, 1992), 195.
58 Paule Marshall, *Praisesong for the Widow* (New York: E. P. Dutton, 1984), 240. Subsequent references are given in the text.
59 Edouard Glissant, *Caribbean Discourse: Selected Essays*, edited and translated by J. Michael Dash (Charlottesville: Caraf Books, 1992), 93.
60 Ibid., 65.
61 Paul Ricoeur, "A Response," in Morny Joy, ed., *Paul Ricoeur and Narrative: Context and Contestation* (Calgary: University of Calgary Press, 1997), xliii, xliv.

3 "LOSS WAS IN THE ORDER OF THINGS": RECALLING
   LOSS, RECLAIMING PLACE IN NATIVE AMERICAN FICTION

1 Edith Wyschogrod, *An Ethics of Remembering: History, Heterology, and the Nameless Others* (Chicago: University of Chicago Press, 1998), xi. Subsequent references are given in the text.
2 Gary Saul Morson, *Narratives and Freedom: The Shadows of Time* (New Haven: Yale University Press, 1994), 6. See also Michael André Bernstein, *Foregone Conclusions: Against Apocalyptic History* (Berkeley: University of California Press, 1994), 1–2. Morson argues that sideshadowing also figures prominently in the novels of Tolstoy and Dostoevsky. Both authors position themselves against the prevailing deterministic and closed views of time existing in nineteenth-century Russia. Sideshadowing allows Tolstoy to convey the contingency of events in *War and Peace* and *Anna Karenina*. For Dostoevsky, sideshadowing functions slightly differently, offering "a concrete image of human freedom" that is connected to his concept of responsibility (6).
3 An almost identical version of Tosamah's journey to Rainy Mountain appears in *The Way to Rainy Mountain* (1969). The two primary differences between the accounts are the change in narratorial voice from Tosamah to Momaday himself and the presence of a counterpointing storyline in *House Made of Dawn* that depicts the suffering of the novel's protagonist, Abel, after a police beating.
4 Louis Owens, *Other Destinies: Understanding the American Indian Novel* (Norman: University of Oklahoma Press, 1992), 20.
5 I take the term "late imperial" from Thomas Biolsi and Larry J. Zimmerman, who employ it as an alternative label to "postcolonialism." Biolsi and Zimmerman reject the latter term because the systems of domination instituted by colonialism continue to function, albeit in fundamentally different ways. "Late imperialism" emphasizes that such systems of domination "have remarkable abilities to appease and contain resistance and to appear (at least to some) as not oppressive." See Biolsi and Zimmerman, eds., *Indians and Anthropologists: Vine Deloria, Jr. and the Critique of Anthropology* (Tucson: University of Arizona Press, 1997), 6. I will use this term to distinguish authors like Momaday who live within cultures whose territories are still occupied by foreign powers from "postcolonial" authors such as Achebe who live in areas that have gained independence.
6 Quoted in R. S. Sharma, "Vision and Form in N. Scott Momaday's *House Made of Dawn*," *Indian Journal of American Studies* 12.1 (1982), 72. Paula Gunn Allen argues that this sensibility is not limited to Momaday but is "a basic assumption for tribal Indians, and estrangement is seen as so abnormal that narratives and rituals that restore the estranged to his or her plane within a cultural matrix abound." See Allen, *The Sacred Hoop: Recovering the Feminine in American Indian Traditions*, 2nd edn. (Boston: Beacon Press, 1992), 127.

7 My argument provides a somewhat different sense of the relationship between the individual and the tribal from that presented by William Bevis. For Bevis, Native American novels like *House Made of Dawn* are structured by what he calls "homing plots" in which protagonists seek to return to tribal past and place. Bevis argues that these plots "all present the tribal past as a gravity field stronger than individual will." See Bevis, "Native American Novels: Homing In," in Brian Swann and Arnold Krupat, eds., *Recovering the Word: Essays on Native American Literature* (Berkeley: University of California Press, 1995), 585. This assessment implies a sort of tribal stability and homogeneity belied by the novels of Momaday, Welch, Silko, and Hogan. On my understanding, their novels focus less on whether the protagonists "return" to a tribal past than on the ways in which their quests provide the means of refiguring tribal culture to accommodate the exigencies of the late imperial situation.

8 N. Scott Momaday, *House Made of Dawn* (New York: Perennial, 1989), 129. Subsequent references are given in the text.

9 See Arlene A. Elder, "Dancing on the Page: Orature in N. Scott Momaday's *The Way to Rainy Mountain*," *Narrative* 7.3 (1999), 275.

10 While Wyschogrod's concept of cataclysm draws upon the tradition established by Adorno that reads the Holocaust as a radical rupturing of history, her use of the term itself appears to draw more upon the work of Maurice Blanchot. In his book *The Writing of Disaster*, Blanchot similarly coins a single term, "*le désastre*" or "disaster," to convey both disparate historical instances of suffering and an existential condition defined by the sense of the absolute alterity of each individual. "The disaster ruins everything, all the while leaving everything intact," Blanchot writes. "It does not touch anyone in particular; 'I' am not threatened by it, but spared, left aside. It is in this way that I am threatened; it is in this way that the disaster threatens in me that which is exterior to me – an other than I who passively became other." See Blanchot, *The Writing of the Disaster*, translated by Ann Smock (Lincoln: University of Nebraska Press, 1986) 1.

11 Several times during the course of *The Names*, Momaday projects himself into the past and interacts with his ancestors. In one such instance, Momaday envisions himself conversing with his grandfather Mammedaty. This conversation allows Momaday to intertwine their lives in an act of mutual genesis: Momaday notes that he is "created in the old man's story" even as the event itself is created by Momaday's narrative. See Momaday, *The Names: A Memoir* (Tucson: University of Arizona Press, 1976), 96–97. This narrative intertwining allows Momaday both to legitimize his writing and to ascribe it to a tribal rather than personal source.

12 Arjun Appadurai, *Modernity at Large: Cultural Dimensions of Globalization* (Minneapolis: University of Minnesota Press, 1996), 31.

13 Charles Jencks, *What is Post-Modernism?* (New York: St. Martin's Press, 1986), 56. Although scholars have become justifiably uncomfortable with such claims, a similar logic can be read to underlie several current theories

of the ethnicity. Anthropologist Michael Fischer, for example, argues that ethnicity is reinvented by each individual. See Fischer, "Ethnicity and the Post-Modern Arts of Memory," in James Clifford and George E. Marcus, eds., *Writing Culture: The Politics and Poetics of Ethnography* (Berkeley: University of California Press, 1986), 195. Hence, ethnicity is not a stable and pure category to which individuals return so much as a "thick concept" that provides a basis for debates over communal identity. Werner Sollors' renowned volume *The Invention of Ethnicity* makes a similar case, arguing that ethnicity represents "widely shared, though intensely debated, collective fictions that are continually reinvented." See Sollors, *The Invention of Ethnicity* (New York: Oxford University Press, 1989), xi.

14 Momaday, *The Names*, 1.
15 Ibid., 1.
16 Appadurai, *Modernity at Large*, 30.
17 N. Scott Momaday, "The Man Made of Words," in Abraham Chapman, ed., *Literature of the American Indians: Views and Interpretations* (New York: Meridian, 1975), 99.
18 Linda Hogan, "Who Puts Together," in Richard F. Fleck, ed., *Critical Perspectives on Native American Fiction* (Washington: Three Continents Press, 1993), 134.
19 Susan Scarberry-García, *Landmarks of Healing: A Study of* House Made of Dawn (Albuquerque: University of New Mexico Press, 1990), 1. Mathias Schubnell's *N. Scott Momaday: The Cultural and Literary Background* (Norman: University of Oklahoma Press, 1985), Scarberry-García's *Landmarks of Healing*, and Louis Owens' *Other Destinies* represent three major examples of works that find Abel to be "reintegrated into the mythic reality of his tribe; he has come home" by the end of the novel (Owens, 127; cf. Schubnell, 85; Scarberry-García, 105). Indeed, the preponderance of Momaday criticism finds Abel healed in the final scenes. Even less optimistic readers like Susan Berry Brill De Ramirez tend to read the possibility of healing. See De Ramirez, *Contemporary American Indian Literatures & The Oral Tradition.* (Tucson: University of Arizona Press, 1999), 56. Larry Landrum accepts that Abel undergoes a "conversion experience" at the end of the novel but considers it to be inconsistent with the novel's critique of modernism. See Landrum, "The Shattered Modernism of Momaday's *House Made of Dawn*," *Modern Fiction Studies* 42.4 (1996), 777. Bernard Selinger represents a notable exception to this trend within criticism, arguing that Momaday's novel disrupts the *bildungsroman* tradition, in which the hero achieves "some sort of identity in accordance with society," by categorically denying Abel healing. See Selinger, "*House Made of Dawn*: A Positively Ambivalent Bildungsroman," *Modern Fiction Studies* 45 (1999), 61.
20 Owens reads the foreshadowing in the prologue somewhat differently, arguing that it establishes a "nonlinear, cyclical time of the pueblo." In so doing, the novel rejects modernism's obsession with ephemerality and fragmentation, defining experience instead "according to the eternal,

immutable values arising from a profound integration with place" (*Other Destinies*, 95). Owens' argument provides a useful corrective to Morson's theory of foreshadowing by pointing to its culture-specific understanding of the linearity of time. However, Owens' theory requires him to read Abel as succeeding in integrating himself with place even in the prologue, an integration that, on my reading, never exists.

21 Abel is running as part of the "runners after evil" ceremony in which a race is connected with the clearing of irrigation ditches in the spring. See Schubnell, *N. Scott Momaday*, 132. Only at the end of the novel do readers discover that Abel is running alone because he has fallen behind the other runners.

22 Selinger makes a similar claim, arguing that Abel's early memories are "not nearly as whole as the narrator claims; they are incomplete, oblique, confusing." See Selinger, "*House Made of Dawn*," 44. Selinger draws a somewhat different conclusion from this, however, arguing that the narrator and Abel work together to make these memories clear and complete.

23 My use of the term "aphasia" is not meant to invoke Jakobson's. Rather, I use it in a metaphorical sense to express Abel's inability to tell stories. Although he is not literally aphasic, Abel almost never speaks. And in a novel that celebrates stories and storytelling, his silence appears not simply as reticence but as a malady that inhibits the imagination.

24 Momaday, "The Man Made of Words," 97.

25 Wyschogrod borrows the term *ficciones* from Jorge Luis Borges, whose fictional works provide a model for historical narratives by the foregrounding of their own "ontological errancy" (32).

26 The significance of Angela's bear story specifically, and whether she represents a figure of healing or corruption generally, is a hotly debated topic in Momaday criticism. Readings of Angela and her function within the novel range from Scarberry-García's claim that Angela functions as a healer and is identified with the mythical figure of the Bear Maiden (*Landmarks of Healing*, 51, 62–63) to Lawrence Evers' argument that "Angela's story is as rootless as a Disney cartoon." See Evers, "Words and Place: A Reading of *House Made of Dawn*," *Western American Literature* 11.4 (1977), 317.

27 A comparison of the Night Chant in the 1989 edition of *House Made of Dawn* (146–47) with Momaday's source, Washington Matthews' transcription, shows that Ben leaves out two lines: the petition "Restore my voice for me" and the repeated final line, "In beauty it is finished." In contrast, the 1968 edition includes the petition line. See Matthews, "Navajo Myths, Prayers, and Songs with Texts and Translations," *University of California Publications in American Archaeology and Ethnology* 5.2 (1906), 54–55. In interpretive terms, the line's inclusion might suggest that the failure of healing in the novel's conclusion is due not to Ben forgetting but to the lost effectiveness of the ritual itself in the late imperial context, though he still forgets to repeat the final line and is noticeably ashamed of performing the ceremony itself. Even the more complete version would be a sacrilege to a traditional Navajo, according to Floyd C. Watkins, whose analysis of the 1968 edition

notes that the novel removes the prayer from its ceremonial context. See Watkins, *In Time and Place: Some Origins of American Fiction* (Athens: University of Georgia Press, 1977), 170.

28 Owens characterizes Tosamah as both "a trickster and fraud" (*Other Destinies*, 108). At turns in the novel, Tosamah is a positive role model who uses nostalgia to reclaim a sense of place and a fraudulent tribal priest who cares nothing for Abel's difficulties.

29 James Welch, *Winter in the Blood* (New York: Penguin, 1974), 175.

30 James Welch, *Fools Crow* (New York: Penguin, 1986), 391.

31 Leslie Marmon Silko, *Ceremony* (New York: Penguin, 1977), 231. Subsequent references are given in the text.

32 For Owens, the opening poem about Thought-Woman signals an epistemological shift away from a Western, modernist notion of the author as originator of knowledge toward the notion of author as "transmitter" of oral traditions (*Other Destinies*, 169). The implication is that such transmissions have the capacity to preserve and disseminate traditions to audiences who may have only limited previous familiarity with such traditions. Owens goes further, claiming that *Ceremony* provides a "cure" for not only Native Americans but also a Western world that has been increasingly "embracing its own fragmentation, deracination, and inauthenticity" (172).

33 Edward S. Casey, *Remembering: A Phenomenological Study* (Bloomington: Indiana University Press, 1987), 284.

34 Rachel Stein similarly argues that Silko recasts the struggle facing Native Americans away from a conflict between races; for Stein, however, *Ceremony* recasts the struggle in terms of conflicting paradigms of storytelling rather than conflicting ethical commitments, as my reading suggests. See Stein, *Shifting the Ground: American Women Writers' Revisions of Nature, Gender, and Race* (Charlottesville: University Press of Virginia, 1997), 122.

35 Momaday, "The Man Made of Words," 97.

36 Ibid., 101.

37 While *Almanac of the Dead* describes the crisis of Native American identity in terms of Marxian language more explicitly than Silko's earlier works did, the novel makes very little direct call for political activism on its readers. The notion of historical inevitability claimed by the novel implies that no one in particular is responsible for effecting change. This becomes apparent when the character Awa Gee describes the coming revolution: "No leaders or chains of command would be necessary" for revolution because everyone will know spontaneously and instinctually when the time is at hand. See Leslie Marmon Silko, *Almanac of the Dead* (New York: Penguin, 1991), 686. Precisely because the revolutionary impulse is felt on a basic, genetic level, political activism to effect change or bring about the revolution is rendered unnecessary.

38 Silko, *Almanac of the Dead*, 749.

39 Linda Hogan, *Solar Storms* (New York: Scribner, 1995), 325.

40 Vine Deloria, Jr., *God Is Red: A Native View of Religion* (Golden: Fulcrum Publishing, 1994), 281.

41 Quoted in Charles L. Woodward, *Ancestral Voice: Conversations with N. Scott Momaday* (Lincoln: University of Nebraska Press, 1989), 38–39.

42 Although Momaday's vision of racial memory does not appear to convey the xenophobia and exclusivism so often associated with ethnic essentialism, it remains unsettling because it appears to challenge the foundational metaphors and assumptions of contemporary ethnic studies. Indeed, Arnold Krupat characterizes the concept of blood memory as "absurdly racist." See *The Voice in the Margin: Native American Literature and the Canon* (Berkeley: University of California Press, 1989), 13. Chadwick Allen rehabilitates the concept to some degree by reading it as a form of constructivism in disguise of essentialism, arguing that it "redefines American Indian authenticity in terms of imaginative re-collecting and re-membering." See Allen, "Blood (and) Memory," *American Literature* 71.1 (1999), 94–95. It nonetheless demands the attention of this study because blood memory might eliminate the need for nostalgia. It suggests that individuals like Ko-sahn could claim memories of events and places of which they have no personal experience. My own sense is that the notion of blood memory does not imply some biological means of cultural preservation; Tosamah's quest to Rainy Mountain would have been unnecessary if he had retained its memory genetically. Rather, blood memory provides an evocative metaphor to describe stories that provide experiences central to how Momaday understands Native American identity.

4 REFIGURING NATIONAL CHARACTER: THE REMAINS OF THE
BRITISH ESTATE NOVEL

1 Evelyn Waugh, *Brideshead Revisited: The Sacred and Profane Memories of Captain Charles Ryder* (Little, Brown and Company, 1945), 5. Subsequent references are given in the text.

2 Quoted in Richard Gill, *Happy Rural Seat: the English Country House and the Literary Imagination* (New Haven: Yale University Press, 1972), 211.

3 If *The Remains of the Day* bears little topical similarity to Ishiguro's previous novels, it does bear a great deal of thematic similarity. Ishiguro's first three novels share an interest in unreliable narration, memory, and characters who are unable either to forget the past or to confront their guilt over past actions.

4 Peter Mandler argues that at the outbreak of World War II, the country house was at its nadir. Between the two world wars, some 5 percent of the estates were demolished and an even larger percentage were in the 1940s and 1950s. See Mandler, "Nationalising the Country House," in Michael Hunter, ed., *Preserving the Past: The Rise of Heritage in Modern Britain* (Phoenix Mill: Alan Sutton Publishing, 1996), 99.

5 The middle-class longing for the grand estates is perhaps best captured by E. M. Forster. "The class which strangled the aristocracy [. . .] has been haunted ever since by the ghost of its victim," he wrote. "It has come into

power consequent on the Industrial Revolution and Reform Bills and the Death Duties. But it has never been able to build itself an appropriate home, and when it asserts that an Englishman's home is his castle, it reveals the precise nature of its failure. We who belong to it still copy the past. [. . .] Our minds still hanker after the feudal stronghold which we condemned as uninhabitable." See Forster, "Mrs. Miniver," in *Two Cheers for Democracy* (New York: Harcourt, Brace and Company, 1951), 299.

6 Virginia C. Kenny, *The Country-House Ethos in English Literature 1688–1750* (New York: St. Martin's Press, 1984), 9.

7 For an excellent analysis of the heritage industry in postwar Britain, see David Lowenthal's *Possessed by the Past: The Heritage Crusade and the Spoils of History* (New York: Free Press, 1996). Two other edited collections, Michael Hunter's *Preserving the Past* and John Corner and Sylvia Harvey's *Enterprise and Heritage: Crosscurrents of National Culture* (London: Routledge, 1991), are also very useful.

8 David Cannadine, *Pleasures of the Past* (London: Penguin, 1997), 100.

9 John Cornforth, *The Country Houses of England 1948–1998* (London: Constable, 1998), 1.

10 I take the phrase "the invention of tradition" from Eric Hobsbawm; for Hobsbawm, nineteenth-century European nationalism was so unprecedented "that even historical continuity had to be invented." See Eric Hobsbawm and Terence Ranger, eds., *The Invention of Tradition* (Cambridge: Cambridge University Press, 1992). While Hobsbawm does not treat the English estate directly in this context, he does analyze the efforts by nationalist movements to restore architectural sites. One of the first examples of an invented tradition that he explores is the rebuilding of the British Parliament chamber (1–2).

11 For an excellent synthesis of Thatcherism and its efforts to reformulate the past, see Peter Clarke's *A Question of Leadership: Gladstone to Blair* (London: Penguin, 1999), 291–324, and *Hope and Glory: Britain 1900–1990* (London: Allen Lane, 1996), 367–79. See also David Childs, *Britain since 1939: Progress and Decline* (London: Macmillan, 1995); Eric J. Evans, *Thatcher and Thatcherism* (London: Routledge, 1997); Joel Krieger, *Reagan, Thatcher, and the Politics of Decline* (New York: Oxford University Press, 1986); and Kenneth O. Morgan, *The People's Peace: British History since 1945* (Oxford: Oxford University Press, 1999).

12 Quoted in James F. Carens, Introduction to *Critical Essays on Evelyn Waugh* (Boston: G. K. Hall & Co., 1987), 172.

13 Mike Petry, in particular, finds irony to be a primary trait of Ishiguro's work, though most studies of Ishiguro invoke the notion. See Petry, *Narratives of Memory and Identity: The Novels of Kazuo Ishiguro* (Frankfurt: Peter Lang, 1999), 102. Brian Shaffer argues that readers understand "representations of oppression masquerading as professionalism" in *The Remains of the Day* through Stevens's ironic narrative. See Shaffer, *Understanding Kazuo Ishiguro* (Columbia: University of South Carolina Press, 1998), 87. And the sense that Ishiguro's work subverts dominant

fictional modes or the "coercive terms" underlying the supposedly benevolent paternalism of colonial Britain requires close attention to Ishiguro's irony. See Susie O'Brien, "Serving a New World Order: Postcolonial Politics in Kazuo Ishiguro's *The Remains of the Day*," *Modern Fiction Studies* 42.4 (1996), 789; see also Salman Rushdie, *Imaginary Homelands: Essays and Criticism 1981–1991* (London: Granta Books, 1991), 244. Even readings that focus on Ishiguro's East Asian influences perceive that his literary contribution is associated with his ironic mode of narration; John Rothfork's argument, for example, asserts that Ishiguro provides a Buddhist critique of Confucian ethics through the use of what he calls "Zen comedy." See John Rothfork, "Zen Comedy in Postcolonial Literature: Kazuo Ishiguro's *The Remains of the Day*," *Mosaic* 29.1 (1996), 82. While I follow this assessment that irony plays a role in Ishiguro's writing, I am suggesting that irony and nostalgia are not opposed but inseparable in *The Remains of the Day*.

14 David Leon Higdon's well-known study of contemporary British literature exemplifies the critical trend that rejects the presence of nostalgia in the work of contemporary literary authors. In Higdon's analysis, nostalgia and escapism are inseparably linked. See Higdon, *Shadows of the Past in Contemporary British Fiction* (Athens: University of Georgia Press, 1984).

15 Homi K. Bhabha, "A Question of Survival: Nations and Psychic States," in James Donald, ed., *Psychoanalysis and Cultural Theory: Thresholds* (New York: St. Martin's Press, 1991), 91, 93.

16 The connection between the English estate and an ethical, if not national, character has precedents in prenovelistic forms, most notably the early modern "estate poem." Ben Jonson's poem "To Penshurst" (1616), for example, praises the estate in order to assert the virtue and character of its lord. Indeed, the imagery used to describe the estate emphasizes the ethos of hospitality and charity (qualities important in a patron), and what finally distinguishes Penshurst from other edifices, those "proud, ambitious heaps," is that it is inhabited by a lord who embodies its *ēthos*: other estates "may say their lords have built, but thy lord dwells," Jonson declares (lines 101–2). Brian Patton makes a similar claim with respect to Andrew Marvell's "Upon Appleton House," arguing that it seeks to reconcile tradition and social stability with social and economic change. See Brian Patton, "Preserving Property: History, Genealogy, and Inheritance in 'Upon Appleton House,'" *Renaissance Quarterly* 49 (1996), 836–37. Kenny argues that such country house poems achieve this reconciliation by depicting the lord as master of self and metaphor for the state (3). In so doing, such poems anticipate the novels of Austen and Forster in that they seek to reconcile national divisions by fusing past, present, and future values.

17 Alastair M. Duckworth, *The Improvement of the Estate: A Study of Jane Austen's Novels* (Baltimore: Johns Hopkins University Press, 1971), ix.

18 Simon Gikandi's *Maps of Englishness: Writing Identity in the Culture of Colonialism* (New York: Columbia University Press 1996) traces how Englishness itself was a product of colonial culture (x). For Gikandi,

Englishness only comes into being in relation to its colonies, and the crisis of identity that increasingly marks Great Britain in the twentieth century is the result of the nation's difficulty in constructing a postimperial identity. From Gikandi's perspective, the prevalent nostalgia within British politics and cultural life reflects an effort to preserve the coherence of national identity even after the loss of its defining aspect, the Empire.

19 For a detailed analysis of Austen's treatment of empire, see Said, *Culture and Imperialism*, 70–97.

20 E. M. Forster, *Howards End* (Bantam Books, 1985), 77. Subsequent references are given in the text.

21 The English estate remains the quintessential icon of nation for Forster despite his commitment to liberal humanism because its existence opposes the threat of mass culture. See Jon Hegglund, "Defending the Realm: Domestic Space and Mass Cultural Contamination in *Howards End* and *An Englishman's Home*," *English Literature in Transition* 40 (1997), 358.

22 Rae Harris Stoll, "The Unthinkable Poor in Edwardian Writing," *Mosaic* 15.4 (1982), 26.

23 Forster's apparent faith in progress should not be equated with a sense of satisfaction with the present. On the contrary, Forster expresses a radical dissatisfaction with society, according to F. R. Leavis. See Leavis, "E. M. Forster," in Malcolm Bradbury, ed., *Forster: A Collection of Critical Essays* (New York: Barnes and Noble, 1966), 35. Philip Gardner makes a similar claim, reading Forster's fiction as an exploration of whether a homosexual could comfortably identify with a notion of Englishness or, in Gardner's terms, come to "possess England." *Howards End*, on this reading, finds "a kind of sexual compromise by means of multiple possession" of the estate at the end of the novel. See Gardner, "E. M. Forster and 'The Possession of England,'" *Modern Language Quarterly* 42 (1981), 176.

24 Alan Sinfield argues that the dependence of the Schlegels on the monetary resources of the Wilcoxes means that their "attempt to 'connect' succeeds only by way of the fantasy collapse of Wilcox resistance." See Sinfield, *Literature, Politics, and Culture in Postwar Britain* (Berkeley: University of California Press, 1989), 41. Likewise, Alistair Duckworth's reading of the novel's epigraph, "Only connect . . ." implies that Forster recognizes the profound difficulty of achieving national reconciliation. The epigraph, Duckworth writes, "might well have been addressed to a whole society in which unionists and nationalists, management and labor, men and women, English and Germans, seemed incapable of reconciliation." See Duckworth, *Howards End: E. M. Forster's House of Fiction* (New York: Twayne Publishers, 1992), 4.

25 George McCartney argues that Waugh differs from modernists such as Virginia Woolf in that the collapse of traditional structures, for Waugh, leads not to self-discovery but to the shallowness of character. See McCartney, *Confused Roaring: Evelyn Waugh and the Modernist Tradition* (Bloomington: Indiana University Press, 1987), 74.

26 Evelyn Waugh, *The Essays, Articles and Reviews*, edited by Donat Gallagher (Boston: Little, Brown and Company, 1984), 575.

27 Ibid., 367.

28 Walter Allen makes a similar argument regarding Waugh's nostalgic vision of Catholicism: "for Waugh, Catholicism is a profoundly romantic thing, the core of a nostalgic dream of an ideal past by which the present is judged and found wanting." See Annette Wirth (citing from Allen's *The Novel Today* [1955]), *The Loss of Traditional Values and Continuance of Faith in Evelyn Waugh's Novels:* A Handful of Dust, Brideshead Revisited *and* Sword of Honor (Frankfurt: Peter Lang, 1990), 97. This valorization of the past, according to John Howard Wilson, allows Waugh to cast history as a process of decline in which the present is condemned for failing to live up to the ideals of the past. See Wilson, *Evelyn Waugh: A Literary Biography, 1903–1924* (London: Associated University Presses, 1996), 171. This vision of history as decline guarantees Waugh's abiding disappointment with Britain, a disappointment that is only exacerbated by his experience in the Army during World War II. Indeed, he was notoriously loathed by the men under his command; his superiors granted him leave to write *Brideshead Revisited* because he was considered such a liability that he needed to be removed from active military service.

29 Waugh describes how *Brideshead Revisited* was inspired by witnessing the deathbed conversion of his friend Hubert Duggan: "It was, of course, all about the death bed," Waugh writes to Ronald Knox in a letter dated May 14, 1945. Quoted in Wirth, *The Loss of Traditional Values*, 17.

30 Intriguingly, Ryder becomes the spiritual heir of the estate only after he loses his opportunity to become the material heir. Shortly before his death, Lord Marchmain rejects his eldest son as heir and names Julia instead. Had Ryder and Julia subsequently married, then Ryder would have become the owner of the estate. When Julia breaks off her engagement with Ryder after Marchmain's demise, Ryder loses this opportunity. He subsequently begins a process of inner reflection that ultimately leads to his own conversion to Catholicism, however, which enables him to link Catholicism and Englishness at the end of the novel. The implication seems to be that Waugh envisions Catholicism to be a necessary but insufficient aspect of national character. For Marchmain rejects out of hand the claim of his eldest son, who is the most orthodox Catholic of his generation, to the estate.

31 David Rothstein, "*Brideshead Revisited* and the Modern Historicization of Memory," *Studies in the Novel* 25 (1993), 329.

32 Quoted in Evans, *Thatcher and Thatcherism*, 96.

33 Patrick Brantlinger, *Fictions of State: Culture and Credit in Britain 1694–1994* (Ithaca: Cornell University Press, 1996), 242.

34 See ibid., 237; Morgan, *The People's Peace*, 489.

35 Although the events of *The Remains of the Day* occur at the nadir of the English estate, Ishiguro writes the novel from the vantage point of its restored fortunes. Indeed, one can speak of the opposite extreme in the past

three decades – the heritage industry of Great Britain since the 1970s and the formation of the Historic Houses Association during the same period have guaranteed the preservation of the estate as tourist attraction. The welfare of the estate has changed so radically that Waugh himself noted in the 1959 edition of *Brideshead Revisited* that his novel might have been a "panegyric preached over an empty coffin." For further information on the state of the estate in the twentieth century, see Peter Mandler, *The Fall and Rise of the Stately Home* (New Haven: Yale University Press, 1997).

36 Quoted in Allan Vorda and Kim Herzinger, "An Interview with Kazuo Ishiguro," *Mississippi Review* 20 (1991/92), 139.

37 See Krieger, *Reagan, Thatcher, and the Politics of Decline*, 77–78.

38 Kazuo Ishiguro, *The Remains of the Day* (New York: Vintage Books, 1989), 28. Subsequent references are given in the text. The struggle to restore national "greatness" became a key theme of Thatcher's election campaign, and the term would still have had wide circulation as Ishiguro was writing *The Remains of the Day.* "Somewhere ahead lies greatness for the country again," Thatcher states on April 30, 1978. "Let us make it a country safe to grow old in . . . May this land of ours, which we love so much, find dignity and greatness and peace again." Quoted in Krieger, *Reagan, Thatcher, and the Politics of Decline*, 77.

39 Žižek argues that Thatcher's government effects "a shift in the center of gravity of 'the real Englishness.'" See *For They Know Not What They Do: Enjoyment As a Political Factor* (London: Verso, 1991), 110. Žižek reads the function of Englishness in somewhat different terms from my own analysis, however. His psychoanalytic focus argues that national identity formation inevitably depends on the fetishization of terms like Englishness that are ultimately empty: "the final answer is of course that *nobody* is fully English, that every empirical Englishman contains something non-English" (110).

40 The negative consequences of the Suez Crisis on Britain remain a debated topic. Childs points to the profound economic effects it had on the country (*Britain since 1939*, 112). Morgan argues that it had powerful but brief social consequences, except on writers like John Osborne and Kingsley Amis, for whom the event becomes a defining moment of governmental betrayal (*The People's Peace*, 156).

41 Interestingly, Harry Smith defers to the perceived expertise of Stevens to counter Dr. Carlisle's argument for granting the colonies independence: "Our doctor here's for all kinds of little countries going independent. *I don't have the learning to prove him wrong, though I know he is.* But I'd have been interested to hear what the likes of yourself would have to say to him on the subject, sir" (192; italics mine).

42 Stevens occupies a highly fraught class position in the novel. Although his status as a servant would incline him to identify with the working class, his efforts at mimicry (when he travels to see Mrs. Benn, for example, he wears Lord Darlington's old clothing) combined with his sense that he is upholding

tradition actually place him in a situation where he identifies himself in opposition to the working class.

43 While Brian Shaffer argues that Stevens returns to his old mentality at the end of the novel (*Understanding Kazuo Ishiguro*, 87), my analysis resembles more closely that of Kathleen Wall, who argues that although Stevens shrouds threatening moments "in layers of more comfortable memory," Stevens himself "unwinds these shrouds." See Wall, "*The Remains of the Day* and its Challenges to Theories of Unreliable Narration," *Journal of Narrative Technique* 24.1 (1994), 29.

44 O'Brien, "Serving a New World Order," 793.

45 In arguing that Ishiguro's narratives connect thick ethical concepts with a concept of nation, I am resisting the critical tendency, identified by Steven Connor, to deny that Englishness is a serious concern in his work. See Connor, *The English Novel in History 1950–1995* (London: Routledge, 1996), 107.

46 Tom Nairn, *The Break-up of Britain: Crisis and Neonationalism* (London: Verso, 1981).

5 APPEASING AN EMBITTERED HISTORY: TRAUMA AND NATIONHOOD IN THE WRITINGS OF ACHEBE AND SOYINKA

1 Reed Way Dasenbrock, "Creating a Past: Achebe, Naipaul, Soyinka, Farah," *Salmagundi* 68–69 (1985–86), 317.

2 Ben Okri, *The Famished Road* (New York: Anchor Books, 1993), 478.

3 Biodun Jeyifo, Introduction to Jeyifo, ed., *Perspectives on Wole Soyinka: Freedom and Complexity* (Jackson: University Press of Mississippi, 2001), xix.

4 Achebe, *Hopes and Impediments*, 29.

5 Wole Soyinka, *The Burden of Memory, The Muse of Forgiveness* (New York: Oxford University Press, 1999), 59.

6 Chinua Achebe, *Anthills of the Savannah* (New York: Anchor Books, 1988), 204. Subsequent references are given in the text.

7 Trauma theory increasingly understands trauma to be experienced by communities as well as individuals. One of the clearest formulations of collective trauma has been made by Kai Erickson. Erickson defines collective trauma as "a blow to the basic tissues of social life that damages the bonds attaching people together and impairs the prevailing sense of communality." See Erickson, "Notes on Trauma and Community" *American Imago* 48.4 (1991), 460. The most salient difference between collective and individual trauma, according to Erickson, is that the former lacks the suddenness typically associated with the latter. Collective trauma works over a process of time as individuals revise their perception of community so that it no longer represents a source of support and safety. Intriguingly, Erickson also suggests that collective traumas can, in some instances, provide the basis of solidarity, noting that "the shared experience becomes almost like a common culture, a common language, a kinship among those who have come to see themselves as different" (461).

8 Shoshana Felman and Dori Laub, *Testimony: Crises of Witnessing in Literature, Psychoanalysis, and History* (New York: Routledge, 1992), 1.

Theodor Adorno most famously takes the position that the "indefatigable self-destructiveness of enlightenment" inculcates trauma. See Max Horkheimer and Theodor W. Adorno, *Dialectic of Enlightenment*, translated by John Cumming (New York: Herder and Herder, 1972), xi. The Enlightenment pursuit of scientific discovery objectifies the natural world and, in so doing, extinguishes self-consciousness (4). Thus, the methodical destructiveness of Auschwitz is not a byproduct of Enlightenment but its logical conclusion and *telos*. For Adorno, history itself ends at Auschwitz – the road to progress follows the tracks leading to the death camps. To live in the aftermath of the Holocaust is to inhabit a traumatized world in which time moves vacuously on.

9 Cathy Caruth, Introduction to Caruth, ed., *Trauma: Explorations in Memory* (Baltimore: Johns Hopkins University Press, 1995), 4.

10 The idea that narrative can facilitate the process of overcoming communal trauma grows out of the sense within psychiatry and psychoanalysis that narrative is crucial in the treatment of personal trauma. Judith Herman, for example, observes that the reconstruction of the past in stories transforms traumatic memories, integrating them into the survivor's life. See Judith Lewis Herman, *Trauma and Recovery* (New York: Basic Books, 1992), 175. A similar notion is implied by B. A. van der Kolk's distinction between *traumatic memory* and *narrative memory*. Unlike narrative memories, traumatic memories have no social component and are not addressed to anyone. The dissolution of the intersubjective aspects of memory effected by trauma precludes the possibility of shared commemoration, which in turn drastically limits an individual's ability to identify with the community's values or dilemmas. See B. A. van der Kolk and Onno van der Hart, "The Intrusive Past: The Flexibility of Memory and the Engraving of Trauma" *American Imago* 48.4 (1991), 431.

11 In a 1969 interview, Achebe asserts that the political conditions of Nigeria, and most particularly the Biafran War, had rendered novel writing impossible: "I can create, but of course not the kind of thing I created when I was at ease," Achebe says. "I can't write a novel now; I wouldn't want to. And even if I wanted to, I couldn't." Quoted in David Carroll, *Chinua Achebe: Novelist, Poet, Critic* (London: Macmillan, 1990), 27.

12 Bernth Lindfors, Introduction to Lindfors, ed., *Conversations with Chinua Achebe* (Jackson: University Press of Mississippi, 1997), x.

13 Dominick LaCapra, for example, opens his study, *History and Memory after Auschwitz*, with a critique of nostalgia. "One particularly dubious phenomenon is the nostalgic, sentimental turn to a partly fictionalized past that is conveyed in congenially ingratiating, safely conventionalized narrative form," he writes. In LaCapra's account, the preoccupation with nostalgia indicates a widespread desire to avoid confronting the needs of the present. See LaCapra *History and Memory after Auschwitz* (Ithaca: Cornell University Press, 1998), 8.

14 Julia Hell, "History as Trauma, or, Turning to the Past Once Again: Germany 1949/1989," *South Atlantic Quarterly* 96.4 (1997), 914.

15 According to Fanon, colonial administrations throughout Africa sought to establish a sense of dependency among African populations that resembled the dynamics of the mother-child relationship. By characterizing Africans as lacking culture or history, the colonial powers promoted the idea that were the European settlers to leave, Africans would "revert" to bestiality. Only the "colonial mother" could check this process and prevent the colonized from reverting back to their essential nature. See Fanon, *The Wretched of the Earth*, translated by Constance Farrington (New York: Grove Press, 1963), 211.

16 For further discussion of Fanon's disillusionment with the politics of figures associated with *négritude*, see Benita Parry, "Resistance Theory/Theorizing Resistance, or Two Cheers for Nativism," in Padmini Mongia, ed., *Contemporary Postcolonial Theory: A Reader* (London: Arnold, 1996), 102.

17 Fanon, *The Wretched of the Earth*, 211–12.

18 Kadiatu Kanneh's analysis of Fanon draws out the tension in his account of the rise of the postcolonial nation. On the one hand, the nation is cast within a progressive time scheme in which national consciousness is born through revolutionary action. On the other hand, Fanon emphasizes the need for "continuous renewal" in the face of new social formations, implying that the nation is the product of a selective return to original group identities. See Kanneh, *African Identities: Race, Nation and Culture in Ethnography, Pan-Africanism and Black Literatures* (London: Routledge, 1998), 85–93.

19 Quoted in Richard Begam, "Achebe's Sense of an Ending: History and Tragedy in *Things Fall Apart*," *Studies in the Novel* 29.3 (1997), 406–7.

20 Chinua Achebe, *Things Fall Apart* (New York: Fawcett Crest, 1969), 168. Subsequent references are given in the text.

21 Chinua Achebe, *Arrow of God* (New York: Doubleday, 1969), 146–47.

22 Chinua Achebe, *The Trouble with Nigeria* (London: Heinemann, 1984), 2. Subsequent references are given in the text.

23 Quoted in Bill Moyers, "Chinua Achebe," in Betty Sue Flowers, ed., *A World of Ideas: Conversations with Thoughtful Men and Women about American Life Today and the Ideas Shaping Our Future* (New York: Doubleday, 1989), 341. The longing to begin the "whole story" of the nation over again can be seen in Achebe's writing for children during the long hiatus between *A Man of the People* and *Anthills of the Savannah*. Indeed, he writes several children's books during the period in which he writes no novels. These stories express a longing for a time before the colonial encounter, "when the world was young" (opening line of *The Drum*). In a number of interviews over the years, Achebe has expressed a sense that children possess a freedom from social constraints and limitations that adults do not (see *Conversations with Chinua Achebe*, 60, 81, 92). "You know, everything is possible to a child," Achebe states. "This is something that children's stories can do for us and that we ought to learn again" (Moyers, "Chinua Achebe," 341). Especially given Achebe's disillusionment with Nigeria's postcolonial leaders, the promise implicit in such a notion of childhood is attractive. This particular hope

remains with Achebe even during the dark years following the Biafran War, as evidenced by his writing for children.

24 *Conversations with Chinua Achebe*, 155.

25 Simon Gikandi, *Reading Chinua Achebe: Language & Ideology in Fiction* (London: James Currey, 1991), 129.

26 On January 15 1970 Gowon declared that Nigerian unity and reconciliation demanded collective forgetting of the Civil War and Biafra:

> The so-called rising sun of Biafra is set for ever. It will be a great disservice for anyone to continue to use the word Biafra to refer to any part of that East Central State of Nigeria. The tragic chapter of violence is just ended. We are at the dawn of national reconciliation. Once again, we have an opportunity to build a new nation.

For a succinct discussion of the traumatic consequences of the Biafran War and postwar government policies, see Amadiume, "The Politics of Memory: Biafra and Intellectual Responsibility," in Amadiume, ed., *The Politics of Memory: Truth, Healing and Social Justice* (London: Zed Books Ltd., 2000).

27 Amadiume, "The Politics of Memory," 47. Although Soyinka condemned the ethnic violence against the Igbo leading up to the Biafran War and the general "Igbophobia" in northern Nigeria, he urged his countrymen not to break away from the rest of the country. After taking a trip to Biafra in 1967, however, Soyinka was imprisoned until 1969 for his purported support of the breakaway region.

28 Biodun Jeyifo, ed., *Conversations with Wole Soyinka* (Jackson: University Press of Mississippi, 2001), 200.

29 Achebe, *The Trouble with Nigeria*, 54.

30 Wole Soyinka, *Art, Dialogue, and Outrage: Essays on Literature and Culture*, edited by Biodun Jeyifo (New York: Pantheon Books, 1993), 19.

31 Caruth, *Trauma*, 5.

32 *Conversations with Chinua Achebe*, x.

33 Moyers, "Chinua Achebe," 337.

34 Gikandi, *Reading Chinua Achebe*, 136.

35 Ibid., 136–37.

36 Achebe, *The Trouble with Nigeria*, 5.

37 Ibid., 5.

38 Quoted in Moyers, "Chinua Achebe," 336.

39 Achebe, *The Trouble with Nigeria*, 15.

40 Ibid., 5.

41 Ibid.

42 Quoted in Romanus Okey Muoneke, *Arts, Rebellion and Redemption: A Reading of the Novels of Chinua Achebe* (New York: Peter Lang, 1994), 163.

43 Over the course of his career, Achebe has repeatedly insisted that the health of the community outweighs that of the individual. One of his most explicit statements in this regard comes in a 1972 interview with Ernest and Pat Emenyonu. "It is the good of these people that is the only good, as far as I am

concerned, not the good of the one man who happens to be the king or priest or what have you" (*Conversations with Chinua Achebe*, 42).

44 Ibid., 11.

45 Quoted in Moyers, "Chinua Achebe," 333.

46 Quoted in Moses, *The Novel and the Globalization of Culture*, 119.

47 Ibid., 120.

48 Achebe, *Hopes and Impediments*, 100.

49 Richard Begam argues that *Things Fall Apart* attempts to undo colonial representation by interweaving multiple forms of history: nationalist, adversarial, and metahistory. Begam's work differs from this study in his focus on the conception of an alternative hermeneutics rather than the articulation of nostalgic worlds as the source for Achebe's critique of empire and rewriting of history.

50 A key moment demonstrating the newly found solidarity among the participants in the naming ceremony comes when Emmanuel, who is President of the Students Union and a wanted man himself, translates the proceedings of the ceremony to Captain Abdul Medani, who was initially assigned to hunt down Chris but decided to try to help him escape instead. Before the ceremony, Emmanuel is justly suspicious of Abdul but during the ceremony he comes to trust him.

51 See Edward W. Said, "Figures, Configurations, Transfigurations," in Anna Rutherford, ed., *From Commonwealth to Post-Colonial* (Sydney: Dangaroo, 1992) 15.

52 Achebe, *The Trouble with Nigeria*, 12.

53 Ibid., 12–13.

54 In "Historical Emplotment and the Problem of Truth," Hayden White suggests that the representation of the Holocaust defies more traditional modes of narrative associated with nineteenth-century realism. Instead, he urges the use of what he terms "the middle voice," which would be distinct from both active and passive voices. According to White, both active and passive voices assume that the subject of the verb is external to the action described; in contrast, when the middle voice is used, "the subject is presumed to be *interior* to the action." See White, "Historical Emplotment and the Problem of Truth," in Saul Friedlander, ed., *Probing the Limits of Representation: Nazism and the "Final Solution"* (Cambridge: Harvard University Press, 1992), 48. Among modern Indo-European languages, there is no grammatical equivalent to the middle voice in ancient Greek; nonetheless, White suggests that the stylistics of literary modernism preserve its function. Indeed, White cites Auerbach's list of distinguishing stylistic characteristics of modernism as the best characterization of "middle voicedness" (51).

55 Neil ten Kortenaar finds the contradictions of nationalism to be reproduced by *Anthills of the Savannah*. Although the novel "calls for radical decentering of the nation [. . .] Achebe has admitted that the novel is addressed to Nigeria's leaders." See Ten Kortenaar, "'Only Connect': *Anthills of the*

Savannah and Achebe's *Trouble with Nigeria*," *Research in African Literatures* 24.3 (1993), 62. The problem of nationalism, for ten Kortenaar, is that it continually evokes "folk" traditions, even as it attempts to impose a modern European social institution. The slippage between a "national" identity and an elite class of citizens can lead to a betrayal of the very people the nation's leaders claim to represent.

56 Wole Soyinka, *The Interpreters* (New York: Africana Publishing Corporation, 1972), 227. Subsequent references are given in the text.

57 Soyinka, *Art, Dialogue, and Outrage.* 17.

58 Soyinka, *The Open Sore of a Continent: A Personal Narrative of the Nigerian Crisis* (New York: Oxford University Press, 1996), 139.

59 Ibid., 139, 140.

60 Soyinka, "A Dance of the Forests," in *Collected Plays 1* (Oxford: Oxford University Press, 1973), 5. Subsequent references are given in the text.

61 Soyinka, *Art, Dialogue, and Outrage*, 179. For an excellent summary of the debates between Soyinka and his leftist Nigerian critics in the 1970s and 1980s, see Brian Crow's essay "Soyinka and His Radical Critics: A Review," in Jeyifo, ed., *Perspectives on Wole Soyinka*, 91–103.

62 Soyinka, *Art, Dialogue, and Outrage*, 128.

63 While Soyinka characterizes iconoclasm as a broad movement, his writings are not specific about who constitutes the movement other than Ouologuem. In his essay "Cross Currents: The 'New African' After Cultural Encounters," Soyinka initially lists Armah under this category, only to distinguish him from Ouologuem for his "careful construction of mythical past as a potential model for the future" (*Art, Dialogue, and Outrage*, 127). In a later essay, "The External Encounter: Ambivalence and African Arts and Literature," it appears that Soyinka's target is less specific literary authors than leftist critics who are too attached to a rigid Marxist framework (179). Soyinka's circumspection here is particularly noteworthy, given that in the same essay he deliberately praises the work of Ngugi, the most famous African novelist to endorse Marxism explicitly.

64 Soyinka, *Art, Dialogue, and Outrage*, 182.

65 Soyinka, *The Open Sore of a Continent*, 127, 128.

66 Soyinka, *Art, Dialogue, and Outrage*, 222.

67 Soyinka's attitude toward *négritude* is complicated both because it has altered over time and because his critique of it is not based on the anti-essentialist account of identity that has figured so powerfully among feminist and American ethnic minority writers. Even in the early 1970s, Soyinka did not deny the existence of what he referred to as "a true, an authentic African spirituality, a religiosity if you like, a Black metaphysical outlook" (*Conversations with Wole Soyinka*, 66). The problem with *négritude*, for Soyinka, is not that it is essentialist but rather that it is the creation of expatriate artists and intellectuals too influenced by Western thinking. Soyinka insists that a black consciousness has always been present among the majority of Africans: "the African people have never lost their negritude,

never" (10). The threat presented by the *négritude* movement, then, is that it might co-opt and redefine the "true" *négritude* in terms of Western philosophical categories. By the 1990s, however, Soyinka demonstrates a preference for *négritude* over the attitudes about Africa demonstrated by African Americans. Rather than rejecting both positions outright for their essentialism, Soyinka critiques the tendency by African Americans to cast Africa as existing in the frozen "nostalgic past, the past as glorious history" – an accusation directed at not only American tourists but even Du Bois's *The Souls of Black Folk* (*The Burden of Memory*, 132). The essentialism of *négritude* differs from that demonstrated by African Americans, according to Soyinka, because its evocations of an idealized past serve to redefine the present reality experienced by Africans who have internalized colonial attitudes toward the continent. The validation of the present, Soyinka concedes in his more recent work, demanded an idea of *négritude* to contest the European denigration of the past.

68 In his book *Twelve African Writers*, Gerald Moore reads *Season of Anomy* as endorsing "a full-hearted espousal of African values or civilizations" and Soyinka himself as proposing that Yoruba society provides the blueprint for the nation as a whole. See Moore, *Twelve African Writers* (London: Hutchinson University Library for Africa, 1980), 226. Moore considers Soyinka to have a fairly naïve vision of historical change, one guided by Yoruba mythology rather than any particular historical insight.

69 Soyinka, *Art, Dialogue, and Outrage*, 222.

70 See Jeyifo, *Perspectives on Wole Soyinka*, xx.

71 Soyinka, *The Burden of Memory*, 194.

72 Jeyifo's Introduction to *Perspectives on Wole Soyinka* provides the most lucid account of the objections raised about the complexity of Soyinka's writings as well as possible responses to such concerns. Jeyifo notes that complexity has historically been associated both with causes of social progress and with efforts to oppress populations. In Soyinka's case, complexity arises from the effort to distinguish his work from both political reactionaries and postmodernist skeptics (xxi). For Soyinka's critics, however, this complexity leads to what Osofisan calls "ideological ambiguity." See Osofisan, "Wole Soyinka and the Living Dramatist: A Playwright's Encounter with a Drama of Wole Soyinka," in Jeyifo, ed., *Perspectives on Wole Soyinka*, 181. In this critical tribute to Soyinka, Osofisan laments the apparent refusal in Soyinka's work to take a formal stand on questions of politics, a refusal that is most apparent in the ambiguity of Soyinka's position toward tradition and the past. As a result, Osofisan finds Soyinka's drama flawed for its inability to convey a clear revolutionary commitment.

73 Amilcar Cabral's critical rethinking of traditional Marxism and its dismissal of culture's role in revolutionary struggles informs Soyinka's own ideas about the political relevance of art. Cabral places culture at the center of national liberation movements. On his understanding, colonialism involves the organized domination of productive forces within occupied territories, and

culture represents one of the most vital forms of these forces. Hence, liberation movements need to cultivate the cultural values of the oppressed in order to establish a vital basis for resistance. Cabral goes so far as to characterize political resistance as an expression of culture: "we may consider the national liberation movement as the organized political expression of the culture of the people who are undertaking the struggle." See Cabral, *Return to the Source: Selected Speeches by Amilcar Cabral*, edited by Africa Information Service (New York: Monthly Review Press, 1974), 43–44.

74 Soyinka, *Art, Dialogue, and Outrage*, 225–26.
75 Nigel C. Gibson's study of Fanon suggests a similar critique of *négritude*. While *négritude* represented for Fanon a new sensibility that could effect an inversion of colonial ideology, Gibson argues that he considered its emphasis on irrationality as preventing proponents from articulating a positive conception of change. See Gibson, *Fanon: The Postcolonial Imagination* (Cambridge: Polity, 2003), 80–1.
76 Soyinka, *The Open Sore of a Continent*, 133.
77 Soyinka, *Art, Dialogue, and Outrage*, 36.
78 Soyinka, *The Burden of Memory*, 194.
79 Dasenbrock, "Creating a Past," 323.
80 Soyinka, *Season of Anomy* (London: Rex Collins, 1973), 2. Subsequent references are given in the text.
81 See *Conversations with Wole Soyinka*, 158.
82 Tobin Siebers, *Morals & Stories* (New York: Columbia University Press, 1992), 186.
83 Ato Quayson, "Realism, Criticism, and the Disguises of Both: A Reading of Chinua Achebe's *Things Fall Apart* with an Evaluation of the Criticism Relating to It," in Isidore Okpewho, ed., *Chinua Achebe's* Things Fall Apart: *A Casebook* (Oxford, Oxford University Press, 2003) 222.

CONCLUSION: NOSTALGIA AND ITS FUTURES

1 Boym, *The Future of Nostalgia*, xiv.
2 Stewart, *On Longing*, 23.
3 Achebe, *Anthills of the Savannah*, 204.
4 Susan Stewart provides a well-formulated version of this critique of nostalgia. She argues, "The realization of re-union imagined by the nostalgic is a narrative utopia that works only by virtue of its partiality, its lack of fixity and closure: nostalgia is the desire for desire" (23).
5 Salman Rushdie, *Shame* (New York: Vintage International, 1989), 90. Subsequent references are given in the text.
6 Salman Rushdie, *The Ground Beneath Her Feet: A Novel* (New York: Picador, 2000), 55.
7 Salman Rushdie, *Step Across This Line: Collected Nonfiction 1992–2002* (New York: Random House, 2002), 336.
8 Ibid., 338.

Bibliography

Achebe, Chinua. *Anthills of the Savannah*. New York: Anchor Books, 1988.
    Arrow of God. New York: Doubleday, 1969.
    Hopes and Impediments: Selected Essays 1965–1987. London: Heinemann, 1988.
    Things Fall Apart. New York: Fawcett Crest, 1969.
    The Trouble with Nigeria. London: Heinemann, 1984.
Allen, Chadwick. "Blood (and) Memory." *American Literature* 71.1 (1999), 93–116.
Allen, Paula Gunn. *The Sacred Hoop: Recovering the Feminine in American Indian Traditions*. 2nd edn. Boston: Beacon Press, 1992.
Alter, Robert. "Modernism and Nostalgia." *Partisan Review* 60.3 (1993), 388–402.
Amadiume, Ifi. "The Politics of Memory: Biafra and Intellectual Responsibility," in Ifi Amadiume, ed., *The Politics of Memory: Truth, Healing and Social Justice* (London: Zed Books Ltd., 2000), 38–55.
Anderson, Benedict. *Imagined Communities: Reflections on the Origin and Spread of Nationalism*. London: Verso, 1983.
Appadurai, Arjun. *Modernity at Large: Cultural Dimensions of Globalization*. Minneapolis: University of Minnesota Press, 1996.
Appiah, Anthony. *In My Father's House*. New York: Oxford University Press, 1992.
Austen, Jane. *Mansfield Park*. London: Penguin, 1966.
Baucom, Ian. *Out of Place: Englishness, Empire, and the Locations of Identity*. Princeton: Princeton University Press, 1999.
Bauman, Zygmunt. *Life in Fragments: Essays in Postmodern Morality*. Oxford: Blackwell, 1995.
    Postmodern Ethics. Oxford: Blackwell, 1993.
Begam, Richard. "Achebe's Sense of an Ending: History and Tragedy in *Things Fall Apart*." *Studies in the Novel* 29.3 (1997), 396–411.
Bernstein, Michael André. *Foregone Conclusions: Against Apocalyptic History*. Berkeley: University of California Press, 1994.
Bevis, William. "Native American Novels: Homing In," in Brian Swann and Arnold Krupat, eds., *Recovering the Word: Essays on Native American Literature* (Berkeley: University of California Press, 1995), 580–620.

Bhabha, Homi K. "A Question of Survival: Nations and Psychic States," in James Donald, ed., *Psychoanalysis and Cultural Theory: Thresholds* (New York: St. Martin's Press, 1991), 89–103.

The Location of Culture. London: Routledge, 1994.

Biolsi, Thomas and Larry J. Zimmerman, eds. *Indians and Anthropologists: Vine Deloria, Jr., and the Critique of Anthropology*. Tucson: University of Arizona Press, 1997.

Blanchot, Maurice. *The Writing of the Disaster*, translated by Ann Smock. Lincoln: University of Nebraska Press, 1986.

Boym, Svetlana. *The Future of Nostalgia*. New York: Basic Books, 2001.

Brantlinger, Patrick. *Fictions of State: Culture and Credit in Britain 1694–1994*. Ithaca: Cornell University Press, 1996.

Brogan, Kathleen. *Cultural Haunting: Ghosts and Ethnicity in Recent American Literature*. Charlottesville: University Press of Virginia, 1998.

Brontë, Charlotte. *Jane Eyre*. London: Penguin Books, 1985.

Cabral, Amilcar. *Return to the Source: Selected Speeches by Amilcar Cabral*. Edited by Africa Information Service. New York: Monthly Review Press, 1974.

Cannadine, David. *Pleasures of the Past*. London: Penguin, 1997.

Carens, James F., ed. *Critical Essays on Evelyn Waugh*. Boston: G. K. Hall & Co., 1987.

Carpenter, Humphrey. *The Brideshead Generation: Evelyn Waugh and His Friends*. Boston: Houghton Mifflin, 1990.

Carr, David. *Time, Narrative, and History*. Bloomington: Indiana University Press, 1986.

Carroll, David. *Chinua Achebe: Novelist, Poet, Critic*. London: Macmillan, 1990.

Caruth, Cathy, ed. *Trauma: Explorations in Memory*. Baltimore: Johns Hopkins University Press, 1995.

Casey, Edward S. *Getting Back into Place: Toward a Renewed Understanding of the Place-World*. Bloomington: Indiana University Press, 1993.

Remembering: A Phenomenological Study. Bloomington: Indiana University Press, 1987.

"The World of Nostalgia." *Man and World* 20 (1987), 361–84.

Chamberlain, Charles. "From 'Haunts' to 'Character': The Meaning of *Ethos* and Its Relation to Ethics." *Helios* 11.2 (1984), 97–108.

Childs, David. *Britain since 1939: Progress and Decline*. London: Macmillan, 1995.

Chow, Rey. *Writing Diaspora: Tactics of Intervention in Contemporary Cultural Studies*. Bloomington: Indiana University Press, 1993.

Ciolkowski, Laura E. "Navigating the *Wide Sargasso Sea*: Colonial History, English Fiction, and British Empire." *Twentieth Century Literature* 43 (1997), 339–59.

Clarke, Peter. *A Question of Leadership: Gladstone to Blair*. London: Penguin, 1999.

Hope and Glory: Britain 1900–1990. London: Allen Lane, 1996.

Colley, Ann C. *Nostalgia and Recollection in Victorian Culture*. New York: St. Martin's Press, 1998.

Condé, Mary, and Thorunn Lonsdale, eds. *Caribbean Women Writers: Fiction in English*. New York: St. Martin's Press, 1999.

Connor, Steven. *The English Novel in History 1950–1995*. London: Routledge, 1996.

Corner, John, and Sylvia Harvey, eds. *Enterprise and Heritage: Crosscurrents of National Culture*. London: Routledge, 1991.

Cornforth, John. *The Country Houses of England 1948–1998*. London: Constable, 1998.

Cowart, David. *Literary Symbiosis: The Reconfigured Text in Twentieth-Century Writing*. Athens: University of Georgia Press, 1993.

Crow, Brian. "Soyinka and His Radical Critics," in Biodun Jeyifo, ed., *Perspectives on Wole Soyinka: Freedom and Complexity* (Jackson: University Press of Mississippi, 2001), 91–103.

Dames, Nicolas. *Amnesiac Selves: Nostalgia, Forgetting, and British Fiction, 1810–1870*. Oxford: Oxford University Press, 2001.

Dasenbrock, Reed Way. "Creating a Past: Achebe, Naipaul, Soyinka, Farah." *Salmagundi* 68–69 (1985–86), 312–34.

De Certeau, Michel. *Heterologies: Discourse on the Other*, translated by Brian Massumi. Foreword by Wlad Godzich. Minneapolis: University of Minnesota Press, 1986.

De Ramírez, Susan Berry Brill. *Contemporary American Indian Literatures & The Oral Tradition*. Tucson: University of Arizona Press, 1999.

Deloria, Vine, Jr. *God is Red: A Native View of Religion*. Golden: Fulcrum Publishing, 1994.

Dimock, Wai Chee. *Residues of Justice: Literature, Law, Philosophy*. Berkeley: University of California Press, 1996.

Doane, Janice, and Devon Hodges. *Nostalgia and Sexual Difference: The Resistance to Contemporary Feminism*. New York: Methuen, 1987.

Duckworth, Alastair M. *Howards End: E. M. Forster's House of Fiction*. New York: Twayne Publishers, 1992.

 The Improvement of the Estate: A Study of Jane Austen's Novels. Baltimore: Johns Hopkins University Press, 1971.

Elder, Arlene A. "'Dancing the Page': Orature in N. Scott Momaday's *The Way to Rainy Mountain*." *Narrative* 7.3 (1999), 272–88.

Eliot, T. S. "Tradition and the Individual Talent," in *The Sacred Wood: Essays on Poetry and Criticism*. London: Methuen, 1960, 47–59.

Emery, Mary Lou. *Jean Rhys at "World's End": Novels of Colonial and Sexual Exile*. Austin: University of Texas Press, 1990.

Erickson, Kai. "Notes on Trauma and Community." *American Imago* 48.4 (1991), 455–72.

Evans, Eric J. *Thatcher and Thatcherism*. London: Routledge, 1997.

Evers, Lawrence J. "Words and Place: A Reading of *House Made of Dawn*." *Western American Literature*. 11.4 (1977), 297–320.

Eysteinsson, Astradur. *The Concept of Modernism*. Ithaca: Cornell University Press, 1990.

Fanon, Frantz. *Black Skin, White Masks,* translated by Charles Lam Markmann. New York: Grove Press, 1967.

The Wretched of the Earth, translated by Constance Farrington. New York: Grove Press, 1963.

Felman, Shoshana, and Dori Laub. *Testimony: Crises of Witnessing in Literature, Psychoanalysis, and History.* New York: Routledge, 1992.

Fisher, Michael M. J. "Ethnicity and the Post-Modern Arts of Memory," in James Clifford and George E. Marcus, eds., *Writing Culture: The Politics and Poetics of Ethnographys* (Berkeley: University of California Press, 1986), 194–233.

Forster, E. M. *Howards End.* New York: Bantam Books, 1985.

"Mrs. Miniver," in *Two Cheers for Democracy.* New York: Harcourt, Brace and Company, 1951.

A Passage to India. San Diego: Harcourt Brace Jovanovich, 1984.

Fowler, Alastair. "Country House Poems: The Politics of a Genre." *Seventeenth Century* 1 (1986), 1–14.

Friedman, Ellen G. "Breaking the Master Narrative: Jean Rhys's *Wide Sargasso Sea,*" in Ellen G. Friedman and Miriam Fuchs, eds., *Breaking the Sequence: Women's Experimental Fictions* (Princeton: Princeton University Press, 1989), 117–28.

Gamble, Andrew. *Britain in Decline: Economic Policy, Political Strategy, and the British State.* Boston: Beacon Press, 1982.

Gardner, Philip. "E. M. Forster and 'The Possession of England.'" *Modern Language Quarterly* 42 (1981), 166–83.

Gibson, Andrew. "Sensibility and Suffering in Rhys and Nin," in Andrew Hadfield, Dominic Rainsford, and Tim Woods, eds., *The Ethics in Literature* (New York: St. Martin's Press, 1999), 184–211.

Gibson, Nigel C. *Fanon: The Postcolonial Imagination.* Cambridge: Polity, 2003.

Giddens, Anthony. *The Consequences of Modernity.* Cambridge: Polity Press, 1990.

Gikandi, Simon. *Maps of Englishness: Writing Identity in the Culture of Colonialism.* New York: Columbia University Press, 1996.

Reading Chinua Achebe: Language & Ideology in Fiction. London: James Currey, 1991.

Writing in Limbo: Modernism and Caribbean Literature. Ithaca: Cornell University Press, 1992.

Gill, Richard. *Happy Rural Seat: The English Country House and the Literary Imagination.* New Haven: Yale University Press, 1972.

Glissant, Edouard. *Caribbean Discourse: Selected Essays.* Edited, translated, and with an Introduction by J. Michael Dash. Charlottesville: Caraf Books, 1992.

Gregg, Veronica Marie. *Jean Rhys's Historical Imagination: Reading and Writing the Creole.* Chapel Hill: University of North Carolina Press, 1995.

Gupta, Akhil, and James Ferguson, eds. *Culture, Power, Place: Explorations in Critical Anthropology.* Durham: Duke University Press, 1997.

Hall, Stuart. "Cultural Identity and Diaspora," in Patrick Williams and Laura Chrisman, eds., *Colonial Discourse and Post-Colonial Theory: A Reader* (New York: Columbia University Press, 1994), 392–403.

Harpham, Geoffrey Galt. *Shadows of Ethics: Criticism and the Just Society.* Durham: Duke University Press, 1999.

Harvey, David. *The Condition of Postmodernity: An Enquiry into the Origins of Cultural Change.* Cambridge: Blackwell, 1990.

"From Space to Place and Back Again: Reflections on the Condition of Postmodernity," in Jon Bird et al., eds., *Mapping the Futures: Local Cultures, Global Change* (London: Routledge, 1993), 3–29.

Hegglund, Jon. "Defending the Realm: Domestic Space and Mass Cultural Contamination in *Howards End* and *An Englishman's Home.*" *English Literature in Transition* 40 (1997), 398–423.

Heise, Ursula K. *Chronoschisms: Time, Narrative, and Postmodernism.* Cambridge: Cambridge University Press, 1997.

Hell, Julia. "History As Trauma, or, Turning to the Past Once Again: Germany 1949/1989." *South Atlantic Quarterly* 96.4 (1997), 911–47.

Herman, Judith Lewis. *Trauma and Recovery.* New York: Basic Books, 1992.

Higdon, David Leon. *Shadows of the Past in Contemporary British Fiction.* Athens: University of Georgia Press, 1984.

Hobsbawm, Eric, and Terence Ranger, eds. *The Invention of Tradition.* Cambridge: Cambridge University Press, 1992.

Hogan, Linda. *Solar Storms.* New York: Scribner, 1995.

"Who Puts Together," in Richard F. Fleck, ed., *Critical Perspectives on Native American Fiction* (Washington, DC: Three Continents Press, 1993), 134–42.

hooks, bell. *Yearning: Race, Gender, and Cultural Politics.* Boston: South End Press, 1990.

Horkheimer, Max, and Theodor W. Adorno. *Dialectic of Enlightenment,* translated by John Cumming. New York: Herder and Herder, 1972.

Huffer, Lynne. *Maternal Pasts, Feminist Futures: Nostalgia, Ethics, and the Question of Difference.* Stanford: Stanford University Press, 1998.

Huggan, Graham. "A Tale of Two Parrots: Walcott, Rhys, and the Uses of Colonial Mimicry." *Contemporary Literature* 35 (1994), 643–60.

Hunter, Michael, ed. *Preserving the Past: The Rise of Heritage in Modern Britain.* Phoenix Mill: Alan Sutton Publishing, 1996.

Hutcheon, Linda. "Circling the Downspout of Empire: Postcolonialism and Postmodernism." *Ariel* 20 (1989), 149–75.

Ishiguro, Kazuo. *The Remains of the Day.* New York: Vintage Books, 1989.

Jameson, Fredric. *Postmodernism, or, The Cultural Logic of Late Capitalism.* Durham: Duke University Press, 1991.

Jencks, Charles. *What is Post-Modernism?* New York: St. Martin's Press, 1986.

Jeyifo, Biodun, ed. *Conversations with Wole Soyinka.* Jackson: University Press of Mississippi, 2001.

Perspectives on Wole Soyinka: Freedom and Complexity. Jackson: University Press of Mississippi, 2001.

Joseph, Margaret Paul. *Caliban in Exile: The Outsider in Caribbean Fiction.* New York: Greenwood Press, 1992.

Joyce, James. *A Portrait of the Artist as a Young Man.* Edited by R. B. Kershner. Boston: Bedford, 1993.

Jussawalla, Feroza, ed. *Conversations with V. S. Naipaul.* Jackson: University Press of Mississippi, 1997.

Kanneh, Kadiatu. *African Identities: Race, Nation and Culture in Ethnography, Pan-Africanism and Black Literatures.* London: Routledge, 1998.

Kant, Immanuel. *Groundwork of the Metaphysic of Morals.* Translated by H. J. Paton. New York: Harper & Row, 1964.

Kaplan, Caren. *Questions of Travel: Postmodern Discourses of Displacement.* Durham: Duke University Press, 1996.

Kearney, Richard. *Politics of Modernity: Toward a Hermeneutic Imagination.* New Jersey: Humanities Press, 1995.

Kennedy, Valerie. "Evelyn Waugh's 'Brideshead Revisited': Paradise Lost or Paradise Regained?" *Ariel* 21.1 (1990), 23–39.

Kenny, Virginia C. *The Country-House Ethos in English Literature 1688–1750: Themes of Personal Retreat and National Expansion.* New York: St. Martin's Press, 1984.

Kincaid, Jamaica. "I Use a Cut and Slash Policy of Writing: Jamaica Kincaid Talks to Gerhard Dilger." *Wasafiri* 16 (1992), 21–25.

Krieger, Joel. *Reagan, Thatcher, and the Politics of Decline.* New York: Oxford University Press, 1986.

Krupat, Arnold. *The Voice in the Margin: Native American Literature and the Canon.* Berkeley: University of California Press, 1989.

LaCapra, Dominick. *History and Memory after Auschwitz.* Ithaca: Cornell University Press, 1998.

Laclau, Ernesto. *New Reflections on the Revolution of our Time.* London: Verso, 1990.

Lamming, George. *The Pleasures of Exile.* London: Allison & Busby, 1984.

Landrum, Larry. "The Shattered Modernism of Momaday's *House Made of Dawn.*" *Modern Fiction Studies* 42.4 (1996), 763–86.

Lawrence, D. H. *Lady Chatterley's Lover.* New York: Signet, 1959.

Lears, Jackson. "Looking Backward: In Defense of Nostalgia." *Lingua Franca* 7.10 (1998), 59–66.

Leavis, F. R. "E. M. Forster," in Malcolm Bradbury, ed., *Forster: A Collection of Critical Essays* (New York: Barnes and Noble, 1966), 34–47.

Levenson, Michael H. *A Genealogy of Modernism: A Study of English Literary Doctrine 1908–1922.* Cambridge: Cambridge University Press, 1984.

Levinas, Emmanuel. *Totality and Infinity: An Essay on Exteriority*, translated by Alfonso Lingis. Pittsburgh: Duquesne University Press, 1969.

Lindfors, Bernth, ed. Introduction to *Conversations with Chinua Achebe.* Jackson: University Press of Mississippi, 1997.

Littlejohn, David. *The Fate of the English Country House.* New York: Oxford University Press, 1997.

Lowenthal, David. *Possessed by the Past: The Heritage Crusade and the Spoils of History.* New York: Free Press, 1996.

MacIntyre, Alasdair. *After Virtue: A Study in Moral Theory.* Notre Dame: University of Notre Dame Press, 1984.

Mandler, Peter. *The Fall and Rise of the Stately Home.* New Haven: Yale University Press, 1997.

"Nationalising the Country House," in Michael Hunter, ed., *Preserving the Past: The Rise of Heritage in Modern Britain* (Phoenix Mill: Alan Sutton Publishing, 1996), 99–114.

Mardorossian, Carine Melkom. "Double (De)colonization and the Feminist Criticism of *Wide Sargasso Sea.*" *College Literature* 26.2 (1999), 79–95.

Marshall, Paule. *Brown Girl, Brownstones.* New York: The Feminist Press, 1981.

The Chosen Place, The Timeless People. New York: Vintage, 1992.

Praisesong for the Widow. New York: E. P. Dutton, 1984.

"Shaping the World of My Art." *New Letters* 40 (1973), 97–112.

Massey, Doreen. *Space, Place and Gender.* Cambridge: Polity Press, 1994.

Matthews, Washington. "Navajo Myths, Prayers, and Songs with Texts and Translations." *University of California Publications in American Archaeology and Ethnology* 5.2 (1906), 21–63.

McCartney, George. *Confused Roaring: Evelyn Waugh and the Modernist Tradition.* Bloomington: Indiana University Press, 1987.

McEwan, Ian. *Black Dogs.* New York: Bantam, 1992.

Mohanty, Satya P. "Can Our Values be Objective? On Ethics, Aesthetics, and Progressive Politics." *New Literary History* 32 (2001), 803–33.

Literary Theory and the Claims of History: Postmodernism, Objectivity, Multicultural Politics. Ithaca: Cornell University Press, 1997.

Momaday, N. Scott. *House Made of Dawn.* New York: Perennial, 1968 and 1989 editions.

"The Man Made of Words," in Abraham Chapman, ed., *Literature of the American Indians: Views and Interpretations* (New York: Meridian, 1975), 96–110.

The Names: A Memoir. Tucson: University of Arizona Press, 1976.

The Way to Rainy Mountain. Albuquerque: University of New Mexico Press, 1969.

Moore, Gerald. *Twelve African Writers.* London: Hutchinson University Library for Africa, 1980.

Morgan, Kenneth O. *The People's Peace: British History Since 1945.* Oxford: Oxford University Press, 1999.

Morley, David, and Kevin Robins. *Spaces of Identity: Global Media, Electronic Landscapes and Cultural Boundaries.* London: Routledge, 1995.

Morrison, Toni. *Beloved.* New York: Plume, 1987.

"Home" in *The House that Race Built: Black Americans, U.S. Terrain.* Edited and with an Introduction by Wahneema Lubiano. New York: Pantheon Books, 1997, 3–12.

Paradise. New York: Alfred A. Knopf, 1998.

"Rootedness: The Ancestor as Foundation," in Mari Evans, ed., *Black Women Writers (1950–1980), A Critical Evaluation* (Garden City: Anchor, 1984), 339–45.

Song of Solomon. New York: Plume, 1987.

Morson, Gary Saul. *Narrative and Freedom: The Shadows of Time*. New Haven: Yale University Press, 1994.

Moses, Michael Valdez. *The Novel and the Globalization of Culture*. Oxford: Oxford University Press, 1995.

Moyers, Bill. "Chinua Achebe," in Betty Sue Flowers, ed., *A World of Ideas: Conversations with Thoughtful Men and Women about American Life Today and the Ideas Shaping Our Future* (New York: Doubleday, 1989), 333–44.

Muoneke, Romanus Okey. *Arts, Rebellion and Redemption: A Reading of the Novels of Chinua Achebe*. New York: Peter Lang, 1994.

Mustafa, Fawzia. *V. S. Naipaul*. Cambridge: Cambridge University Press, 1995.

Naipaul, V. S. *A Bend in the River*. New York: Vintage International, 1989.

The Enigma of Arrival: A Novel. New York: Vintage Books, 1988.

Finding the Center: Two Narratives. New York: Alfred A. Knopf, 1984.

A House for Mr. Biswas. New York: Penguin Books, 1992.

The Mimic Men. New York: Vintage International, 2001.

The Return of Eva Perón with The Killings in Trinidad. New York: Alfred A. Knopf, 1980.

Nairn, Tom. *The Break-up of Britain: Crisis and Neonationalism*. London: Verso, 1981.

Newton, Adam Zachary. *Narrative Ethics*. Cambridge, MA: Harvard University Press, 1995.

Nussbaum, Martha C. *Love's Knowledge: Essays on Philosophy and Literature*. Oxford: Oxford University Press, 1990.

O'Brien, Conor Cruise, Edward Said, and John Lukacs. "The Intellectual in the Post-Colonial World: Response and Discussion." *Salmagundi* 70–71 (1986), 65–81.

O'Brien, Susie. "Serving a New World Order: Postcolonial Politics in Kazuo Ishiguro's *The Remains of the Day*." *Modern Fiction Studies* 42.4 (1996), 787–806.

O'Callaghan, Evelyn. "The 'Pleasures' of Exile in Selected West Indian Writing Since 1987," in Glyne Griffith, ed., *Caribbean Cultural Identities* (Lewisburg: Bucknell University Press, 2001), 73–103.

Okri, Ben. *The Famished Road*. New York: Anchor Books, 1993.

Osofisan, Femi. "Wole Soyinka and the Living Dramatist: A Playwright's Encounter with a Drama of Wole Soyinka," in Biodun Jeyifo, ed., *Perspectives on Wole Soyinka: Freedom and Complexity* (Jackson: University Press of Mississippi, 2001), 172–86.

Otten, Terry. "Horrific Love in Toni Morrison's Fiction." *Modern Fiction Studies* 39 (1993), 651–68.

Owens, Louis. *Other Destinies: Understanding the American Indian Novel*. Norman: University of Oklahoma Press, 1992.

Palmer, Frank. *Literature and Moral Understanding: A Philosophical Essay on Ethics, Aesthetics, Education, and Culture.* Oxford: Clarendon Press, 1992.

Palumbo-Liu, David. "The Politics of Memory: Remembering History in Alice Walker and Joy Kogawa," in Amritjit Singh, Jr., Joseph T. Skerrett, and Robert E. Hogan, eds., *Memory and Cultural Politics: New Approaches to American Ethnic Literatures* (Boston: Northeastern University Press, 1996), 211–26.

Parry, Benita. "Resistance Theory/Theorizing Resistance, or Two Cheers for Nativism," in Padmini Mongia, ed., *Contemporary Postcolonial Theory: A Reader* (London: Arnold, 1996), 84–109.

Patey, Douglas Lane. *The Life of Evelyn Waugh: A Critical Biography.* Oxford: Blackwell, 1998.

Patton, Brian. "Preserving Property: History, Genealogy, and Inheritance in 'Upon Appleton House.'" *Renaissance Quarterly* 49 (1996), 824–39.

Perl, Jeffrey M. *The Tradition of Return: The Implicit History of Modern Literature.* Princeton: Princeton University Press, 1984.

Perry, Donna. *Backtalk: Women Writers Speak Out.* New Brunswick: Rutgers University Press, 1993.

Petry, Mike. *Narratives of Memory and Identity: The Novels of Kazuo Ishiguro.* Frankfurt: Peter Lang, 1999.

Quayson, Ato. "Realism, Criticism, and the Disguises of Both: A Reading of Chinua Achebe's *Things Fall Apart* with an Evaluation of the Criticism Relating to It," in Isidore Okpewho, ed., *Chinua Achebe's* Things Fall Apart*: A Casebook* (Oxford Oxford University Press, 2003), 221–48.

Ramchand, Kenneth. *An Introduction to the Study of West Indian Literature.* Middlesex: Thomas Nelson, 1976.

Redding, Arthur. "'Haints': American Ghosts, Ethnic Memory, and Contemporary Fiction." *Mosaic* 36.4 (2001), 163–82.

Reyes, Angelita. "Reading Carnival as an Archaeological Site for Memory in Paule Marshall's *The Chosen Place, The Timeless People* and *Praisesong for the Widow*," in Amritjit Singh, Jr., Joseph T. Skerrett, and Robert E. Hogan, eds., *Memory, Narrative, and Identity: New Essays in Ethnic American Literatures* (Boston: Northeastern University Press, 1994), 179–97.

Rhys, Jean. *The Letters of Jean Rhys.* Edited by Francis Wyndham and Diana Melly. New York: Viking Penguin Books, 1984.

  Voyage in the Dark. New York: W. W. Norton & Company, 1982.

  Wide Sargasso Sea. New York: W. W. Norton & Company, 1966.

Ricoeur, Paul. "A Response," in Morny Joy, ed., *Paul Ricoeur and Narrative: Context and Contestation* (Calgary: University of Calgary Press, 1997), xxxix–xliv.

  "Memory and Forgetting," in Richard Kearney and Mark Dooley, eds., *Questioning Ethics: Contemporary Debates in Philosophy* (London: Routledge, 1999), 5–11.

  Time and Narrative, translated by Kathleen McLaughlin and David Pellauer, 3 vols. Chicago: University of Chicago Press, 1984–1988.

Riley, Joan. *The Unbelonging*. London: The Women's Press, 1985.

Rody, Carolyn. "Toni Morrison's *Beloved*: History, 'Rememory,' and a 'Clamor for a Kiss'." *American Literary History* 7 (1995), 92–119.

Rosaldo, Renato. *Culture & Truth: The Remaking of Social Analysis*. Boston: Beacon Press, 1993.

Rosen, George. "Nostalgia: A 'Forgotten' Psychological Disorder." *Clio Medica* 10.1 (1975), 28–51.

Rothfork, John. "Zen Comedy in Postcolonial Literature: Kazuo Ishiguro's *The Remains of the Day*." *Mosaic* 29.1 (1996), 79–102.

Rothstein, David. "*Brideshead Revisited* and the Modern Historicization of Memory." *Studies in the Novel* 25 (1993), 318–31.

Rubenstein, Roberta. *Home Matters: Longing and Belonging, Nostalgia and Mourning in Women's Fiction*. New York: Palgrave, 2001.

Rushdie, Salman. *The Ground Beneath Her Feet: A Novel*. New York: Picador, 2000.

   Imaginary Homelands: Essays and Criticism 1981–1991. London: Granta Books, 1991.

   Shame. New York: Vintage International, 1989.

   Step Across This Line: Collected Nonfiction 1992–2002. New York: Random House, 2002.

Said, Edward W. *Culture and Imperialism*. New York: Alfred A. Knopf, 1993.

   "Figures, Configurations, Transfigurations," in Anna Rutherford, ed., *From Commonwealth to Post-Colonial*. Sydney: Dangaroo, 1992.

   "The Intellectual in the Post-Colonial World." *Salmagundi* 70–71 (1986), 44–64.

Sale, Maggie. "Call and Response as Critical Method: African-American Oral Traditions and *Beloved*," in Barbara H. Solomon, ed., *Critical Essays on Toni Morrison's* Beloved (New York: G. K. Hall, 1998), 177–88.

Scarberry-García, Susan. *Landmarks of Healing: A Study of* House Made of Dawn. Albuquerque : University of New Mexico Press, 1990.

Schubnell, Mathias. *N. Scott Momaday: The Cultural and Literary Background*. Norman: University of Oklahoma Press, 1985.

Selinger, Bernard. "*House Made of Dawn*: A Positively Ambivalent Bildungs-roman." *Modern Fiction Studies* 45 (1999), 38–68.

Shaffer, Brian. "An Interview with Kazuo Ishiguro." *Contemporary Literature* 42.1 (2001), 1–14.

   Understanding Kazuo Ishiguro. Columbia: University of South Carolina Press, 1998.

Sharma, R. S. "Vision and Form in N. Scott Momaday's *House Made of Dawn*." *Indian Journal of American Studies* 12.1 (1982), 69–79.

Siebers, Tobin. *Morals & Stories*. New York: Columbia University Press, 1992.

Silko, Leslie Marmon. *Almanac of the Dead*. New York: Penguin, 1991.

   Ceremony. New York: Penguin, 1977.

Sinfield, Alan. *Literature, Politics, and Culture in Postwar Britain*. Berkeley: University of California Press, 1989.

Soja, Edward. *Postmodern Geographies: The Reassertion of Space in Critical Social Theory.* London: Verso, 1989.

Sollors, Werner. *The Invention of Ethnicity.* New York: Oxford University Press, 1989.

Soyinka, Wole. "A Dance of the Forests," in *Collected Plays 1.* Oxford: Oxford University Press, 1973, 1–78.

    Art, Dialogue, and Outrage: Essays on Literature and Culture. Edited by Biodun Jeyifo. New York: Pantheon Books, 1993.

    The Burden of Memory, The Muse of Forgivenesss. New York: Oxford University Press, 1999.

    The Interpreters. New York: Africana Publishing Corporation, 1972.

    The Open Sore of a Continent: A Personal Narrative of the Nigerian Crisis. New York: Oxford University Press, 1996.

    Season of Anomy. London: Rex Collins, 1973.

Spillers, Hortense J. "Chosen Place, Timeless People: Some Figurations on the New World," in Marjorie Pryse and Hortense J. Spillers, eds., *Conjuring: Black Women, Fiction, and Literary Tradition* (Bloomington: Indiana University Press, 1985), 151– 75.

Spivak, Gayatri Chakravorty. "Three Women's Texts and a Critique of Imperialism." *Critical Inquiry* 12 (1985), 243–261.

Starobinski, Jean. "The Idea of Nostalgia." *Diogenes* 54 (1966), 81–103.

Stein, Rachel. *Shifting the Ground: American Women Writers' Revisions of Nature, Gender, and Race.* Charlottesville: University Press of Virginia, 1997.

Stewart, Susan. *On Longing: Narratives of the Miniature, the Gigantic, the Souvenir, the Collection.* Durham: Duke University Press, 1993.

Stoll, Rae Harris. "The Unthinkable Poor in Edwardian Writing." *Mosaic* 15.4 (1982), 23–45.

Sugg, Katherine. "'I Would Rather Be Dead': Nostalgia and Narrative in Jamaica Kincaid's *Lucy.*" *Narrative* 10.2 (2002), 156–73.

Suleri, Sara. "Naipaul's Arrival." *Yale Journal of Criticism* 2.1 (1988), 25–50.

Taylor, Patrick. *The Narrative of Liberation: Perspectives on Afro-Caribbean Literature, Popular Culture, and Politics.* Ithaca: Cornell University Press, 1989.

Ten Kortenaar, Neil. "'Only Connect': *Anthills of the Savannah* and Achebe's *Trouble with Nigeria.*" *Research in African Literatures* 24.3 (1993), 59–72.

Tiffin, Helen. "Post-Colonialism, Post-Modernism and the Rehabilitation of Post-Colonial History." *Journal of Commonwealth Literature* 23.1 (1988), 169–81.

Van der Kolk, B. A., and Onno van der Hart. "The Intrusive Past: The Flexibility of Memory and the Engraving of Trauma." *American Imago* 48.4 (1991), 425–54.

Vorda, Allan, and Kim Herzinger. "An Interview with Kazuo Ishiguro." *Mississippi Review* 20 (1991/92), 131–154.

Walcott, Derek. *Omeros.* New York: Farrar Straus Giroux, 1993.

Wall, Kathleen. "*The Remains of the Day* and its Challenges to Theories of Unreliable Narration." *Journal of Narrative Technique* 24.1 (1994), 18–42.

Walter, Eugene Victor. *Placeways: A Theory of the Human Environment.* Chapel Hill: University of North Carolina Press, 1988.

Watkins, Floyd C. *In Time and Place: Some Origins of American Fiction.* Athens: University of Georgia Press, 1977.

Waugh, Evelyn. *Brideshead Revisited: The Sacred and Profane Memories of Captain Charles Ryder.* Boston: Little, Brown and Company, 1945.

The Essays, Articles and Reviews. Edited by Donat Gallagher. Boston: Little, Brown and Company, 1984.

Welch, James. *Fools Crow.* New York: Penguin, 1986.

Winter in the Blood. New York: Penguin, 1974.

Werman, David S. "Normal and Pathological Nostalgia." *Journal of the American Psychoanalytic Association* 25.2 (1977), 387–98.

White, Hayden. "Historical Emplotment and the Problem of Truth," in Saul Friedlander, ed., *Probing the Limits of Representation: Nazism and the "Final Solution"* (Cambridge: Harvard University Press, 1992), 37–53.

Williams, Bernard. *Ethics and the Limits of Philosophy.* Cambridge, MA: Harvard University Press, 1985.

Wilson, John Howard. *Evelyn Waugh: A Literary Biography, 1903–1924.* London: Associated University Presses, 1996.

Wilson-Tagoe, Nana. *Historical and Literary Representation in West Indian Literature.* Gainesville: University Press of Florida, 1998.

Wirth, Annette. *The Loss of Traditional Values and Continuance of Faith in Evelyn Waugh's Novels:* A Handful of Dust, Brideshead Revisited *and* Sword of Honour. Frankfurt: Peter Lang, 1990.

Woodard, Charles L. *Ancestral Voice: Conversations with N. Scott Momaday.* Lincoln: University of Nebraska Press, 1989.

Woolf, Virginia. "Mr. Bennett and Mrs. Brown," in *Collected Essays.* New York: Harcourt, Brace and World, 1953, 319–37.

Wyschogrod, Edith. *An Ethics of Remembering: History, Heterology, and the Nameless Others.* Chicago: University of Chicago Press, 1998.

Žižek, Slavoj. *For They Know Not What They Do: Enjoyment as a Political Factor.* London: Verso, 1991.

The Sublime Object of Ideology. London: Verso, 1989.

Index

Lightning Source UK Ltd.
Milton Keynes UK
14 January 2010

148577UK00001B/144/P